SILVER
THREAD

SILVER THREAD

The Ups and Downs of a
Mennonite Family in Mission (1895-1995)

JOSEPH C. SHENK

Good Books

Intercourse, PA 17534

Photography Credits

All photographs from the Joseph C. and Edith Shenk family collection except the following: Page 109, top, Lancaster Mennonite Historical Society, Joanne Hess Siegrist collection; Pages 109, bottom, 166, bottom, 167, top and bottom, and 168, Eastern Mennonite Missions; Pages 135, bottom, 166, top, 200, 202, top and bottom, 203, 230, 231, top and bottom, 232, and 233, Daniel and Erma Wenger family collection; 201, Mennonite Central Committee.

All scripture references in Books One and Two from the King James Version of the Bible unless otherwise noted. All scripture references (unless otherwise noted) in Book Three from the HOLY BIBLE: THE NEW INTERNATIONAL VERSION, © 1973, 1978, 1984 by the International Bible Society, used by permission of Zondervan Bible Publishers.

Design by Dawn J. Ranck

SILVER THREAD: The Ups and Downs of a Mennonite Family in Mission (1895-1995)
Copyright © 1996 by Good Books, Intercourse, Pennsylvania 17534
International Standard Book Number: 1-56148-207-2
Library of Congress Catalog Card Number: 96-23958

Library of Congress Cataloging-in-Publication Data

Shenk, Joseph C.
    Silver thread : the ups and downs of a Mennonite family in mission, 1895-1995 /
Joseph C. Shenk.
        p. cm.
    ISBN: 1-56148-207-2
        1. Mennonites--Missions--Africa, East. 2. Mennonites--Mission--Nicaragua.
3. Shenk, Joseph C.--Family. 4. Shenk family. 5. Barge family. 6. Landis family.
7. Mennonites--Biography. 8. Missionaries--Biography. 9. Christianity and culture.
10. Missions--Theory. I. Title.
BV2545.S44 1996
266'.97'0922--dc20
[B]   96-23958
                                                                                     CIP

On the cover:

Top left: Clyde and Alta Shenk in the 1960s with Tanzania Mennonite Church leaders, Kashan Kawira (left) and Ezekiel Muganda (right).

Top right: Joseph C. Shenk (author) with his four daughters on a family outing in the Ng'ong Hills, Kenya in 1974. (Left to right) Joyce, Rosemary, Rebecca, and Dianne.

Bottom: Danny Wenger (1989) presents the Mennonite Central Committee philosophy as part of his food distribution work during his year as an MCC worker in Nicaragua.

Table of Contents

Introduction

In 1896 most Mennonites lived either in Russia or the United States. When they gathered for worship, most spoke either German or Dutch. By 1996 Mennonites worshiped in well over 100 languages with churches in some 60 countries. Some of this spread happened through migration, but much more of it happened through the missionary efforts of the Dutch and North American Mennonite churches.

From 1963 to 1981, my wife and I were missionaries in East Africa. During the last five years of that experience, I represented Mennonite Central Committee in Uganda, Kenya, and Tanzania. Workers and visitors from North America were constantly coming and going. Those visitors who spent time with the African church were often puzzled, sometimes critical. The church which the missionaries planted didn't feel like the church back home.

I began to hope that an African Mennonite could tell the story of the coming of the missionaries, recount how the Gospel was received, and show how the church took shape. Then in 1983, I spent three months with the first Mennonite bishop in East Africa, Zedekia Kisare, helping him to tell his story, *Kisare, a Mennonite of Kiseru*.

I came to believe the story of the "new Mennonite"–Kisare's story–needed to be balanced by the story of the missionaries. Mennonites didn't just show up in Africa and South America and Asia. What happened in the North American churches which produced these people? How did they do their work? How did being in mission change them and change what they did? *Silver Thread* addresses these questions.

The idea that what took place in the particular reflects what was happening generally has guided the collecting of these stories. The particular stories are of two families–a Landis/Wenger family and a Barge/Shenk family–who were pioneer missionaries in Tanganyika, East Africa. Patterns seen in the stories of these families are similar to the patterns of any Mennonite family in mission during the same time period.

Gathering this material has not been difficult because my own story forms a part of the mosaic. In 1938 I was born in Tanganyika, third generation in the Barge/Shenk part of the tapestry. Further, in 1970 my family was joined by marriage to the Landis/Wenger family when my father, J. Clyde Shenk, married Miriam Landis Wenger. Each had buried first spouses in Tanzania, formerly Tanganyika.

During the 100 years which this saga covers, the way in which cross-cultural mission was understood and done changed dramatically. Nevertheless, there is a constancy in the story–faithfulness in witnessing to the gospel of Jesus Christ. It's the story of real people struggling to be faithful while doing what hadn't been done by Mennonites before. And it is the story of these people's profound transformation, leading to changes in the North American Mennonite church as well.

I want to thank my stepmother, Miriam, for hosting me in her home during the months that I did research for this book, for telling me what she remembers, and for sharing of her diaries and letters.

Many, many others also helped me. I am grateful to them. I would like to thank the Mellinger Christian Service Sunday school class, and especially their president, Ruth Hollinger, for arranging a fund raiser for this project and for those from the Mellinger, Millersville, Rohrerstown, Strasburg, and Stumptown congregations who contributed financially. I thank Omar Eby and Rose Shenk for guiding the shape of the finished manuscript. I thank Rose for editing much of the "Middle Voices."

Prologue

EDITH

The story begins where it ends, with a Nicaraguan Mennonite pastor's family. The Vado family of Nicaragua is part of a recent phenomenon, the multi-racial, multi-language Mennonite church. In 1974 the Vado family became Mennonite. Arnulfo, the husband and father, became an ordained Mennonite leader of a new congregation five years later. Like many first generation Mennonite leaders around the world, Arnulfo began his Christian life as a member of another church. Mrs. Vado tells us her family's story.

A dream jolted me awake. Something about it filled me with foreboding. In my dream I was sitting in a big evangelical church. Three brides in white wedding gowns were walking down the aisle toward the altar at the front of the church. Each of the young women wore a sparkling tiara instead of a wedding veil. One of the girls stopped and turned back before getting to the altar. But the other two kept walking slowly toward their destiny. The altar was covered with bouquets of flowers so that it felt more like a funeral than a wedding.

As soon as it was morning, I went across the street to tell my sister-in-law about my dream. Her daughter Maria and my daughter Edith were both teenagers. These cousins, Edith and Maria, acted like sisters.

Many years earlier, an old Costa Rican man had told me that if I ever dream about a wedding, then there will be a death. I told my sister-in-law what the old man had said. She said that it might be my mother who would die. My mother was sick at that time. My sister-in-law said I should prepare myself for Mother's death.

My husband, Pastor Arnulfo, has had a lot of bad accidents. So I have become a fearful woman, always expecting something bad to happen. By now Mother was an old woman. Old people die. Why would I be warned of her death? Hadn't the dream been of young women, beautiful girls? The days passed and Mother got well. I began to forget my dream.

In Arnulfo's first accident, a heavy object fell on his leg, smashing it. During the six months that he was hospitalized, no one from our church–the Apostles & Prophets Church–went to visit him. They only came to see him after he was home from the hospital. By then Arnulfo was disgusted with the Apostles & Prophets.

"I won't belong to a church that doesn't visit members in the hospital," he grumped. So we stopped going to their church.

At that time I met Alfred Friesen, an Evangelical Mennonite missionary from Canada, from Manitoba. Pastor Friesen invited us to a vigil, an all-night Christian party. At evening time people gather in a home or church hall for visiting, singing, and preaching. This goes on till past midnight. In the wee hours of the morning we eat together. After the meal we go on singing and preaching until sunrise when we all go home.

Arnulfo couldn't go to the vigil because of his leg. I went and when I got home, I told Arnulfo that we should become Mennonites. He agreed that we would attend the Mennonite church. This is how we became Mennonites. It was 1974.

At once the Mennonites got us involved in church work. They opened a new worship place near our home, and Arnulfo was chosen as pastor of this new church, the Los Cruces Mennonite Church. Lester Olfert, another Evangelical Mennonite from Manitoba, ordained him. Then, in 1979 all of the missionaries left Nicaragua because of the socialist revolution when the Sandinistas overthrew the Somoza dictators.

Arnulfo continued to pastor the Los Cruces Mennonite Church. Because the congregation is too small and too poor to support a full-time pastor, Arnulfo also works for CEPAD, a Nicaraguan agency formed by all the evangelical churches in our country. CEPAD does development work and distributes material aid relief from Canada, the United States, and Europe to refugees and poor people. The Mennonite Central Committee (MCC) brings material aid into Nicaragua through CEPAD.

God blessed Arnulfo and me with four daughters. Our third daughter Edith was eighteen years old when I had my dream. Edith was a slim, beautiful, bright-eyed, generous, quick-to-notice, caring, friendly, and industrious girl. God's Spirit was with her.

At Christmas time in 1989 Edith decided to have a party for the children in our town. She made a pinata for the party. The children had lots of fun and laughter at Edith's party! Edith began to give away some of her personal things that Christmas. I asked her, "Why are you giving away your clothes?"

"I don't need these clothes anymore," she said.

At that time she noticed that her father and I were tired and hassled by so much activity and so many responsibilities at the church. On the way to church she took my hand and comforted me. "Don't fret, Mother," she told me.

Just before the New Year's celebrations, Edith told Arnulfo and me that we must take a break. This seemed strange to me that an eighteen-year-old girl wasn't thinking of her plans and parties but was thinking of her parents. This was the Spirit of Jesus in her. Edith wanted us to get away, for even half a day, before the Sunday services on New Year's Eve 1989.

"Go to the beach Saturday morning," she urged. "Take a picnic lunch. You need some time to be together, to be away from all the other people coming and going." She promised to do the Saturday housework so we could go. She urged us three times, "Sit together on the sand, get away from town, take a swim."

On the Saturday morning before New Year's Eve, we did get away for a few hours. My husband and I sat together on the sand watching the waves washing the shore. "Arnulfo," I said softly, "Edith has been so thoughtful and caring. Whatever would we do if something happened to her?"

"Hush you now!" I heard him say sharply. "Get that out of your head."

An overnight youth retreat was planned for Saturday evening through Sunday breakfast. The retreat site was 30 miles from where we live in Corazo. The youth from our church were leaving that afternoon for the retreat. I was restless at the beach, uneasy. "Let's go home," I said to Arnulfo. We started home from the beach by 2:00 p.m. We were on my husband's little motorbike. I rode sidesaddle, my arm around Arnulfo's waist.

As we turned into the lane leading to our house, we met Edith hurrying out to the main road where the youth from our church were piling into the back of a Toyota, double-cab pickup for their trip to the retreat. Edith waved to us and shouted, "I've done the Saturday cleaning." Then, as we passed, she turned and called after us, "I'll see you in the morning."

The leaders of the youth group had arranged for the MCC pickup to take them to the retreat. The designated driver was from the North, from the United States, an MCC volunteer. He had been living and working in our country for some months. Already he spoke Spanish fluently. He was a development worker. He had helped the women's group at our church to begin a clothing project. He was a young man, a Mennonite, just a few years older than Edith.

When we got to our house, Arnulfo set the bike up on its stand and I untied our picnic basket from the carrier. Everything was quiet. The air was still in the afternoon sunshine. There were no sounds of birds or crickets—just stillness. We went into the house. Then we heard an ambulance siren piercing the afternoon stillness. My heart jumped. Looking out the window toward the highway, I saw the ambulance going up the road toward Jinotepe.

A neighbor boy came running, gasping for breath through his words. "The ambulance was coming just after the accident. It rolled over and over. The pickup with the youth, it landed with the wheels in the air. They are all dead. Everyone is scattered all over the road. The ambulance took them to the hospital."

Arnulfo rushed outside, kicked the motorbike into life, and roared off down the lane to the main road. I was frantic waiting for Arnulfo to come back. Edith and two of our other daughters were on the pickup. I was praying aloud, looking out the window toward the road. Soon I saw Arnulfo coming back. He called for me to come, to get on the cycle. "Adella, we are going to Jinotepe, to the hospital," he shouted.

On the way to the hospital, Arnulfo was yelling to me above the noise of wind and cycle, telling me what had happened. "It is only about a mile from our house to the place where the pickup rolled over," I heard Arnulfo say. "When I got there, a crowd was gathering. People were helping to put the last of the injured into a truck. There was a man telling what he had seen.

"We were walking along the road, my wife and I," the man was saying. "The youth from the North, red hair, he was thrown into the air and landed upside down into the barbed wire fence, head down with legs dangling over the fence. The rolling truck whacked into him. The open door on the passenger side slammed him into that tree. Then the truck rocked back onto its roof and the youth crumpled onto the ground. As the truck rolled over, all the youth standing in the back were flung out all over the road. The ambulance was coming just then. This is a miracle that the ambulance was coming when the pickup rolled over. The ambulance took the unconscious ones to the hospital in Jinotepe."

Another man too was telling what had happened. "I was riding my motorbike," he was saying excitedly. "I was going at top speed, about 50 kph (32 mph). The truck with many youth standing in the back passed me. It began to sway and went out of control. The pickup rolled over twice, leaving bodies scattered everywhere. I had to stop quickly to avoid running over any of them."

When Arnulfo and I got to the hospital, we were told that four of the youth were very seriously injured and were unconscious. All four were in the same emergency room. They let us into the emergency room. Edith was there! When I saw my daughter, I began to be hysterical. They took me out.

Arnulfo was with Edith as she died. Next Magda died. Magda wasn't a member of our church. She had been invited along to the retreat as a guest. Then Daniel, the MCC worker, died. Edith died about an hour after the accident. Magda and Daniel died in the next hour following Edith.

Nineteen youth were in the accident. Sixteen recovered. Maria, Edith's cousin, had severe head injuries. Maria was in a coma for two weeks. But she turned back from the flower-covered altar of death. Of the three girls who were seriously injured—Edith, Magda, and Maria—only Maria turned back.

The youth from the North, Daniel, I am told that his grandfather was buried in Africa. But they took Daniel's body—Ann Hershberger of the MCC took Daniel's body, took it back to the United States. He was not buried here in Nicaragua.

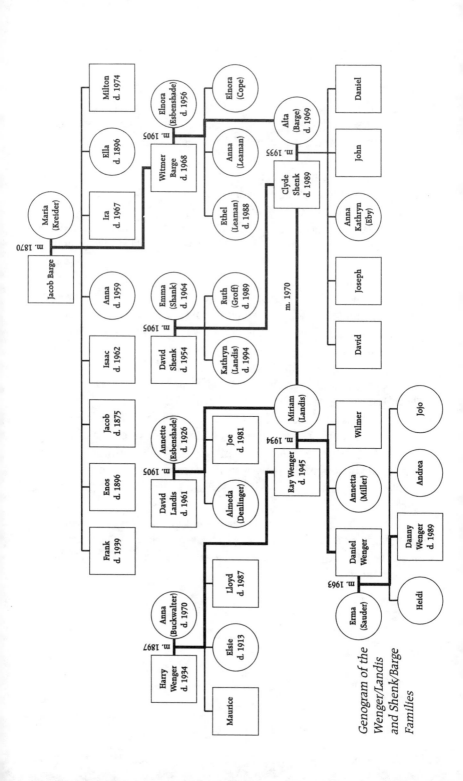

Genogram of the Wenger/Landis and Shenk/Barge Families

BOOK ONE

Old Voices
Beginnings

1.

Missionaries

"We shall not all die, but we shall all be changed. . ."
    —I Corinthians 15:51 (NEB)

Out to Africa

Half a century before Danny Wenger's death in Nicaragua, his grandparents, Ray and Miriam Wenger, were rookie Mennonite missionaries, discovering a slice of the world beyond their eastern Pennsylvania homeland.

The work song the men were singing sounded to Miriam like *"Oscar rom da veta hoot."* They were off-loading the *S.S. Njassa*, a German ship, docked at Port Sudan on the Red Sea. Their Islamic clothing looked to her like dresses cut off at the knees. Pity and care welled up in Miriam's heart for these black men carrying freight on their backs. They looked so thin and worn and humble as they sang their mournful song under those heavy loads. How helpless she felt as she watched from the *Njassa's* deck high above them. She could do nothing to lessen their burden, couldn't even understand a word of their strange language.

Miriam was hearing so many strange languages on her journey—German, Italian, and Arabic in Algiers and Tangier, Portuguese in Lisbon. She couldn't understand or even read any of it. Miriam began to think of her friend Alta Shenk who had preceded her to Africa. Alta had already been in Africa for two years. Certainly by now she would be able to understand an African tongue, be able to tell Africans about Jesus.

This day, the day of the laboring black men singing their unintelligible lament, was Alta's 26th birthday, March 24, 1938. On March 26 Miriam would be 24. "Perhaps, in another year, we can celebrate our birthdays together," Miriam breathed in a silent prayer.

Two years earlier, Ray and Miriam had decided not to go to Clyde and Alta Shenk's commissioning and farewell service at Millersville Mennonite Church near Lancaster, Pennsylvania. The missionary spirit was at a fever level among Lancaster Conference Mennonites. Many young couples were wondering if they would be called; wondering what they would say if they were called.

Miriam wanted to keep a level head about this. She was afraid that the emotionalism of the packed church, the stirring testimonies, powerful preaching, rousing singing, and the finality of the commission being laid on the Shenk couple would confuse the quiet voice of the Spirit in her heart. She didn't want to go. She didn't tell Ray why. Maybe he felt the same way. He agreed that they wouldn't go. They spent that evening quietly together in the upstairs sitting room of their home.

The confident enthusiasm with which Lancaster Mennonites sent out the missionaries had been building for a generation. This was a youth movement, drawing its direction and energy largely from men and women who were not ordained. The official church leaders were men chosen by the "lot" and they were ordained for life.

In the 1890s, Lancaster Mennonites were mostly of Swiss-German background. Their knock-about language was Pennsylvania Dutch; they worshiped–singing, praying, and preaching–in German. A strong youth movement began encouraging singing in English. Then there was English preaching at evening services, attracting young people in droves. Sunday schools, in English and held on Sunday afternoons, became tremendously popular. Young people began to experience "personal salvation" and sympathetic pastors began to baptize them into church membership, while they were still teenagers and before they got married. Then when they did marry, many wanted their marriages to be in church instead of in homes and on lawns as before. Lancaster Mennonite young people also developed consciences against the raising of tobacco, their parents' main cash crop.

Institutions and publications were springing up to service the new day–a publishing house, English hymn books, church newspapers, Sunday school quarterlies, colleges, mission and service societies. Later women's societies formed under the guise of sewing circles. Still later church grade schools and high schools were opened. It was a wild and wonderful time, this unleashing of youthful energy in the service of the church.

The old, established leaders became a little nervous about all the changes. In the old days when married couples joined church–often two or three years after the wedding–the woman would put away her jewelry and her English, or non-Mennonite, clothing and begin to dress in the plain Swiss-German, Mennonite style.

No one, or no group of people, sat down and figured this out, but as the missionary fervor increased, the youth movement and the ordained leadership developed an accommodation which dictated that young girls would begin to dress plain as soon as they were "saved" or went forward in a revival meeting. It soon developed that boys and men, if they were serious about their relationship to the church, would also dress plain (a collarless coat, buttoned at the neck) after baptism. This putting on of plain clothing by the youth involved in the exciting new revival movement kept the bond of trust intact between the young people and the official church leadership.

* * *

It happened as Ray and Miriam had each silently and privately expected. One afternoon about a year after the Shenks had sailed for Africa, the phone rang. Miriam, at home alone, answered. Henry Garber, president of Eastern Mennonite Board of Missions, wanted to know when Ray would be home from work. Henry wanted to see them about something.

Later that afternoon, in the living room of the Wenger home, Henry Garber explained the situation. The fledgling Mennonite Mission in Tanganyika was now three years old. Four stations had been opened, about a dozen missionaries were at work, and the mission's finances had become a big mess. The accounts had to be straightened out and maintained properly.

Ray's academic training was in accounting. His accounting work at Armstrong Floor Coverings (now Armstrong World Industries) was flawless. Ray would be ordained and would be the pastor in charge of one of the mission stations. He would also be charged with the responsibility of treasurer of the Tanganyika Mennonite Mission.

Picture them, then, on February 23, 1938, standing in their blue-black Mennonite garb against the railing of the enormous passenger liner, the *S.S. Queen Mary.* They smiled and waved to the crowds of Mennonite well-wishers dockside below. Tiny, muscled tugboats strained to slip the three-stacked behemoth backward out of its Manhattan berth into the Hudson River.

Neither Ray nor Miriam Wenger, nor anyone else, considered that they might be too young to be sent off into the unknown–too inexperienced, too untrained. Miriam, tall, slender, black-haired, shy, head bowed slightly downward to the left, noticed everything. Her dark, smiling eyes saw, remembered each upturned face. A strong bond of love and trust bound her–the open faced, guileless girl-woman high at the deck railing–to the dark-clad Mennonites on the wharf.

Ray was 27, starched, erect, athletic with a boyish grin on his face–a banker who knew his accounts, a straight arrow, that smiling face unclouded by ambiguity–no puzzlement with him.

An air of finality hung in the widening space between ship and well-wishers. Ray and Miriam had promised that, if God so willed, they would be missionaries–for life. This commitment, like their marriage vows, allowed no turning back.

That night, out on the Atlantic Ocean, Miriam wrote in her diary, "At about 11:30 a.m. our final farewell service was held and Abe

Martin, Sem Eby, Menno Brunk, Amos Rutt, Aaron Groff, and Uncle Landis spoke, followed by Ray and me. I spoke on 'The Love of Christ Constraineth Us' and 'To Them That Believe, He Is Precious,' and indeed He is."

Being farewelled in the *Queen Mary's* crowded tourist-class library by speeches from six men felt intense and wearying, and so it was. Yet this was similar to what Ray and Miriam had been experiencing since the evening of Henry Garber's visit.

To get some Bible training, they were enrolled in Eastern Mennonite College for the 1937 fall semester. The semester ended in January, but they got so busy outfitting and packing and visiting churches and friends that they didn't go back to school after the Christmas break.

During the 53 days from New Year's Day 1938 to departure, they had church appointments on the average of one every two days and as many farewell dinners in homes.

Their tiny tourist-class cabin on the *Queen Mary* overflowed with reminders of the interested, praying friends and relatives they had left behind–five bouquets of flowers, for example, and lots of candy, cookies, nuts, even celery, plus cards and letters, many with dates on the envelopes stipulating when the letter was to be opened.

The world was big in 1938. It would be 47 traveling days before Ray and Miriam would meet Clyde and Alta Shenk in Tanganyika. Miriam loved the stormy winter crossing of the North Atlantic–salted spume of seawater flying; sliding tables, chairs, and dishes in the dining hall; staggering, jerky sea-legs bumping into other passengers and things.

The formal Sunday Episcopal worship service in the cabin-class lounge left Miriam cold. Back in their tiny cabin, she asked Ray for a sermon which for text he chose, merriment in his eyes, "Young women should be sober" (Titus 2:4).

England was different from Lancaster County but not so different as to be beyond the reach of Miriam's experience. "People eat backwards," she observed, "wear high hats, carry canes, and sell flowers on almost every street corner. I wonder," she asked herself over the crown jewels on display in the Tower of London, "how beautiful heaven must be with all its gold and precious stones."

Sailing from Southhampton on the German liner, *S.S. Njassa*, moved the young couple into a world radically different from anything they had experienced before. Miriam especially felt this distance. She had decided to follow Christ. She was committed to serving others, and she wanted to witness to everyone that Jesus saves from sin and futility. Yet, how in the world would she do this? Even on shipboard the white people were talking German and acting differently from anything she had experienced before. How ever would she relate to Africans? The way through, she began to find, was to pray about it. She tried to notice the good and beautiful that was mixed in with all the other stuff.

About the passengers and crew on the *Njassa*, she lamented, "There is much drinking and smoking. Most of them are German. They are so impolite and just stare and stare at us. We don't mind their staring, though, because we can very easily tell by their countenances and actions that they are not Christians and do not know the Lord. When we retired, it sounded as though half of them were drunk. Dear Lord, send the revival fire down upon this world that these souls might be saved. Give us a greater prayer burden for them."

They went ashore in Algiers, Algeria. "Many shops sold pastries which . . . made one's mouth water," Miriam noted. "We saw Arabs, Muslims," she continued. "The women were dressed in all white–faces covered except for the eyes. In the shops we saw lovely dress materials. Dirty men were lying sleeping in the streets and doorsteps with little or no clothing on. One fish market smelled simply terrible. Toilets were open right out on the streets. Poor people sat in the streets begging. Oh, God, help these people to know Thee as Thou art."

It was 1938 and Hitler's Germany was preparing for what would become World War II. The young couple steaming every day farther from the safety of their Lancaster home could feel from passengers and crew the fearful intensity of the German will to dominate the earth. One day in the area of the Mediterranean Sea north of Egypt, a German battleship came into view over the horizon. In awed respect, the *Njassa* stilled its engines. All on board crowded to the

side and sang patriotic songs as the battleship passed. One day it
was announced that Germany had annexed Austria. Again everyone stood at attention and sang patriotic songs extolling the
Fatherland.

Miriam was with child, in her first trimester. She and Ray hadn't
told anyone. They didn't want their parents to worry or make a
fuss. On those mornings when she couldn't face the dining room
with its heavy German fare, Ray would bring a tray of selected foods
to their cabin, and her heart would overflow with love and tenderness for this strong, sensitive man who was husband to her. And
she would breathe a quiet prayer (for such things were not spoken
aloud) of thanksgiving and praise to the Lord for His wonderful
goodness to her.

As the *Njassa* steamed south around the Horn of Africa toward
the Equator, the weather got hotter. How hot would it be living in
Africa? The missionaries began to wear their sun helmets whenever they were on deck–even when they were under the ship's can-
vas awning.

The drunkenness of the Germans got on Miriam's nerves. There
was very little fresh water on board. It was difficult to get even a
bucket of fresh water for bathing and shampooing, let alone laundry. Yes, life on the *Njassa* was getting even older than it had been.
One afternoon during siesta time, Miriam took to relieving the
tedium by trying to kick Ray from the bunk bed above her. After
three shots from below, Ray called for a ceasefire.

On March 31 about 4:30 p.m. the *S.S. Njassa* tied up to a wharf
in Mombasa Harbor, Kenya. "To Ray and me," Miriam exclaimed,
"it was an experience that never will be forgotten! Before us was
Africa and this was the port where we were to leave ship and begin
our travels inland to Mugango which would be our future station."

Getting off the *Njassa* and onto the train in Mombasa in 1938
was like getting back into England. "We had a lovely two-passenger
sleeper compartment all to ourselves!" Miriam exulted. "During
the night we were to climb 4,000 feet as we traveled 300 miles
inland to Nairobi, Kenya's capital.

"Before long a steward passed along the hallway outside our
compartment, striking a gong announcing dinner in the dining car.

Imagine our surprise when we discovered the dining car to offer the traditional five-course English dinner served on tables covered with damask tablecloths and set with china and silverware, no flatware but silver engraved with the moniker EARH for East African Railways and Harbors. Each table was graced by a small bouquet of carnations. This was our introduction to colonial Africa, from the European perspective.

"After dinner the steward brought bed rolls and made up our bunks for us. That night we affirmed with the Apostle Paul, 'He hath done exceeding abundantly more than we were able to ask or think!' Our hearts were so full of joy just to know that we were nearing our field of labor that we found sleeping rather difficult.

"Morning found us puffing across the Athi River plains east of Nairobi. We could lower the glass in our window to get a clearer view of the passing herds of zebra, antelope, gazelle, scattered giraffe, and occasional coveys of guinea foul and partridge.

"Leaving Nairobi, the train continued to climb to about 8,000 feet before dropping off into the Lake Victoria basin. It was dusk as we pulled into Kisumu, Kenya's lakeport, 3,200 feet above sea level.

"Arrangements had been made to have us met by an African Inland Mission (AIM) missionary, a Mr. Skoda, an American.

"Mr. Skoda had a rickety car with a canvas-covered back where Ray crawled in among our stowed luggage. It was dark by the time we pulled out onto the dirt road. It rained terrifically on the way up to the AIM Ogada Mission, situated in the tropical forest up on the escarpment to the north of Kisumu. Such a rainstorm I never saw; lightning flashed, hail dropped, but above all the rain poured. We all got wet but Ray especially got soaked in his Mennonite suit which he had worn for our arrival in the missionary world. He was all rumpled and wet when we pulled up in front of the Skoda home. Mr. Skoda just laughed about the rain. I was impressed that he must be adjusted.

"Mrs. Skoda showed us to our room. Soon we had bathed–in a large tub with plenty of hot water(!), changed into dry clothing and enjoyed a delicious meal with fellow Americans.

"When morning dawned it was beautiful and we found it hard to realize that we were in Africa. The scenery was simply gorgeous.

In the distance to the south, we could see Kisumu Bay, an extended arm of the lake, with the town nestled around the eastern end of the bay. All around the Skoda home were lawns, flowers, fruit trees, shade trees. A large brick church dominated the compound of scattered buildings.

"I believe Africa is about the most beautiful spot in the whole wide world, but then it should look good to us for it is here that the Lord has called us.

"It was Sunday that first day we were at Ogada Mission and we eagerly looked forward to worshiping in a church with other evangelical Christians–a first since leaving home a month and a half ago. As it turned out, we couldn't understand a thing–singing, Scripture reading, prayers, exhortations, all were in a tongue of which we couldn't understand a word. How I longed to know what people were saying! I felt as though I was blind.

"During the several days we were at Ogada it seemed routine that I could not eat breakfast. Maybe it was partly the 4,000 foot altitude. One morning I was sitting on the veranda after Ray and Mr. Skoda had left to attend to errands in Kisumu. Dear Mrs. Skoda brought a tray of breakfast to me–poached egg, toast, jam, and coffee. I enjoyed that very much and my heart went out in love to this woman, veteran missionary, and I wondered how it would be with me as over the coming years, for me too, this land would become home.

"We were at Ogada Mission a week. On Saturday afternoon we boarded the lake steamer for an overnight voyage south to Musoma in Tanganyika. We were to dock at the Musoma wharf at about noon on Sunday. I was not able to go with Ray to breakfast that morning, but I was up on deck watching the scenery. The steamer was sailing along not far offshore. The farther we sailed, the more apprehensive I felt. Musoma-land was a lot different from Kisumu. The climate was drier, fewer trees, no escarpments in the distance, just scrubby hills pocked with granite boulders.

"As we pulled into the Musoma wharf, the breezeless noonday felt hot and oppressive. The inability to understand any of the shouted noises of arrival and docking filled me with even greater despair. Was this it? Was this place to be hometown for me, for Ray, and for our child? There were no white faces in the crowd swarming about dockside. That is better, I thought, that no one is here to meet us for surely I would weep.

"Then Ray joined me, and my spirit brightened. Soon we saw John Leatherman pushing his way through the crowd, shirt sleeved, waving, beaming beneath his sun helmet. John's casual attire made us feel strange and over-dressed: me in Mennonite cape dress and black stockings, prayer covering with strings, and Ray in his buttoned Mennonite coat over white long sleeved shirt. That moment of waved greeting soon passed and we became busy with our bags–porters carrying things out to the mission's pickup truck.

"Soon we were on our way along a dirt, rain-soaked road to the Bukiroba Station where John and Catherine Leatherman lived. The station, six miles east of Musoma, is on a hillside overlooking Mara Bay. The lake-view from the station is beautiful.

"Catherine had a delicious dinner waiting for us. In the afternoon Clyde and Alta Shenk came from their station, Bumangi, eighteen miles inland from Bukiroba. Their firstborn, David, at eleven months, was a lively crawler, as was Leatherman's year-old daughter, Lois. Africa must be the place for children, I thought. I could see that Alta was expecting another child in a few months. It was good to be with the Shenks again. As we sat there in the Leatherman living room recalling past times, we could almost think that we were back in Lancaster County."

Both of these Mennonite couples were married in 1905. David and
Annette (Esbenshade) Landis (above) had not yet been baptized or become
members of the church. (They were the parents of Miriam Landis Wenger.)
Witmer and Elnora (Esbenshade) Barge (facing page), had been baptized
and joined the church. (They were the parents of Alta Barge Shenk.) These
wedding photos demonstrate the struggles many Mennonite young people
were having during those years with the question of plain dress.

This photo of the David and Annette Landis family in 1917, twelve years after their wedding, shows how much their style of dress changed after they joined the church. They are seen with their three children: (Left to right) Miriam, Almeda, and Joe.

The Witmer and Elnora (Ella) Barge family in 1935. (Left to right) Anna, Ethel, Witmer, Elnora, Ella, and Alta. This photo was taken around the time of Alta's wedding to Clyde Shenk, less than a year before she left for Africa.

Clyde and Alta Shenk (above) on their wedding day in 1935. Ray and Miriam Wenger (below) before leaving for Africa in 1938. These young people were deeply affected by a strong missionary movement among Lancaster County Mennonites in the 1930s. Within several years after their respective weddings, both couples made commitments to become missionaries for life. They served together in Tanganyika (later Tanzania).

Mugango

*Ray and Miriam arrived at their new home, the
Mugango mission station, near the end of April 1938.*

The first order of business for the new missionaries was to visit
the stations of the Mennonite Mission. There were four in 1938.

First Ray and Miriam visited the Shirati station to the north of
Bukiroba and located on a long, sloping hillside a mile back from
the lake. Although only some 30 miles away, this northern station
was hard to get to from Bukiroba because of rivers and lake bays.
After trying for several days by car, they gave up. High water had
made the river crossings impassable.

So the Wengers went to Shirati by dhow, an Arab-type sailboat.
The dhow left Musoma Town in the evening and was to arrive at
the Shirati jetty by early the next morning. But they were becalmed
that morning while still some distance from Shirati. Miriam was
the only woman on the dhow. There were no on-board toilet facili-
ties which posed no problem for the men who seemed to be everywhere. It soon got hot under the tin roof which provided the
dhow's only shelter. Miriam's usual morning sickness grew to full
pitch. Terrified of making a white-woman scene in that black man's
world, she sat very still and munched on some dry biscuits and,
somehow, managed to hold onto both bladder and stomach until a
breeze picked up and took them to land.

After Shirati they returned to Bukiroba by road, visiting Clyde
and Alta's station, inland from the lake, some eighteen miles
southeast of Bukiroba. "We had such good meals at Bumangi,"
Miriam wrote, "but I guess they were no better than the ones we
enjoyed at Bukiroba and Shirati. One thing that I liked very much
was boiled peanuts, raw freshly harvested peanuts, boiled in the
shells in salt water, then shelled at the table and eaten."

While they were at Bumangi, John and Catherine Leatherman
and year-old Lois had been invited out from Bukiroba for David
Shenk's first birthday party. Miriam baked and decorated the cake.
"One of the dishes Alta was having was baked fish and just as she
was calling us to supper, the African cook let the whole thing crash

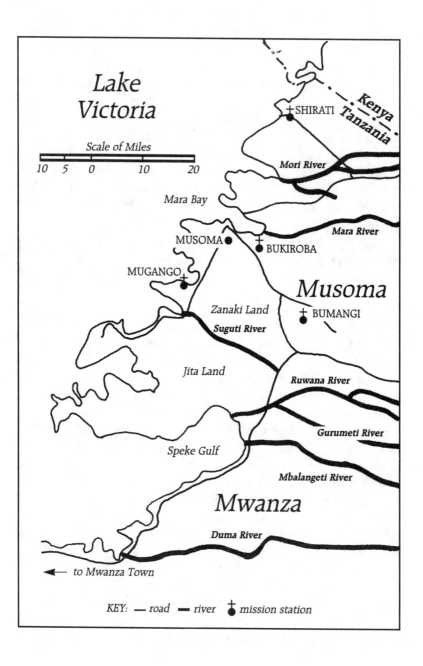

to the concrete floor," Miriam wrote. "Alta was almost heartbroken, but we had plenty without it. Clyde scooped up what he thought didn't have glass in it so we still had a taste."

After visiting Bukiroba, Shirati, and Bumangi, Miriam was beginning to feel that she could handle living in Musoma District. "It is far more beautiful and nice," she confided to her sister, "than I expected it would be. The roads are fairly good. We were surprised to see how nice the missionary homes are. We found that they have window panes in all the Bumangi windows and, by the way, I hear most of the stations are putting them in. Stauffers at Mugango don't have them yet. The floors are of cement and the walls are the color of mud for that is what they are, sun-dried, earthen brick plastered with mud. The outside is white-washed and is very clean looking and cool. The roofs are of corrugated, galvanized iron sheeting. Ceilings are of celetex to protect against the sun's heat on the roof. They are quite livable and I know I shall like our little mud house."

Miriam also wrote to her sister, describing what it was like relating to the Africans. "Folks from home write and ask us how we feel. Some think that the foreign missionary makes such a great sacrifice. But thus far we have not found it so. Home ties do tug at the heart strings, yet overall the Lord has been exceedingly faithful.

"All the missionaries are jolly," was her observation. "They have a sense of humor."

Even though several months pregnant, Miriam was enjoying motoring over the dirt roads. "We have a Ford pickup truck with one front seat and the back bed," she wrote. "You should see us when we go on safari. Three get in the front seat and usually there are two Europeans—all white folk are 'European' in Africa—to sit on the back bed. Natives usually want to go along and sometimes the entire back is full of people. It is one grand merry ride too. Over bounces, through streams and mud holes, stopping until the cattle and goats decide to move off the road to let you pass, and then away we go until our final destination is reached."

Soon it was time for the new missionary couple to be taken to their future home, Mugango. This fourth and most recently opened station was eighteen miles south of Musoma Town.

Mugango was on Lake Victoria, set back a half mile from the Mugango Bay.

While the four mission stations–Shirati, Bukiroba, Mugango, and Bumangi–were located in an area just 40 miles across, they were home to four different ethnic groups, four different languages. Shirati was located among the Luo people. The Luo were a Nilotic people whose ancient roots were in the southern Sudan. The other three stations were located among Bantu peoples whose ancient roots were in West Africa. The people around Bukiroba were Roba, those around Bumangi were Zanaki, and those around Mugango were Ruri. (Later a fifth station was opened, Nyabasi, inland from Shirati, among the Kuria, also a Bantu people.)

Nowhere else in East Africa were so many ethnic groups found in such a small area. A slightly larger circle on the map, say 100 miles, brought even more ethnic groups into the picture–the Jita, Ikoma, Nata, Ngurimi, Issenyi, Simbiti. Why were the Mennonites building mission stations in Musoma District? And why was a mission station being built at Mugango?

* * *

In 1934 Musoma District was the only populated area in Tanganyika where no Protestant mission agency was working. The area was shunned by the Lutherans, Episcopalians, and African Inland Mission (AIM) because there were too many different kinds of people in such a small area. Not that the area was overpopulated in 1934, no. Only some fifteen percent of the land was cultivated at any one time. It was just that every several miles a different ethnic group spoke a different language and expressed its own unique traditional faith and culture.

The agency in the coastal capital city, Dar es Salaam, whose business it was to assign territory to missions, urged the Mennonites to take Musoma District. And God must have smiled. Imagine a regional Mennonite Church assembly, say Lancaster Conference's annual general meeting, where the delegates came from a dozen different ethnic groups. Certainly God's eye twinkled when the peace church Mennonites sent to "spy out the land" headed out of Dar es Salaam for Musoma District.

The Wengers were going to the Mugango location because the Mennonite Mission had received 41 baptized Christians, scores of unbaptized believers, and eight little bush schools (grades one and two or one to four) from the African Inland Mission (AIM). This gift to the Mennonites lay out the back door, so to speak, of the Mugango station.

By the time the Mennonites arrived in 1934, the Tanganyika AIM missionaries had been evangelizing for 30 years among the Sukuma people, a large "tribe" south of Lake Victoria. Mwanza, a lake-port and rail terminal, was the hub of their work. Through the efforts of African teachers and evangelists, the AIM work had grown northward from Mwanza into the area south of Mugango. So, although there were no missionaries living in the area, there were AIM churches in Musoma District among the Jita people, whose territory bordered the Ruri people surrounding Mugango. It seemed to both the AIM and Mennonite missionaries that these Christians in Musoma District should become Mennonites.

Letters to Eastern Mennonite Board of Missions from the leader of the Mennonite Mission at Mugango, Elam Stauffer, explained what was happening:

> July, 1936: The Jita-land field will be taken over for care upon our entering Mugango but it becomes quite evident that much of the final deciding will be done by the natives themselves. They constantly accuse the AIM missionaries for selling them to the Mennonites, and since they see no personal advantage in changing, they feel sure there must have been an ulterior motive in it. We are trying to go cautiously and leave nothing for them to hang their suspicion on and the final outcome remains to be seen.

> October, 1936: From July 31 to August 5 Mr. Sywulka (the Mwanza-based AIM leader, an American and a "Defenseless Mennonite") and I were in Jita-land together telling the natives of our plans and asking the schools separately what their desire is. I took the names of all 41 Christians and many unbaptized believers and from then on they are considered to be under our care. As

soon as the work at Mugango is under way, there will need to be some more work done in this field. It is a very promising field of over 22,000 people.

Earlier in 1935: On the border of Mugango and Jita-land is a tsetse fly belt about fifteen miles wide running inland from the lake. Few natives live in the tsetse fly belt. The tsetse are the carrier insect for the deadly sleeping sickness. It is felt that the Mugango mission station is well located relative to the people in Jita-land to be cared for.

* * *

While Mugango was just eighteen miles from supplies and mail in Musoma Town and easily accessible even by bicycle over the dirt road, Ray Wenger's primary mission focus was to be among the former AIM Christians in Jita-land, fifteen miles beyond Mugango on the other side of the tsetse fly zone.

In 1990 looking back across half a century of time, Miriam remembered the Mugango mission station as a place of mosquitoes, biting ants, and baboons. Her life would be profoundly shaped there–a place she would grow to love.

Two large granite outcroppings–large enough to be called mountains–stood as sentinels, looking northward across Mugango Bay. The 35-acre Mugango mission station compound lay between them. Like a slung hammock, the land sloped gently from each mountain's base toward the center of the space between them. Driving to Mugango from the main road, one came around the base of Mt. Chamakaya. Mt. Nyangoma, on the other side of the compound, was where the baboons lived. Local folklore had a story about the baboons.

"Long, long ago," the myth declared, "an old, old woman lived on Nyangoma, the baboon mountain. In fact, she was a witch, an embodied evil spirit. Her eyes were pussy and scabbed. One day she summoned the local clan of people and asked them to pass before her one by one. She asked each one as they came before her to restore her sight by licking her eyes clean. Each person in turn refused. Finally one man accepted to do as she wished. Then the old woman enriched this man and his family. She established them as the Ruri clan in that area and made them very rich. Everyone else she turned into baboons."

The tsetse fly zone began just behind the Nyangoma Mountain. The baboons would flee for refuge into the tsetse fly zone whenever they were attacked.

Miriam and Ray moved to Mugango at the end of April 1938. Three missionaries were already living on the 35-acre compound–Elam and Elizabeth Stauffer and Phebe Yoder. Three buildings had been constructed–a grass thatched church which doubled as a school room, a two-room house where Phebe lived, and the Stauffer's two-bedroom house. Ray and Miriam moved in with the Stauffers. All five missionaries had their meals together in the Stauffer house.

Elizabeth, with African servants, managed the household. Phebe, a registered nurse, taught in the little primary school and ran a small clinic. Elam did church work and the Wengers studied Swahili.

Miriam had thought Mr. Skoda at Kisumu to be "adjusted" when he made light of the soaking they had endured inside his rickety car. The time had now come for Miriam to become adjusted to Mugango. What an adventure that would be!

Mission policy required that new missionaries spend at least five hours a day studying Swahili until they passed the first and second exams. Then they were allowed to vote in mission business meetings. They were required to continue to spend three hours a day until the third and final exam had been passed.

In the beginning, Swahili seemed impossibly difficult. Everything was book work, no African tutors. After three months of effort, Miriam's journal still cried out, "Swahili, Swahili, Swahili! Where art thou? Not in my head anyway."

But slowly, slowly the new language took shape in their minds. The first exam consisted of twenty questions on grammar, eighty entences of English to be translated into Swahili, twenty sentences from Swahili to English, fifteen sentences translated orally into Swahili and taken down by the examiner, and fifteen sentences read by a native to be translated into English. "The latter for me was the hardest," Miriam wrote, "but the grammar part I enjoyed."

Elam administered and scored the exam. Both Ray and Miriam passed this first exam on their first try. Success put the missionaries into a celebrative mood. Elam and Miriam were natural vocalists. Ray could not carry a tune. That evening, Elam and Miriam got out the Mennonite *Life Songs #2* and sang and sang with Elizabeth and Ray as their audience. They sang by the light of the kerosene lamp until nearly 11:00 p.m.

When Miriam wasn't studying Swahili, she practiced it in Phebe's school. This led to her first experience with a jigger.

"I had a rather sore toe but I did not know what ailed the dumb thing," she wrote. "Since I had been in the school daily in all that dust, I thought it might be a jigger. But it did not feel quite like a jigger was described to feel. Visitors from the home board were coming, and I didn't want to be hobbling around when they were here, so at bedtime on the day before the guests were to arrive, I asked Ray to look at my swollen toe.

"Ray watched while I stuck a needle into the toe along the edge of the nail. Some watery juice came out. We thought that was it, and Ray went to get the iodine bottle. While he was getting the bottle, I accidentally stuck the head of the needle under the toenail and there, behold, was a nest of hundreds of jigger eggs. I picked and picked and squeezed and squeezed, and still jigger eggs came forth. Two hours later, I thought it was time to stop, and went to bed with a small hole where the dirty things came from."

An already short night was to be further interrupted. Phebe's house was invaded. At about 3:00 a.m. Phebe awoke, startled, unable to figure out why she was awake. Then she felt something on her arm and reached for her flashlight to see if she had brought a bed bug home with her from one of her visits in local homes.

"Light on the subject revealed along the top of my mosquito net, down the side and across my pillow, a safari of quite large black ants," Phebe wrote. "My first thought was, 'Well, praise the Lord that they are not biting ants!' First I thought that I would put my pillow at the other end of my bed and try it until morning. But there were so many that I decided to vacate the bed. No sooner had my feet touched the floor than I realized that my little house was full of them, and I soon discovered that they were biting ants.

"They may be on your body five minutes or more before they start tasting, although they have no set of by-laws regulating their actions. Sometimes they wait until they reach your head to grab a hold. I opened my door and flashed the light about. Behold, I saw numbers of roads and crossroads heavily laden with ant traffic.

"I decided to call Bro. Stauffer and see whether it would be wise to start war or peaceably vacate. Soon everyone was up and we saw that the ants were at the doors and windows of Stauffer's house too. There was no way to get them out of my house, but Ray and Elam brought dry grass and burned it at the door steps of their house to keep them out. Hot ashes or fire seem to be the only check on their travels. That house secured, I moved in with the Stauffers and Wengers for the rest of the night. By morning when I went back to my house every ant had left."

That morning–June 23, 1938–someone from Bukiroba brought the Eastern Mennonite Board of Missions deputation visitors to Mugango. This was the first deputation from the Mission Board in the States and, as it turned out, the last official visit for nearly a decade due to the war in Europe which made international travel almost impossible. There were three in the group of visitors–Henry Garber, Eastern Board's chairman, his wife Ada, and Bishop Henry Lutz.

Phebe, a highly motivated, well-trained teacher and nurse, had carefully laid plans in anticipation of the deputation's coming to Mugango and visiting Jita-land. But the premature birth of Joseph Shenk took Phebe off the station at that most crucial time.

* * *

The morning of June 23 dawned with Clyde in bed at Bumangi, down with malaria. The deputation had just been to Bumangi. It had been an intense, busy time–especially for Alta who was eight months pregnant.

About mid-morning, Alta went into labor. She and Clyde, with toddler David, were the only white folks around. Clyde got up, with his 103° fever, packed the pickup, and they set out for Musoma Town where there was a hospital. By the time they got to Bukiroba, labor had progressed to where it seemed unwise to go the remaining six miles to Musoma. They pulled in to the Leatherman house. The mission's builder, Clinton Ferster, took off for Musoma to bring the British doctor.

Clinton found that the British doctor was also down with malaria. So he got the Asian doctor and returned, flying along the dirt road to Bukiroba. In the meantime, the baby's face appeared, strangled and blue. This was caused, the doctor said later, by the umbilical cord being stretched tightly around the baby's neck.

It was a frantic, desperate situation. The missionaries had no idea what to do. Clyde had been praying as he paced helplessly about. Now he left Alta's side and went into John's study where he could see the road. He prayed fervently that when he got to the window he would see the pickup coming up the road, and so it was–trailing a plume of dust.

No one had thought to prepare soap and water for the doctor to wash. He went immediately to work, loosened the cord, bringing a flush of pink to the little face.

"Another two minutes," the doctor said, "and all would not have been well."

Meanwhile, John Leatherman had dashed off in the Bumangi pickup to Mugango to get Phebe Yoder the nurse. He came clattering into the Mugango station, shouting for Phebe to come "as fast as possible." Elizabeth and Miriam packed Phebe's suitcase for her "any old way" and in less than ten minutes, Phebe and John were off.

* * *

That evening the missionaries at Mugango and their deputation guests were wondering if the ants would come back. Safari ants are known to strike three nights in a row.

"Just about dark we went out with our flashlights to check on what was happening," Miriam wrote with a grin, to her sister. "Here they were coming back full force. This was something new for our guests and they didn't seem to sense the need of keeping out of harm's way. I wish you could have seen it. We all laughed until tears came. The two Henrys were walking around with their flashlights when suddenly, up to the knees went one of Lutz's pant legs, then both of Garber's. Sometimes they had both hands in their pockets so they could, with a little more modesty, get these crawling, biting creatures. Finally they both walked out into the darkness where they could get these pests in privacy.

"Elam and Ray secured the houses as they had done the night before by burning grass around the outside along the foundations. After supper, we made ready for bed. Elam and Ray set up cots on the screened porch. Elizabeth and I took the Stauffer bedroom, the Garbers had our bedroom, and Bro. Lutz went over to Phebe's vacant house.

"Before long a high wind and rainstorm came up and this, of course, made our boys move off the porch. In the excitement, Ray upset his basin of water and had a wet pair of pajamas in which to sleep."

It was mission policy that mission funds be used to put glass in only the dining room and office windows. Any additional glass was the expense of the individual missionaries. Elam and Elizabeth, being the missionary leaders, were toughing it out and had not bought glass for their bedroom windows.

"The poor visitors didn't know what to do," Miriam continued. "The wind blew the rain in the windows full force and wet Henry Garber's bed and clothes. Finally he came to the door so helpless in his pajamas and said, 'Elizabeth, what shall I do? It's wet in here!' She quickly went in and lowered the storm curtain while Elam ran across to Phebe's house where Bro. Lutz was sleeping to help him out of his troubles, for he had the string in a knot that lowered the rain curtain by his bedroom window.

"Ray and I think now that the Mission Board will decide that glass should be put in all the windows at mission expense.

"The next morning I asked Bro. Lutz how he had slept, and he said, 'Fear hath torment' (I John 4:18), showing that his rest was none too sweet.

"The following day, all the men pulled out for Jita-land," Miriam wrote. They spent the weekend there visiting the churches received from AIM. On Monday the Fersters came from Bukiroba to take the delegation back with them.

For a final experience before their return to Bukiroba, a hunting trip for the purpose of gathering meat had been arranged. It was a party of nine–the Garbers, Stauffers, Fersters, Wengers, and Brother Lutz.

They left about one o'clock in the afternoon in two pickup trucks. By about four o'clock, they began seeing animals grazing on the plains. They shot two Thompson's gazelles, a topi, a zebra, and a wildebeest. On the way home, they shot three rabbits by the lights of the car's headlights. Ray Wenger described the expedition in a letter and concluded by saying, "So we had eight animals in all, and plenty of meat."

"Eight animals," Miriam wrote, "meant that Elizabeth and I had quite a chore canning and preserving it. The meat almost stuck out our eyes! We did five pressure cookers full and gave the natives a lot besides as well as cut up a lot for drying.

"It is amazing to me what the natives eat," she continued. "The stomachs and intestines of a freshly killed animal are a delicacy for them. The staple food for the people here is a heavy mush and dried fish. They use meat when they can get it. Fruits, sugar, salt are considered *maridadi*–ornamental or nonessential."

* * *

At Bukiroba Henry Lutz came down with a malicious strand of malaria. For a while his recovery was in doubt. He was laid up for three weeks. The departure of the deputation had to be pushed back because he was unable to travel.

Before the deputation's departure for the States, a baptism service was held at Bukiroba. After the Sunday morning service, everyone walked a mile down to the lake where Elam baptized four believers. It was quite a procession going to the lake with everyone singing. A man walking beside Phebe confided, "Nurse Yoder, this makes much joy in my heart. It seems that we are walking right on to heaven this morning." In her own heart Phebe was thinking of the joy it would be to march through the pearly gates among a group of "our dear African brothers and sisters."

That afternoon at Bukiroba, there was a communion service and Elam Stauffer was ordained as bishop over the Tanganyika work. Phebe wrote, "Since this was the first ordination service our people had ever seen, they were much interested and deeply impressed. Will you remember to faithfully pray for our bishop? There are many problems and heavy responsibilities resting upon the shepherd of a flock in this land."

Henry Garber's parting comment to the Wengers was that they would sink or swim. At about that same time, Elam and Elizabeth Stauffer returned to the States for a furlough. This left Phebe and the Wengers in charge of the station work at Mugango.

What did it feel like to be young, inexperienced, and in charge? At first it was mostly a matter of the missionaries and Africans getting to know each other and of developing ways to communicate.

"Since the deputation has left, we have had the experience of being in charge of the station here at Mugango," Ray wrote in a prayer letter. "Because of the impossibility of depending on another missionary to interpret for us, we have been forced to use the Swahili we know, which is still limited. The Africans with whom we speak exercise great patience and certainly fulfill their part in helping us assemble words into thoughts. Once when I wanted to use the word 'shelter' (kibanda) I said 'ulcer' (kidonda).

"These folks, although unable to read or write, are keen observers of people, especially of Europeans," Ray continued. "They will, whenever the opportunity is theirs, put the new missionary to the test–the test of patience, of judgement, of discipline, and of love toward them. After they have completed their observations, the evening campfire finds them gathered around deeply absorbed in the conversation of their new findings of what these strange people will or will not do. To our dismay, they speak in the Jita vernacular which we cannot understand even in part.

"Once they were conversing in Swahili about white people. Maybe they had the intention of being overheard. They were discussing heads. 'They think that Africans have hard heads,' the Africans said of us missionaries. 'Heads that are good for carrying heavy loads. Hard heads don't get tired, neither do they feel the sun. The white man's head does feel the sun so he wears a big hat. When we are in school, the white people think we can't learn well because of our hard heads. They think we are good for doing work like carrying heavy loads and building houses.'"

Teaching in the little Mugango primary school helped Miriam to get to know some Africans. She sensed that teaching would be the way to win them for Christ and train them in Christian ways. "How we yearn to be able to reach these dear children," Miriam wrote for the prayer letter. "Their little round, dusky faces are a real challenge to us to be diligent in our language study. As they look up into our faces with bright shining eyes, they seem to say, 'Make haste with the Gospel story, we have not heard it yet.' Unless it is taught them and unless they accept of His precious atoning blood, their souls will be lost. Pray for these precious ones, that they might be enlightened and made to be partakers of the joy, peace and satisfaction of living that you and I are enjoying daily. When one sees the sin and filth in which these children are living, one can realize in a new aspect the cost of our redemption and its wonderful cleansing power.

"Little Rei, named after Ray Wenger, is a new baby at the native village. He is now less than seven weeks old, and has been a regular attendant at our afternoon school. He does not have a carriage softly blanketed and protected from insects in which he is wheeled to the school room, nor does he have a large layette, but regardless of his limited supply of possessions, he is a happy little fellow and sleeps soundly while tied on the back of Ochere, his little nurse maid, who I think must be about eight years of age. As she sits in her place writing the vowels and numerals on her slate, she gently rocks to and fro in cradle-like manner to keep her charge from disturbing the rest of the group. In spite of his diet of thick, sour milk with an occasional feeding of sweet milk, he is thriving nicely.

"Thirty-eight are enrolled in the school now. They range from Rei, the youngest, to about 40 years of age. They have such cheery faces and their eyes fairly sparkle when their answers are given correctly. Each one who can afford to purchase a slate brings it, but less than half are able to own these, so when the period of writing comes, they bend over and draw the vowels on the dirt floor of the classroom. Still others write on their legs. Any pointed scratcher, such as a dry straw, makes a white mark on their skin. Of course the teacher places a check mark on the leg, too, if the lesson is correctly written. Some of them are quite good artists."

One day during singing class, Miriam tried to "show them how to beat time. Hands flew in all directions. I took one fellow's wrist to get him in the right swing, but when I wanted him to beat to the left, he went to the right. On the upstroke, he went down. I think teaching Western rhythms to Africans is a hopeless endeavor."

October came and Miriam, heavy with child, turned her attention toward preparation for the baby. "I have my sewing just about finished now," she wrote to her sister, "but I didn't make as much as I would have at home lest I should have to be disappointed. I made only what was necessary and no more–three dozen diapers, five shirts, three bands, four kimonos of outing cloth, and about one half dozen outing cloth blankets."

Miriam hadn't told her sister or father that she was expecting until a month before the baby was due. Part of the silence was the natural shyness of that time. People noticed these things by observation, but they were not talked or written about. But part of Miriam's silence was also due to her not wanting her situation to impose any uneasiness on her family. She tried to explain this, somewhat awkwardly, to Almeda, her sister.

"I wrote a letter to Father this evening and told him the news about our expectation next month," Almeda read in the letter she got from Miriam. "Now please don't be provoked that I didn't tell you earlier. You told me before we left home that you were just going to worry and worry, and I did not want to add any more on you, so I did not tell you before, even though I could have before we left the States."

Miriam and Ray went to the mission hospital at Shirati in late October to wait for the arrival of their firstborn. Ray was with Miriam when she gave birth to a son whom they named Daniel Landis. He was born on November 10, a big, healthy baby.

Thinking about going back to Mugango gave Miriam a tired and apprehensive feeling. For one thing, she still hadn't finished language study. And, with Elizabeth Stauffer gone, Miriam now had all the domestic responsibilities. This was pretty scary, especially when there were a lot of missionary guests. Besides that, Elizabeth's African cook had also left Mugango. Miriam would need to find and train new household servants.

Ray's work was also piling up. A second missionary house was to be built at Mugango. This new house would be "the Wenger house." Phebe would move into the old "Stauffer house." Ray was also still studying Swahili. Then, after mastering Swahili, he was supposed to learn the Jita vernacular as well. With Elam gone, he was responsible for the station activities at Mugango, and he needed to make a lot of weekend trips to Jita-land. Besides all that, he was treasurer and accountant for the Mennonite Mission. These responsibilities meant that he had to go to Musoma and Bukiroba from time to time. He was 28 by then, and Miriam was still 24.

But Daniel was born. All was well. And Ray and Miriam had to return to their responsibilities on the Mugango station.

Miriam had begun to see teaching as her mission. Within a week of her return to Mugango, she went back to the school room to teach vowels and sums and to tell the children about Jesus. Her class was scheduled for when Daniel was having his afternoon nap.

Managing the house servants was more difficult than teaching in the school. "Since I have returned," Miriam wrote, "I have had full charge of the kitchen and house servants. It is rather a problem sometimes to know what to cook and how to supervise the servants, two teenage boys. They can be most trying at times. Yesterday when I went out to the kitchen, a room separated from the rest of the house by a breezeway, they had the dust pan on top of the trays they serve our food on. The tea towels they were using looked as though they used them for wash-off cloths.

"One evening after I had given Daniel his bath, I called Chai and told him to empty the tub of water. It was just about supper time, and so he asked if he could use the water to wash the dishes. I told him that I thought it would be better to put it on the newly planted trees instead.

"Sometimes the boys can be most accommodating. Today I sent Chai to the tiny country store down by the main road for salt. I wanted it for dinner because we had baked fish and our other salt was finished. I told him to hurry. He told me that he was tired, but I told him I wouldn't accept that excuse. Imagine my surprise when he returned shortly, having run the whole distance. I should think it was three miles round trip. He came into the kitchen, sweat streaming down his face."

News of the war in Europe gave Miriam the feeling of being cut off. "Mussolini has annexed Ethiopia and threatens to move into Kenya," she wrote. "Tanganyika was a German colony up to the end of the Great War [World War I], and some fear that Hitler plans to retake it. An English government official from Musoma paid us a reassuring visit one afternoon. He then stayed for dinner which really made Chai nervous.

"I used my silverware, of course, and had Chai bring the food. Afterwards he told me, 'Mama, the work is good when it's just you, Pastor, and Daniel. But I am afraid of guests.' The lad always gets excited when we have guests. One time he brought in the bread and then came with his tray full of our dessert. He was very much embarrassed too."

Little Daniel became a bridge, bringing the missionaries and Africans closer together. "Chai says he has much work," Miriam laughed, "because he has to make beds, set the table, do laundry for Daniel everyday, everyday, everyday. The laundry I think he enjoys thoroughly. Today I saw that he had three of his buddies to help him with the diapers. After they were finished, they threw white suds on each other.

"It seems that these black folk have a curiosity about whiteness. Yesterday in school, some of the girls wiped their faces on the whitewashed walls. I thought they looked more like ghosts than anything else. In subtle ways we can feel that there is a warm place for us in the hearts of the youth with whom we interact. Last week Chai said to me, 'Mama, when you and Pastor go to America, leave Daniel here. I'll feed him millet mush, fish, eggs, and milk. I'll tend him well for he is my friend.'

"The first Sunday I took Daniel to church, the women said that I didn't know how to hold him. But I held him as I chose. Soon I saw a mother who was sitting in front of me holding her little girl over her shoulder and patting her just as I was doing. She sneaked a look at me several times to see how it was done. That morning I had been no sooner seated when an old woman dressed in traditional skins reached out both hands to take Daniel. I smiled but held him securely to my heart."

The Mugango people speculated on what language young Daniel would learn. "Some say he will speak English," Miriam wrote, "because he is European. Others say he will speak Luo because he was born at Shirati, our Luo station. Others say he will speak Chijita, the Jita vernacular. Others say it will be Ruri, the language spoken around the Mugango station, and still others say he will speak Swahili, the East African trade language. There are six different languages represented at our weekly Sunday services at Mugango."

The building of the "Wenger house" moved into full swing as soon as the Wengers returned from Shirati. The mission's building couple, Clinton and Maybell Ferster, moved to Mugango in November. With their arrival, living arrangements in the old "Stauffer house," now that there was a baby in residence, were tighter than ever.

The work on the new two-bedroom house progressed slowly through year-end into 1939. By the beginning of February, the house was ready for roofing. Clinton had asked Clyde Shenk to come over from Bumangi to help with this part of the building. On Monday of the week when they planned to put on the roof, Miriam was weak and a bit dizzy as she struggled to hold up under a siege of too many missionary guests and too much malaria.

"These past weeks have been rather hectic ones," she wrote to her sister Almeda in mid-February. "People have been coming and coming. We were glad for every visit too. Dr. Noah and Muriel Mack with Dr. Lillie Shenk spent some time here. Then John and Catherine Leatherman with Lois came and John and Ruth Moseman. The Fersters came to build our new house, and they moved in with us in November already of last year. Finally Clyde and Alta Shenk with Joseph came. Then Dr. Mack and John Moseman were back for another visit. Eby and Elva Leaman were here. You might well imagine that this two-bedroom house was filled just about to capacity. To top it all off, I came down with malaria. The quinine we take for it really makes your head spin. The fever leaves you weak and wobbly.

"Then this past Monday, Clyde came to help Clinton get the roof on the new house," Miriam continued. "Alta and her boys stayed at Bukiroba. On Wednesday morning Ray was involved with a station *shauri*. *Shauri* is a Swahili word that cannot be expressed in English except that it means that someone has a problem that needs to be discussed. While Ray heard the *shauri*, Clyde and Clinton, along with several African workers, went over to the new house, on the baboon mountain side of the mission compound, to put up the scaffold for the roof. When they were ready to begin working on the roof, they sent a lad to get Ray.

"Before going up on the framework, Clyde called the men together for a brief prayer. Later Clyde said that on the drive down from Bukiroba on Monday he couldn't shake a premonition that he would be hurt and incapacitated.

"The house is square with a peaked roof. The main ridge timbers had been precut and in a few minutes Clyde was nailing at the peak, fifteen feet above the concrete floor. Ray was on the wall. Clinton and two Africans were on the scaffolding about five feet lower than Clyde. Clyde looked down and saw Clinton walking along the scaffold. Some sixth sense told him to shout, 'Don't step on that board!' but he suppressed the urge, thinking it a queer notion. As Clinton stepped on the board, it broke, bringing the scaffolding down along with the four men. Ray, on the wall, was safe.

"Nurse Phebe was teaching nearby in the station's primary school. Hearing the commotion, she ran immediately to the scene and found the men conscious. Clyde had fallen the most distance. He landed on his feet, and it seemed that his back was broken. Immediately a messenger was sent by bicycle to Musoma to ask the government English doctor, Dr. Edmundson, to come and to inform Alta at Bukiroba and the others there of the accident.

"Dr. Edmundson believed Clyde to have crushed a vertebrae in his lower back and advised several days of bedrest followed by normal, although non-strenuous activities, for three months.

"That evening Ray drove in to Bukiroba to get Alta and her boys. The next day Ray went to Shirati to bring the Mennonite mission's Dr. Mack for an American opinion.

"Dr. Mack got Phebe's bed in her two-room house. The rest were in what had been the Stauffer house. Phebe, Alta and I tied Ray's and my two beds together, and we three used that with me sleeping on the ridge between the two beds. Clyde was in a small sewing room screened off from us three women by a blanket and sheet. Daniel was in his usual bed, Joseph in a tub in the bathroom, 22-month-old David on a bedroll on the bathroom floor. Clinton and Maybell were in their normal place, the house's second bedroom. Ray set up a cot in the study or office."

Dr. Mack advised that Clyde be examined in Mwanza. So that Sunday Clyde was taken to Musoma on a cot in the station pickup. There the Shenk family got on the lake steamer for Mwanza, Tanganyika's third largest city, a lake-port and railhead at the southern end of Lake Victoria. Mwanza was where the African Inland Mission had its headquarters. From the AIM mission station in town Alta wrote, "We are now here in Mwanza. Clyde is at the hospital getting very good care. I am staying with Mrs. Emil Sywulka who is a dear motherly woman. We have nothing but praise in our hearts to our kind heavenly Father when we think of all the things that might have happened but did not."

Clyde, somewhat resentful of "American medical opinions," was put in a body cast and spent three months on his back in bed at Bumangi. The English doctor would have had him up and about. Clyde, a 27-year-old American farm boy, regarded his casted incarceration as a physical and spiritual wasteland.

One year and four months after leaving the United States, Ray and Miriam, with seven-month-old Daniel, finally moved into their still unfinished home. "During this time," Miriam wrote on June 21, 1939, "the Lord had many lessons to teach us and we are thankful the house was not ready before. We have two bedrooms, an office, kitchen, and one large room which is used as a dining room and a living room combined."

Behind the Wenger house to the west lay Nyangoma, the baboon mountain, with its troupes of marauders. The outhouse sat a hundred paces off to the south. The house faced east overlooking the station, but that view was mostly blocked by an enormous fig tree. To the north lay Mugango Bay and Lake Victoria.

This Later House

*The new missionaries began to discover that being a
Christian in Lancaster, Pennsylvania, was not the same
as being a Christian in Jita-land.*

At first, Ray and Miriam didn't know very much about what was
going on in the hearts and minds of the Ruri and Jita people. They
saw with Lancaster County eyes and heard with Lancaster County
ears.

The Mennonite missionaries who were being sent to Africa from
Lancaster, Pennsylvania, were commissioned to teach and preach
the "all things" of the gospel. The phrase "all things" came from
Jesus' Great Commission to his disciples in Matthew 28:19,20.
"Teaching them to observe *all things* whatsoever I have command-
ed you." How were the missionaries to know what these "all
things" were?

* * *

Miriam's father, David Landis, was a Lancaster County preacher,
one of the Mellinger Mennonite Church preachers. He was
ordained in 1911 and continued preaching until his death in 1961,
a span just a few months short of half a century. Preacher Dave was
not excited about Ray and Miriam being appointed to missionary
service in Africa. He didn't try to persuade them not to go. But he
never encouraged them in that direction. Preacher Dave and his
second daughter Miriam represented two different worlds in the
Mennonite Church.

Preacher Dave was a patriarch. Church meant peoplehood. All
the people of similar religious heritage gathered together for worship; a body of disciplined, Christian believers, rooted in history
and in geography–this was the church. Peoplehood was what was
important. The physical and spiritual health of the body as a whole
was what mattered. The individual was important because the
individual was part of the body.

Ray and Miriam thought about these things a bit differently.
They were inclined toward a new spirituality which emphasized

"salvation." For them the individual's personal relationship to God was the basis for church. The individual became a member of the church by experiencing salvation through faith in Jesus Christ.

Because the Mennonite young people who were experiencing this new spirituality were wearing plain clothing, it wasn't easy, on the surface of it, to understand that they were seeing things differently from the traditional leadership of the church. Mennonite clothing became a common denominator which held together both ways of understanding salvation and church. Mennonite clothing became symbolic of the "all things" of the Gospel.

During Preacher Dave's boyhood years, Mennonite clothing was a minor issue in the church. But as changes came—English preaching, Sunday schools, four-part singing, personal salvation—clothing came to be the glue that held things together.

Preacher Dave accommodated himself to the new way of thinking—that Mennonite peoplehood could be shown through a standard way of dressing. Ray and Miriam also accepted that personal salvation through faith in Jesus Christ was to be expressed by wearing plain coats, cape dresses, and black stockings. The Lancaster Conference leadership expected that as Africans became Mennonites they would show their faith in the same way the missionaries were being commissioned to show it, by how they dressed.

In the beginning the missionaries followed the home pattern and challenged each other if anyone became careless. Miriam had a light blue Mennonite dress with long sleeves. The dress material had dark blue and white dots which were about four inches apart. This was considered a "large print" and wearing such a dress was pushing the boundaries of the "all things." Miriam was challenged by a fellow missionary sister. It was not good, Miriam was told, to wear such a dress.

However, in Africa this way of thinking could not hold. Slowly, over time, the missionaries began to see that Africans weren't wired the same way they were. The Lancaster way of expressing the gospel was not scratching where Africans itched.

* * *

A year before the Wengers arrived at Mugango, Elam Stauffer had gone to Jita-land to hold communion services for the Christians received from AIM and to baptize new believers. At each worship place, Elam interviewed the Christians individually before the service. To his amazement, nearly all of them had tangled up marriage confessions to make. The situation was so different from what he had expected that he decided not to hold any communion service, let alone any baptisms, in Jita-land. Instead, he and Elizabeth, along with another missionary couple, went to Mwanza to consult with Emil Sywulka, the AIM missionary through whom the Jita-land Christians had become Mennonites. John Moseman, the Mennonite mission secretary, wrote to the home board about this trip.

"Possibly the question which will give rise to the greatest problems in our native church will be this one of marriage in all its varied complications," John wrote on April 15, 1937. "The social structure of our entire field is different and is based on different principles than our own."

Elam also wrote to the home board about his trips to Jita-land and to see Sywulka in Mwanza. His letter indicated that he expected the Lancaster Conference of Mennonites in its 1937 spring session to discuss the problem and give instructions on how the missionaries were to proceed.

Everything in Tanganyika, as was true in much of Africa, had meaning in terms of the village. The village was the circle of dwellings where the family of one man lived. The primary good was that the village flourish, that it have large fields, many houses, large granaries, many strong young men, many daughters. Because it was ultimately the ancestors who looked after the prosperity of the village, ancestor veneration was a central part of traditional religion.

In Tanganyika evil was anything which attacked the village, anything which made the village weak and sterile. The witches were bad. They worked secretly at night to bring troubles and quarreling into the village. The job of witch doctors was to find and neutralize the witches. Witch doctors were good.

The Tanganyika people used cattle to keep the struggle honest, the struggle to strengthen the village. When a man married, he gave cattle to his bride's father. By this exchange, it was agreed that the bride's life force would go toward the strengthening of her husband's village. Any children which she bore or any enterprise in which she engaged contributed toward the strengthening of her husband's village.

The bride's father in turn used the cattle which he received to get another wife for himself or to get a woman for his son to marry. Whether the bride's cattle were used so Dad could get another wife or to get a wife for Brother, either way, Dad's village was strengthened. So, when a woman was married, her husband's village and her father's village were both given a boost.

Among the Zanaki people around Bumangi where Clyde and Alta Shenk worked, the bride-wealth or dowry was high, up to 40 head of cattle. There was very little divorce among the Zanaki people because of the large amount of "glue" (up to 40 head of cattle) which held a Zanaki marriage together. If a woman left her husband, it was his right to demand the cattle back from her father. So Dad would be very upset if Daughter came home. If a husband dismissed his wife, he got to keep her children, but he was out of pocket by up to 40 head of cattle. So marriages among the Zanaki were very stable.

There was also polygamy among the Zanaki. A man wanted many wives so that he would have many children to help keep his village strong. But, understandably, a Zanaki man would usually not have enough cattle to marry a second wife until after one of his daughters had been married. So Zanaki polygamists were usually older men. The missionaries found it especially distressful that old men married young women, usually girls still in their teens.

Marriages among the Jita people followed the same dowry rules as did Zanaki marriages. But for a Jita the dowry gift to his bride's father was much smaller. It was often as low as two or three head of cattle. Consequently, there was much more divorce among the Jita than among the Zanaki. If a man divorced his wife, her children still belonged to his village and he was out of pocket only two or three head of cattle. So, losing a wife was not as serious with the Jita. Also, because of the low dowry, a Jita man might become a polygamist while he was still young, maybe in his twenties.

In both the Zanaki and Jita societies, a child born to an unmarried woman belonged to her father's village. However, most African societies did not want their daughters to have children before they were married because a husband would consider his wife more highly if she was a virgin when they got married.

Sexual intercourse was regarded differently by the traditional, pre-Christian European peoples than by the traditional, pre-Christian African peoples. The European peoples regarded the sex act itself as the primary bond between a husband and wife. The marriage was consummated by the act of sex. But the African peoples regarded the dowry gift as the primary bond between a husband and wife. There was no marriage where there was no dowry. These differences existed before the coming of Christianity into either culture.

In his letter to the home board, Elam Stauffer gave two Jita case studies:

> Case 1: Maragesi is a fine young man whose marriage was arranged by his parents in the usual way. While yet a heathen young man, he put his wife away for one of the usual reasons. She was soon married by another and has children to him. Maragesi married another and these two later believed in Christ under the teaching of the AIM and have been sufficiently taught to be baptized.
>
> Maragesi's second wife too has been married to him as her second husband, and her first husband has married again.
>
> These folks have come to the teachings and understand the way of salvation sufficiently to be baptized, I believe. To get their former partners back is impossible to them. All these remarryings took place ere they had heard of the way of salvation. What can we tell them or do for them?
>
> Case 2: Manyama married long ago. His first wife died and he married two others. Under these circumstances the parents of the deceased wife usually give a sister of the deceased to the husband in place of the former one. The sister of this first wife was yet too young, hence the

marrying of two others first. The sister, having grown up, comes to the village and steps into the place of the first woman, the deceased wife, and so is head or big or first wife, as they call them. In the eyes of the tribe, she is his first and big wife since she takes the place of her dead sister who was the first one married, though she is actually fourth married.

About this time Manyama hears the gospel and believes, and so puts wives number two and three away, and retains the head wife who actually is fourth married. Because the community of Manyama lacks a teacher to further instruct and carry on 'follow-up work,' Manyama lags and drifts back again and marries wife number five, and lives with these two.

About this time, we came along and took over this field and put a teacher in his community, and Manyama again returns, rejoicing that a teacher has come to them. He put away wife number five, and lives with only wife married fourth but in the native eyes she is number one, for she was given in place of her sister who had been number one and died. He is now believing for a period of about one year and is looking forward to being baptized soon. The wife given him in place of the first one believed soon after marrying him, and has been steadfast ever since, and is now ready for baptism if she can be accepted. She was asked to remain back this last time because I was not sure what should be done in such a case.

I give you these two cases that are very typical to better give you an idea of the problem before us. You will readily see that there should be some kind of an answer to these folks ere long for those who were asked to remain back cannot be put off indefinitely for it will tend to tire these folks to whom baptism is a big thing and very disappointing if put off for what they cannot see is a good reason. I told them we possibly could give them an answer of some kind by the time of our June Conference, and I trust we shall be able to do so.

Elam's letter to the home board went on to explain another marriage problem, the fact that Christian youth (male) in Jita-land were not able to marry Christian "girls."

"Further I would say," Elam wrote in 1937, "the tribal custom of arranged marriages where the girl is still a child at the time of her first marriage is so shameful and heathen that a Christian or believer would not think of trying to get a girl not yet married because she would not be available unless taken at a very young age, and then would be under the control of the parents who would insist on the heathen marriage ceremony which they think is necessary. There are no Christian parents in this tribe yet having girls ready for marriage. These believers find it easier and far less tempting and heathen to take a woman already left by her first husband for they are not then bound to participate in the heathen ceremony for first marriages. To get an unmarried girl here at present means to marry a heathen one and then to fall into sin by participating in the heathen marriage ceremony. The girls are hard to reach and save in Africa."

So, it gradually became clear that even if plain clothing had meaning in Lancaster, it had no meaning, no witness, to the village-based African traditional religion. The missionaries' concerns about plain clothing did not speak to the life questions which concerned the African people.

What visible difference then should the gospel make in the life of a missionary if it wasn't distinctive dress? Wasn't this missionary question also the African question? Africans phrased it differently. They asked the question this way: "If the purpose of a faithful life wasn't to build up the village, then what was life about?"

* * *

Ray and Miriam slowly became more aware of the traditional culture and religion of the Ruri people living around Mugango and the Jita people in Jita-land. Then one day the Lord gave Ray a vision. The vision came from Haggai 2:9. "The glory of this later house shall be greater than the former and in this place will I give peace."

This vision which captured Ray's spirit was that God was creating a "new house," a new way of life, for both missionary and Ruri-Jita, that would be better than, of more glory than, the former way.

Rebekah-the-Beaten

An African woman teamed up with Miriam to begin a Christian ministry which addressed marriage and threatened the traditional village system.

An attractive youthful woman, maybe twenty years older than Miriam, came regularly to the worship services on the Mugango station. As Miriam's continued study of Swahili opened her ears and loosened her tongue, she was able to begin a hesitant conversation with this woman. Her name was Rebekah Mtemwa (Rebekah-the-Beaten).

Rebekah was of the Jita people. It was in Jita-land that she heard the preaching of AIM evangelists and became a Christian. Her husband was not pleased that she had joined the Christians and been baptized. Because the Jita people's marriage dowry was small, divorce was relatively easy.

Rebekah's displeased husband set her things outside his house and told her to go away. She gathered up her few possessions and returned to her father's house. After a year, she became discouraged with living at home and being a Christian. She moved in with another man. No dowry was exchanged, so this wasn't an official marriage.

One day Rebekah became deathly sick. Neighbors thought she was dying and began the traditional wail for the dead. There on her deathbed she had an out-of-body experience. She saw herself on the edge of a deep pit. In the pit were two men holding out their hands urging her to jump in. Two other men at the top were trying to push her into the pit.

As Rebekah-the-Beaten struggled to escape, she was suddenly confronted by a Holy Spirit from God who told her that the decision was hers. It was her sin which was pushing her into the pit. She could decide to embrace her sin and disappear into the pit, or she could leave her sin, turn to God, and be free.

She pledged to the Holy Spirit that her choice was to return to the salvation in Jesus which she had known. When she became well, she left the man with whom she was living and dedicated her life to prayer and Christian witness.

Rebekah and Miriam became soul sisters. From the beginning of the AIM work in Jita-land, the primary school had been the main evangelizing tool. The Mennonites at Mugango also adopted this approach and set up their school. This school had very little to offer girls. And what could be offered was available only to the girls who lived nearby.

Rebekah and Miriam began to think and pray about opening a home where teenage girls from a distance could come to live, learn about Jesus, and develop domestic skills. Elam Stauffer, back from furlough, became aware of Rebekah and Miriam's vision to develop a ministry which would prepare teenage girls to be the wives of Christian men and to become mothers in Christian homes. He encouraged Ray to consider the matter of a girls' home. A mud and stick hut was built. Rebekah-the-Beaten was engaged as matron, and it was announced in the Jita-land congregations that girls could apply.

The month before Daniel's first birthday, four girls moved into the home. "They brought their possessions," Miriam wrote. "Some of you may wonder what possessions a teenage African girl has. One girl came with only the clothing she wore—a dress and a cloth she tied on her head. There was nothing else she could have brought for she owned nothing obtained by money. However she did come with a sweet smile and a lovable disposition. If these girls could suddenly peep into some wardrobes of young girls at home, there would be much astonishment."

By November 1939 the home's enrollment had swelled to seven. Three of the girls were in tatters and had to have something to wear. Miriam took them to the store down by the main road to have them measured by the tailor. "I wish you could have seen their faces when they were measured for the dresses," Miriam wrote to her sister. "Actually they could hardly stand still for joy. The dresses are very simple ones. I like to buy all white for these girls because as much as they are in the sun, their others fade so soon. With their white prayer coverings pinned on neatly and their black faces shining, then the clean white dresses make them look like angels. Indeed it will be a glorious day when I see some of these girls, among whom I have the privilege to work, over yonder. I feel as though they are my children."

The youngest of the seven girls would wander over to the Wenger house to check on the ways of white folk. This gave Miriam the opportunity to check on the ways of small black folk.

"All the time I was writing this," Miriam wrote of her guest, "there was a little black girl standing by my side. First she asked to look at pictures, then she asked me to give her a 'covering' or piece of cloth, then it was a slate for school. Becoming bored, she said that one of her friends, who is bigger than she, is crying and she asked that I permit her to go see her friend. But before going off she began to lick the metal screening in the screen door–an attractive taste? Or was it the odor? Or the texture in the material? She is one of the seven in the girls' home. She might be four years old. I am sure she is no more, and she has memorized the first six verses in John 15 and several hymns!"

Some of the girls came to the home as runaways from arranged marriages which they didn't want. One of these runaways, Sara, was in a forced polygamist marriage to an older man. Her husband would come to Mugango and take her home. She would run away again and come back to Mugango. Once when she saw her husband coming for her, she ran into the Wenger house and hid under Daniel's crib.

Eventually, Sara was able to get free from her polygamist marriage and was married to a Christian man. A half century later, her brother became the pastor at Mugango and her husband an elder of the Musoma Mennonite Church.

At first, though, it took some persuasion to get parents to allow their daughters to come to the home. But the home's reputation spread and in several years there were 30 to 40 in residence at any one time. They ranged in age from young children to the upper teens and early adults.

It would never have been possible to run the girls' home without Matron Rebekah. She gave her life to the home. She earned the trust of the girls' parents. In traditional African society, teenage girls often live with their grandmothers who are given the responsibility of preparing them for marriage. Matron Rebekah became a Christian "grandmother" to the girls. Young Christian men began to look for wives among the older girls at the home.

One morning Miriam heard loud, angry words "coming from the direction of the girls' house. I went to the open window of our home to hear better what was going on. Immediately I recognized the voices of Nyabise, the first girl to enter the home, and Magunira, one of the boys who lives in the Christian village. But all those words!! What were they saying? A group of youths had gathered, listening to the fight. It made me shudder as I pieced together what had happened.

"The boy, Magunira, had started it by teasing, 'Nyabise, you have feet just like a duck,' and she had retorted, 'You, Magunira, are the blackest of all the black men.'

"The young man took this retort as a low blow, and flashed back angrily that he would beat Nyabise if it weren't for the white woman. 'I could beat you till you die,' he ranted. Nyabise burst into tears. Matron Rebekah brought the pair to me for adjudication."

What was the meaning of these insults? Because an infestation of jiggers in the toes caused pain when walking barefoot, a person with jiggers would turn the foot outward when walking, like a duck, so that anything in the path would hit the side of the foot instead of the toes. A base insult among the Jita was to observe that one walks "like a duck" meaning, "you have jiggers," which implies an unkempt, dusty home.

The Jita are a brown people. The English colonial rulers of Tanganyika based social status on skin color with the whitest of women being suited for lives of ease and luxury whereas the blackest men were suited for the more demeaning laboring tasks. The blackest of men would of course never be able to provide well for a wife and family. A second layer of insult also inferred that the "blackest of men" was not really a Jita, who are brown.

Nyabise was so devastated by the boy's insults that she could hardly talk through her sobs. Miriam wrote, "The two tried to forgive each other but for weeks, yes even months, there was friction between them."

A year passed. Late on an afternoon Magunira came calling, *"Hodi,"* at the Wenger door. When an African went calling, he announced his presence verbally saying, *"Hodi,"* at the door. Knocking was the announcement of an intruder or thief. The voiced "knock" identified the caller to the homeowner. Miriam recognized by the *"Hodi"* that it was Magunira who was standing at her door.

Miriam responded with the traditional, *"Karibu,"* (Draw near) as she left her work and went to greet her caller.

"May I talk with you about a personal matter?" Magunira asked nervously.

Miriam welcomed him into Ray's small office, and they both took seats. During the previous several months, both Magunira and Nyabise had had an "experience with their Lord that had meant heart cleansing." Miriam wondered if this visit related to Magunira's conversion experience.

"I wish to marry Nyabise," he stated.

Miriam smiled inwardly, remembering that back in Lancaster, some young men also had strange ways of letting a girl know that she was attractive. She resisted asking if he had thought of an improvement over his duck-waddle compliment. Instead, she asked if Nyabise knew that he wished to marry her.

"No."

"Then you need to ask her," Miriam said. "I'll send someone to bring her here."

When Nyabise came, Miriam excused herself, giving them some privacy to discuss Magunira's proposal. And he was successful.

Nyabise consented, "Yes, I can accept that you marry me."

The next step was for Magunira to contact the girl's father. Probably Magunia made the initial inquiry through an intermediary. Nyabise's father accepted. Then the dowry needed to be agreed upon and exchanged. It took more than a year for everything to be arranged. A church wedding celebrated their union.

It became an almost normal routine for Christian men to announce first to Miriam that they had fallen in love with one of the young women in the home.

Those early years of Mennonite mission work were heady and exciting times for the African young people. The church was becoming an alternative to the village-oriented traditional way. No one paused to philosophize about where this would lead. One of the unexpected things that happened was that some of the young men from Clyde and Alta's Zanaki station began to notice the Ruri and Jita girls in the Mugango Girls' Home. Inter-tribal marriages would fly in the face of everything the village-based system stood for.

Phebe Yoder wrote the details of one of these inter-tribal love stories:

The wedding of Nyamisi, a girl of the Jita people, and Nathaniel Warioba, a Zanaki Christian boy, occurred on the afternoon of April 21, 1945. There have been other weddings at Mugango in the recent past, but this one is of special interest to us because God's power was so definitely manifested in breaking down every attempt of the enemy to hinder it.

Nathaniel, a Zanaki-man, had come from Bumangi to Mugango to go to school. The Mugango school by then was offering up to grade four. Nyamisi, a Jita girl, was living at the Girls' Home. In the spring of 1943, Nathaniel asked to marry Nyamisi. For many months, refusal from the girl's family made the wedding seem impossible.

Then in January 1945, hindrances began to be removed. Mikael, Nyamisi's full brother, had the final authority in Nyamisi's marriage. Mikael is a Mennonite Christian. For a long time, Mikael had stood as a hindrance to the wedding. He now began to accept and to agree to the amount of the dowry.

This freed Nathaniel to make trips into Jita-land to inform all the relatives of his sweetheart, according to native custom. March 14 was set as the wedding day.

Fifteen cattle and Shs. 120/= [120 shillings or about $30] had been agreed upon for the dowry, this being a compromise between the Zanaki dowry of 30-plus cattle and the Jita dowry of two to four head of cattle. After the dowry had been delivered by Nathaniel's family to Nyamisi's village, then the Christian ceremony would be observed in the church.

Well, March 14 came and passed, but no cattle arrived. Instead, Stefano, Nathaniel's Christian brother, came from Bumangi and reported that the cattle were delayed because the British colonial government required the cattle be vaccinated before being transferred from Zanaki-land to Mugango.

Meanwhile, the bride-to-be's little mother (Nyamisi's real mother had died) raised her objections to having Nyamisi 'sold off ' to a tribe with a much higher dowry than the Jita's customary dowry. To her it seemed 'her child' was being sold as a slave to the Zanaki people. A quarrel ensued between the little mother and brother Mikael. Eventually, Mikael changed his mind and absolutely refused that the marriage take place.

This came as a terrible blow, not only to the bridal couple, but to praying ones. The disappointed groom-to-be hastened to Zanaki-land to inform his brother Stefano not to bring any cattle. He then returned to Mugango where he is attending school in grade four.

Meanwhile the bride-to-be was begging her brother Mikael to reconsider and accept the marriage plans. But then the groom-to-be became discouraged for the first time during the many long months of waiting and many difficulties of arranging for this cross-tribal marriage. He wrote a letter to his sweetheart, Nyamisi, telling her that he was calling off their marriage plans.

Then brother Mikael did change his mind and said that they shall go ahead and have the wedding as soon as possible. April 14 was agreed upon as the new date for the marriage.

So the groom-to-be went off once more to Zanaki-land to inform his brother. Nathaniel found Stefano weary of the changeableness of the Jita. Nathaniel was weary too of his many long foot journeys–some 34 miles cross-country between Bumangi in Zanaki-land and Mugango. The two brothers decided to call it quits. Then groom-to-be Nathaniel returned to Mugango and announced that indeed the marriage was off for sure.

Then, by God's appointment, Mikael (the bride's

brother and negotiator) and Stefano (the groom's brother and negotiator) bumped into each other in Musoma
Town. They negotiated an agreement which God per-
mitted to be carried through.

April 21 was then set for the marriage. On the morning of that day the cattle and shillings arrived and in the
afternoon the marriage was performed.

Nathaniel went on to become a certified school teacher, a grad-
uate of the Mennonite Theological College, and an ordained
Mennonite pastor. In 1991 he and Nyamisi were pastoring the
Musoma Mennonite Church.

Although exciting and liberating, the movement away from traditional ways was complicated and difficult. It required great
courage. Jonah, another young Zanaki-man from Bumangi who
married a Ruri girl from Mugango, told Clyde Shenk that "he
doubts if missionaries are able to understand what struggles
Africans go through if they want to really take a stand for Christ.

"For instance," Jonah said, "if a young man wants to stand for the
Lord, his parents will start to scorn him and poke all kinds of fun at
him and will force him to do things he doesn't want to do. If he still
persists, they will try to drive him away from home. If he hasn't
another place to go to sleep, he is apt to become 'conquered.' If he
does resist these minor persecutions, his folks tell him that they will
bewitch him, and if he still stands true, he will be considered to be
a man who does not have any intellect, sense, or wits."

Jonah was hated by the Zanaki people because he left their village-based traditional religion, became a Christian, and married a
Ruri girl. He did other things too which showed disrespect for the
village system. So the Zanaki people put a curse on him and dug a
grave to symbolize his death.

Jonah was ordained at Bumangi in 1956 as the first Zanaki pastor. Throughout his life only one other person from his large
extended family–a woman–left the traditional religion and became
a follower of Jesus. From his youth, Jonah was alone in his decision
to become a Christian.

When Jonah was in his late 50s, he began to reconsider his
youthful decision to leave the village system and become a follow-

er of Jesus. He felt that his Ruri wife from Mugango had raised their children as Ruri people rather than as Zanaki people. Jonah feared that when he died there would be no Zanaki children to venerate him and preserve his life in the other world through ceremonies done at his grave. So he secretly gave the required dowry in cattle for a Zanaki wife. After a few years, he married a second Zanaki wife. He then had three wives. The Zanaki wives did not live in his main home with his Ruri wife. Jonah continued to be a Mennonite pastor, but his ministry lost power and Sunday attendance dropped to fewer than ten worshipers.

Eventually the situation was discovered and after a long process, Jonah was excommunicated. By then the missionary era was over and it was an African bishop who excommunicated him.

Jonah was a broken man. He had no place. The traditional system wouldn't accept him, and the church had excommunicated him. After several years, he repented and returned to the church. He died as a communicant member.

Boundaries

Missionaries and Africans struggled over where the boundaries would be set regarding the ownership that African Mennonites would have in the American support system which maintained the missionaries.

Along with the home for girls, Miriam began a weekly meeting for women who lived within walking distance of the Mugango station. The meeting, modeled after sewing circle in the States, consisted of a Bible lesson and sewing hour.

Miriam wrote, "These meetings are always a joy to me for it is in them that I really learn to know the women and to understand their problems. Sometimes it seems as though we have not even begun to learn to know or understand our people."

From the beginning of Miriam's work with the home and women's meeting, there was a struggle with defining boundaries. The girls in the home and the women coming to meeting had never experienced anything like this before; neither had Miriam. This was a first for both the missionaries and the Africans. Each side approached the situation from its own perspectives, and neither understood where the other was coming from.

Miriam wanted to help the women, but she didn't want to help too much. To help too much would make them dependent. To the African women, receiving help from a foreigner was wonderful. But why, they wondered, did Miriam help with some things and not with other things? How did she choose what not to help with? There were many occasions like this where the missionaries and the Africans saw things differently.

In her second year at Mugango, Miriam wrote about some of these misconceptions. "Yesterday there were fifteen present at women's meeting. Some of the folks are sewing children's clothes, others are sewing for themselves. They take much joy in doing the sewing, but when the time comes for them to bring the cents to contribute toward the material used, there are many words. We can't give the garments free to these women or they would become dependent. Many think that it is up to me to give until there is nothing left to give.

"Another thing the girls in the home can't understand is why people are punished. They think that we teachers of Christianity must just forgive, forgive, and forgive–which we do. But they think if because of disobedience they are asked to do extra digging in the school garden, then they are not forgiven.

"One of the Christian women here at Mugango was turned out by her husband, divorced. Having nowhere else to go, she moved into her brother's village. This brother has three wives, and he doesn't want his sister around because if she is in his village, the British government will require that he pay her head tax. In the meantime, a man who is not a believer asked her to move in with him. He promised to give her money for clothes, etc.

"This woman came here to our house and asked me for advice on what to do. It isn't difficult to know what is the right thing to do, but how could we help her earn the cents she needed to survive alone? These people will soon learn how to beg if we begin giving them gifts.

"One Sunday I was visiting in a village near here. In this village there was a new little baby girl. I was no sooner seated until they informed me that the baby's name is Mama Wenger. They then asked for a dress for her, but I am reluctant to give them one as I don't want them to become dependent on me. Yet I am afraid that if I don't give the baby a dress, they will feel that the baby is not blessed by its spiritual namesake and may unknowingly neglect it in ways which will cause it to die of an intestinal or respiratory infection, as do so many new babies. Little Rei, named after Ray did die recently.

"It is the many, many problems like these that make us look old before we really are. Muriel Mack told us that Ray and I aged more by the end of our first year than any of the others, even though they have been here longer.

"When I was in America, I learned how to be still so that the Lord could meet me and be my peace. Here in Africa, there are times when things pile up and then, if I can find just five minutes to be quiet, He brings a Peace that nothing else ever could, and my day goes on smoothly. If it weren't for this fellowship with the Lord, even the strongest person couldn't stand the strain."

It wasn't just in women's work that the problem of boundaries was surfacing. As early as 1938, the mission secretary wrote to the home board: "At each mission station we have selected a few of the elder natives to sit in council with the white pastor on various church problems. The missionary must, of course, do the suggesting and guide the discussions. However, by this means, we hope to have them develop an understanding of the magnitude and weightiness of the work of God's kingdom, and at the same time see God's wonderful sufficiency for every need."

A year later–1939–the mission secretary wrote further on this matter to the home board: "We have realized very keenly the need of doing everything in our power to break down grounds for the suspicion that can so easily exist between the black and white man, and which so effectively hinders the work of the Spirit in the church. We feel that especially this year, the Lord blessed richly in our efforts in this direction by holding the native and European conferences separately."

By 1941 the issue of discrimination, which up until that time had only been alluded to, broke out into the open. The mission secretary wrote a very long letter to the home board about it. This short excerpt explained the gist of the problem:

> The event of outstanding note during the quarter was the native church conference, August 26-29, 1941.
>
> There were big problems such as circumcision and the marriage questions which needed to be discussed. However, the African elders presented a matter which they insisted should be given priority in the discussions nor were they of a mind to give consideration to the other problems until this one was settled. Since there was no concrete reason to object, their desire was granted, and the problem they had to present was couched in these words: 'The separation between the black and white man.'
>
> It gradually became clear that this had to do with the question why the primary school teachers do not receive allowances from the mission as the missionaries do.

The Africans maintained this was discrimination. The missionaries insisted that it was unscriptural for teachers and elders to be paid from mission funds. After endless discussion, the Africans walked out of the conference saying that other missions would support them if the Mennonites wouldn't.

"The situation was a critical one," the secretary continued, "and the missionary pastors spent considerable time in prayer asking the Lord's guidance and His undertaking in the matter. We attribute all credit to Him that by the next day, the Africans had relented in their demands and were willing, after much discussion, to adopt the tithe as a systematic method of contributing for the support of local church and school work."

Of course, if no money came from the mission, would the mission be able to control the schools and churches? "We contemplate this prospect [loss of control] with no little degree of apprehension. We call upon our home constituency to pray very specifically for the successful issue of the indigenous church here," the secretary concluded.

The African interest in receiving some sort of salary or wage for school teachers and church elders from mission funds would not go away. Relying on fees paid by students and money collected in the offering on Sunday was too erratic and uncertain for the emerging African leaders. In response to the African concern, a number of missionaries began to feel badly about their financial security. Every month Ray, as mission treasurer, saw to it that each missionary got an envelope containing the monthly allowance from the home board in cash. It seemed too easy in light of the struggle the Africans were having.

So a number of missionaries asked that they receive only designated funds; that is, money designated by a giver in the States for a specific missionary. The missionary would not get any money from the general Tanganyika fund. Those missionaries who requested this arrangement felt this would be a step of faith, putting them on a more equal footing with the emerging African leaders.

The home board wasn't happy with such an idea. It had plenty of money in its Africa account for missionary support. The board wished for all the missionaries to receive the allowances which had been budgeted for them. But those missionaries wishing to take this faith step were not persuaded.

So it was decided that all missionaries would get their regular monthly allowance *plus* any designated funds contributed specifically for them. Then at the end of the year, it was up to the individual missionary to return the regular monthly allowance money to Ray, the mission treasurer, for recycling the next year.

Not all of the missionaries who took the faith pledge got as much money as they needed. One family did not have enough money to buy the boat tickets when it was time for them to go on furlough. In this case, another missionary wrote to his parents in the States asking that his and his wife's savings be given to the Mission Board, anonymously, as funds designated for the furlough travel expenses of the family that was short.

While the problem which concerned African Mennonites was not fully addressed by the faith pledge, the pledge was a way for missionaries to do something about one of the things they believed in. A number of the missionaries quietly lived by the pledge through their first furloughs.

Clouds

*Some hard questions were asked. How good an idea
was it anyway to be in this missionary venture?*

During the first years of missionary work, things seemed to go
fairly well. But slowly the real issues were defined and many
Africans stopped coming to church. The missionary families were
growing, too, which meant more work, and more tiredness, especially for the missionary mothers. There were no furloughs because
of World War II. International travel by civilians dried up after
December 7, 1941, when Pearl Harbor was bombed and the United
States entered the war. The missionaries needed to live indefinitely on their mission stations.

In 1945 Miriam Wenger wrote, "Today I read in the *Overcomer* a
sentence that I can truly agree with: 'Through the effect of five years
of the European War, nerves have been strained to the utmost. Let
us bear in mind this may not be for want of trust in God, but often
proceeds from physical infirmity.' I firmly believe that the effects of
a war with spiritual darkness can and do bring about the same
thing."

The results of the work in evangelization and church planting
were often discouraging. During the first two years at Bumangi in
Zanaki-land, over 60 people confessed Jesus as Saviour and were
registered in the catechumen book. But by the middle of 1939, Alta
Shenk wrote, "There are only five still recorded as believers and
there is reason to doubt the genuineness of two or three of these."

Again and again the most promising of the missionaries' students left the mission stations to find work in the towns. Alta
wrote from Bumangi on April 5, 1941, "Recently three seemingly
faithful boys left here to seek employment. They need our earnest
prayers."

Laments such as Alta's about people leaving the mission stations
are repeated over and over in the correspondence. One missionary
suggested that this outward flow be discouraged by changing the
curriculum in the mission schools to subjects less useful in finding
employment in the towns.

The girls attending school and worship services were also dropping out and getting married. This, too, caused a drain in congregational membership. In 1943 Alta wrote, "At present there appear to be no women or girls with whom I can fellowship in the Lord."

These problems were in sharp contrast to the enthusiasm which Alta felt at the dedication of the Bumangi church in 1937. At that time she wrote, "The new church building was used for the first time on Sunday morning, October 16, 1937. As the school bell gave out the invitation to come, the people began to gather. By the time to start the Sunday school classes, the building was seated full. People kept coming all during the Sunday school and a few kept coming in during the church services. . . . There were at least 475 people present."

From Mugango Miriam wrote in 1939: "Satan is very busy and by his power is trying to snatch those who are talented members of the church. One of the most promising members of our church, and possibly the best trained native brother in the church, was found guilty of making arrangements to marry another wife."

Discipline problems kept cropping up among the Mugango station workers and among the school students. There were problems with rebellious residents in the girls' home. When Ray asked their advice, the African church elders in Jita-land urged him to physically beat the girls who were misbehaving.

* * *

The underside, the secret side, of the African Traditional Religion was witchcraft. It became clear that the work of the missionaries was undermining Africa's ancient religious ways. It would be natural for Africa to fight back with witchcraft. Sometimes missionaries wondered if they were the targets of witchcraft.

"In the early days of our work, I was sleeping soundly one night," Clyde wrote from Bumangi. "Suddenly I was wide awake with a fearful vision on my mind. It was as though I saw an old pagan man standing by our bedroom window who, sensing my awakening, crouched and grunted as he slipped into the night. I found myself to be full of great fear.

"I lay there wide awake for some time. Many thoughts went through my mind. What does this mean? Lord, didn't you send us here? Lord, do you not have more power than all the powers of darkness? And, of course, I prayed earnestly that the Lord would save me from whatever this experience was or whatever the meaning of it would be.

"Then, again, rather suddenly, I awoke and the morning sun was shining! The Lord had put me to sleep again. He had taken away my fear and he had caused me to sleep overtime that morning."

Many of the missionaries struggled, sometimes questioning their own spirituality. Their efforts seemed so fruitless. "The needs seem so many around us," Miriam wrote, "and I am convinced that some of the trouble must be in our own lives or there would be more liberty of the Spirit. Lord, teach us–teach me, Lord, teach me more concerning your holiness. I feel my utter need of casting myself wholly upon you."

Spiritual problems and physical problems, the missionaries discovered, were intimately related. Mugango had mosquitoes, the anopheles which stands on its head and injects people with malaria. The Wengers frequently were sick with fever, vomiting, and diarrhea caused by the malaria blood-parasite. The medication of the day was quinine, which was taken after you were sick rather than as a preventative. Miriam, who was especially susceptible to malaria, was sick every several months. Each time she would need to take a course of quinine.

Quinine when combined with a high fever caused giddiness and hallucinations. The medicine itself was terribly bitter. Children hated it. To give quinine to a baby, parents smashed a half tablet in a teaspoon, dissolved it with a bit of water, lay the baby on its back, held its nose shut, and, when the child opened its mouth to breathe, poured in the quinine. Because nursing babies have the reflex to swallow before breathing, they did not choke.

Miriam sent some of the quinine powder, wrapped up in a bit of tissue, to her sister. "Be sure you taste it," she said. "It's sweet," she lied. "When my fever was highest, I got 25 grains, or 25 spoonfuls."

Ray and Miriam's two-year-old daughter, Annetta, was sick for a month with a heavy chest cold in addition to fever. There was no car on the Mugango station to take her to Musoma. (Those were the war years when gasoline for civilian travel was rationed to two gallons per vehicle per month. Without fuel some stations got along without a car.) Miriam put mustard plasters on Annetta every four hours for three days during the time her congestion was at its worst. Over one 24-hour period, all Annetta took in was two ounces of milk. At another time, Annetta had dysentery, and Miriam spent five days with her in the Musoma hospital.

Once when Daniel was sick and vomited over the supper table, Miriam was so tired herself that she could scarcely clean him up. One of Daniel's illnesses lasted three weeks. It was probably typhoid. They took him to Musoma for medication.

These illnesses drained Miriam's physical strength. Aesthetically she was being drained too. All her early life, she had access to a piano and would often play in her father's home. She loved music. She never realized this was something she should give thought to when moving to Africa. The only source of familiar music for Miriam at Mugango was her own voice.

The Shenks at Bumangi had brought with them a portable, foot-pumped organ. One day when Miriam and Ray were visiting Bumangi, she sat down at the organ and played. The music was so overwhelmingly beautiful to her music-starved spirit that she wept.

* * *

Travel was so difficult during the war years that the missionary bishop, Elam Stauffer, could not regularly visit the five stations. So it was decided to ordain a second bishop and divide the work. Ray was chosen by lot to be the second bishop. He traveled over the dirt roads on a little German motorbike which ran on kerosene but needed a snifter of real gas in the carburetor to get started.

Ray's bishop responsibilities took him away from Mugango for extended periods of time. With no telephones, there was no way for him to let Miriam know if he would be home later than planned. Once she wrote in her diary, "Ray was here for six whole days!" It was always a great joy and relief to her when he returned from one of his trips.

Ray, too, got the fever from time to time. In those days when quinine was the only remedy and when white people got malaria recurrently, they would get black water fever. This happened when the malaria parasite, in combination with quinine, would cause a kidney disintegration, diagnosed by blood in the urine. Reddish-black urine meant that you had "black water" fever. The combination of malaria and uremic poisoning killed people.

An owl used to sit at night on the Wenger house roof and do her mournful hooting. The Africans said that owls were messengers sent by witches carrying notices of death. Miriam wrote, "One of these birds perches itself on top of our house frequently and coos out his weird song."

* * *

The third Wenger child, Wilmer Ray, was born in the Musoma hospital on March 18, 1943, five years after they had left the United States.

The war in Europe continued to drag on, and no one knew when it would be possible to travel internationally again. Eastern Mennonite Board of Missions had decided that after five years on the field, missionaries should get three months of leave somewhere in Tanganyika. This was to give them a bit of a break, instead of furlough.

The Wengers arranged to spend their three months in Dar es Salaam, Tanganyika's harbor city and capital. Wilmer was just six weeks old. Unfortunately, their time at the coast was even more exhausting than life at Mugango had been. The guest house where they stayed was run by English "spinsters" who didn't like children.

Ray wrote about one of the things that happened which made the managers uptight. "Soon after our arrival, four-year-old Daniel went into the bathroom, next to our bedroom, and locked the door. He began to explore and find out the marvels of a modern bathroom. He tried the faucet to the wash bowl and washed his hands, then he opened the faucet to the bathtub and found it all was very interesting. Then he climbed into the bathtub, dressed in his best suit and saw a knob to be turned. He quickly turned same, activating the shower, and immediately began to cry furiously. He was so frightened that he could not get the door unlocked for some time."

Baby Wilmer became persistently fussy. Miriam was acutely sensitive to the attitude of the English ladies toward children's disturbances. She and Ray spent many a night pacing the floor with Wilmer and trying to keep him quiet. In time Miriam discovered he had mango worms. (The larvae wiggle under the skin and appear as pimples until they mature and pop out.) The woman who did their laundry had been spreading Wilmer's diapers to dry on the ground under a mango tree.

Even though Ray wrote of their three-month extended leave in Dar es Salaam as helpful with pleasant sea breezes, Miriam was more exhausted than ever when they returned to Mugango. During the half year that followed Wilmer's birth–March to September, 1943–Miriam had come down with malaria six times, on average once a month. In early September, the doctor prescribed a new drug. Miriam found the side effects of the new drug made her even more giddy than had the standard quinine.

Near the end of the required course of medication, Miriam felt that the new drug was pushing her over the edge, and she begged Phebe to stop the course. But Phebe insisted that the doctor's prescription be followed to the last pill. Then, boom, the next weeks were a haze through which Miriam remembers nothing.

Daniel, Annetta, and Wilmer were scattered to the Shirati and Bukiroba stations. Miriam was indeed very sick and some were fearful that she would die. Ray took her to Bumangi for its cooler, mosquito-free, higher elevation.

At Bumangi the Lord gave the missionary family Psalm 70 as a prayer and promise to rally their faith: "Make haste, O God, to deliver me; make haste to help me, O Lord. Let them be ashamed and confounded that seek after my soul: let them be turned backward, and put to confusion, that desire my hurt. Let them be turned back for a reward of their shame that say, Aha, aha. Let all those that seek thee rejoice and be glad in thee: and let such as love thy salvation say continually, 'Let God be magnified.' But I am poor and needy: make haste unto me, O God: thou art my help and my deliverer; O Lord, make no tarrying." A bedside anointing service was held. Slowly Miriam began to recover.

After a while she was strong enough that Wilmer could rejoin his parents. Three months later at Christmas time, Ray and Miriam were still at Bumangi. A spiritual life conference was to be held at Bumangi and this gave Matron Rebekah and four of the girls from the Mugango Girls' Home a good excuse to walk the 34 miles, cross country, from Mugango to Bumangi. "It was such a treat to me to have prayer fellowship with Rebekah again," Miriam wrote. Following the spiritual life conference, Rebekah and Miriam continued for the next week to have a ministry in meetings held at Bumangi for girls and women.

When she was ready to return to Mugango, Miriam wrote in the missionary prayer letter about her illness. "Perhaps a number of you have heard of my physical collapse in September. I am grateful to my Lord for restoration and am happy to again take over some duties. The Lord has been so gracious in supplying my every need and through all the experiences of these past months, I can see His leading. 'Bless the Lord, O my soul: and all that is within me bless his Holy Name. Forget not all his benefits: who healeth all thy diseases' (Psalm 103).

"We have had several very restful months here at Bumangi. Just now we are trying to put all the possessions we have here at Bumangi into suitcases so that we will be ready for our trip back home to Mugango tomorrow, January 1, 1944."

After a month at Mugango for Ray to catch up a bit with his pastoral and administrative work, Ray and Miriam spent two months in Songhor, Kenya, on an English settler farm which had a guest house. Miriam recovered fully. Returning to Mugango, they resumed their normal responsibilities.

The Way

The East African Revival provided a way for the Gospel to take root in African soil.

It was 1970. I was visiting Mwanza where I met a Mr. Chagu, the African personnel manager of Lake Press, a large firm owned and operated by the African Inland Church, successor to AIM.

"Did you say that your name is Shenk?" Chagu asked, shaking hands warmly.

"Yes," I replied. "Joseph Shenk. Why do you ask?"

"I heard the name Shenk from my father," the personnel manager explained. "When I was a boy, my father was an AIM evangelist. In 1943 he was invited by the Mennonite mission in Musoma District to preach in several of their spiritual life conferences. Whenever he came home from a preaching tour, we children would linger around the table after supper, and Father would tell us about his adventures.

"'Listen to this,' he told us after he had been to Zanaki-land. 'On this trip, for the first time in my life, I ate with a white family in a white man's home. This white man's name was Shenk, Pastor Shenk.'"

"My gracious!" I exclaimed, remembering back to when I was four years old. "I do remember your father! His name was Methuselah."

"Yes," the personnel manager grinned, "Methuselah Chagu."

"But it wasn't in my dad's house where your dad first ate with white folks. It was in the Wenger home, Ray and Miriam Wenger's home at Mugango. There was an annual African Conference. Your father, as guest speaker, ate with the missionaries. A table stretched across the Wenger dining room with benches on both sides, where we sat, missionaries and their children. Your father was the first African I had seen sitting among us eating our food, in a missionary house.

"We had tomato soup. I watched wide-eyed to see how he would eat his soup, for I had never seen a black person before taking food in any way other than with his fingers or by drinking from a cup or bowl. Your father, I was so amazed, he dipped his spoon backward in the bowl as I had seen the English people do in the guest houses where we went for local leave.

"He also came to Bumangi later. This was a local conference with no other white people there except our family. That is when he was in my dad's house.

"You know, Mr. Chagu," I continued, "It is more than eating soup that I remember of your father. He was a man of God. I remember a sermon he preached at Bumangi, and that was before I went to school. He preached on 'The King of the Wilderness,' the anti-God who kept the Children of Israel in the desert for forty years. 'The King of the Wilderness' did not let the Children of Israel enter the Promised Land which flowed with milk and honey. 'The King of the Wilderness,' Methuselah said, 'is our own selfish pride. We won't let God be God. We want to be god ourselves and manage our own affairs. And that spirit keeps us in the desert, keeps us far away from the good place where God wants us to live.'"

There we were, two young men, both around 35 years old, sons of that first generation which planted the church, lost in boyhood memories.

* * *

"Last week, August 1943," Clyde Shenk had written 27 years earlier, "a visiting native evangelist spent a few days here at Bumangi. He had been at our native conference at Mugango also. One evening while he was at Bumangi, I went to the native prayer meeting, which was held in the house of Jonah, who is the native church elder on the station. I was a little late and found that this visiting evangelist was seated in a corner wrapped in a blanket, his face lit by the reddish light of a kerosene lantern, speaking on John 3:30, 'He must increase, but I must decrease.'

"He stressed death to the 'old man' and 'newness of life' in Christ Jesus. To see him was to understand that he lived as he spoke. I wish you could have been with me to see the faces of those who were sitting on the floor and on various boxes, bags, etc. It was a humble group of about twenty in all."

How was it that in 1943 an AIM evangelist from Mwanza was

preaching among the Mennonites in Musoma District? Methuselah Chagu had been invited by the missionaries because of what had happened in 1942. The missionaries had become convinced that their preaching and teaching just wasn't connecting with the Africans.

The mission secretary put it in an interesting way: "The African native accepts our 'religion' on the same mental basis that he would any of the other religions afloat in the land, which means that his heart has not been touched and the great sin problem has not been faced and solved. Outwardly, he asserts submission to the church rules and order, but inwardly he is a heathen, with his heart lusting after the same things that the so-called 'non-religious' native lusts after."

Miriam said it in another way: "Just recently," she wrote, "one baptized Christian and another believer left the Mugango compound because of sin. Another Christian at this time is living in a very rebellious and openly defiant attitude. We are not rejoicing in these defeats."

At first the missionaries tried harder to get the gospel message across. But gradually, they began to see it as a spiritual problem. They began to pray more. At Mugango a prayer house was built on the Chamakaya Mountain, at the eastern edge of the station. Here missionaries, and others, would gather in the morning, often while it was still dark, to pray.

The missionaries began to ask themselves to what extent they themselves had been saved. They began to be as much concerned about their own salvation as about the salvation of Africans. Slowly they began to feel that God would soon do something.

The spiritual breakthrough came in a way that no one expected. God began to answer their prayers through the ministry of two women–Rebeka Makuru (not Rebekah Mtemwa of the Mugango Girls' Home) and Phebe Yoder. Rebeka Makuru lived in Mwanza. She was an old sister, a member of an AIM congregation. Rebeka heard of sin among the Mennonites in Jita-land who had earlier been AIM people. She began to pray for these Mennonites. Rebeka couldn't read or write and she was a slow speaker, but God gave her the spirit of discernment.

When Phebe Yoder visited in Mwanza, she heard Rebeka speak in a prayer meeting. Phebe knew immediately that God would use Rebeka to answer the prayers of the Mugango missionaries. When Phebe got back to the station, she urged Ray Wenger to invite Rebeka to come to Mugango. Ray wrote a letter asking Rebeka to come.

It was planned that Phebe and Rebeka would visit the women's groups in the churches in Jita-land. Ray couldn't go with them because he had to go to Bukiroba for a finance committee meeting. The women, with others, walked from Mugango to Jita-land–eighteen miles to the *nearest* meeting place. It was war time, and there was no fuel for vehicles so they walked.

* * *

A young man, Ezekiel, had joined the church through the work of AIM evangelists and become a church leader and evangelist in Jita-land. By 1942 Ezekiel had become Mennonite and was living with his family on the Mugango station. He objected to Rebeka's coming to Mugango because she couldn't read or write and because she was a woman.

At the Bukiroba finance committee meeting, Ray asked his fellow missionaries to pray for God's blessing on the work which Phebe and Rebeka had set out to do. He also asked for special prayer that Ezekiel would not take it into his head to follow the women to Jita-land. Ray was sure that if Ezekiel went to Jita-land, he would disrupt the work the women were doing. Phebe and Rebeka, knowing of Ezekiel's spiritual darkness, were praying that he *would* follow them to Jita-land.

He did. Ezekiel got on his bicycle and went to Jita-land. There Rebeka confronted him about sin in his life. Ezekiel was so convicted by what Rebeka said to him that he fell over and had to be carried out of the meeting. That day Ezekiel confessed many things which were wrong in his life. From then on, he was a changed man. (Later he was one of the first two native pastors ordained for service in the Mugango/Jita-land churches.)

Phebe and Rebeka were in Jita-land several weeks. They visited all the churches. Everywhere they went it was as though light flooded the darkness. Ray, Miriam, and Phebe sent a brief note to the home board following what had happened in Jita-land. Their note sounds as though they were having trouble explaining what they were experiencing:

"'GLORY, PRAISE, AND HONOR unto GOD, who has promised ALL things, WHATSOEVER ye shall ASK in prayer, BELIEVING, ye SHALL RECEIVE,' and who has marvelously fulfilled," they wrote. "The hearts of the three of us at Mugango are overflowing with joy in gratitude for the Spirit's burning among us–in our own hearts and in the hearts of a number of our native brethren and sisters. From the faces of those who have shed tears of penitence, there is glowing forth a radiance of victory and His indwelling presence. We praise Him for assurances that He will continue to do His work until only Christ is magnified.

"To you who have been laboring with us in prayer for the work at Mugango, may this working of the Spirit strengthen your faith in HIS FAITHFULNESS. Continue in prayer and praise to His glory."

What the Mennonites were experiencing was what later became known as the East African Revival, an awakening which impacted all the Christian denominations in Uganda, Kenya, and Tanganyika.

When Africans talked about what happened in 1942, they spoke of it differently than the traditional missionary way of talking about revival. Africans talked about what was happening in a way which connected with their traditional village system. When an African got revival, he or she saw that God, through Jesus, was bringing men and women into a new village, the village where God was "father," the Village of God. This meant that races, tribes, and clans were becoming sisters and brothers in a new family.

Seen this way, revival actually changed the definition of sin for Africans. In the traditional village system's understanding of sin, sin was what hurt your father's village. Thus, stealing from an out-group or clan, for example, was not sin. But if God was "father," then hurting any other human being, even people outside of one's own village, was sin.

When revival came, Africans began to use their traditional ideas of "covenant" to understand what happened when Jesus was crucified and rose from the dead. The old village system was a covenant system. The exchange of cattle was how two families made a marriage covenant. Animal sacrifice was also used in covenanting ceremonies. The Africans saw that Jesus' blood was the covenanting power that made it possible for men and women of whatever race or clan to become members of God's New Village.

For example, when Africans spoke of being "crucified with Christ" (Romans 6:6), they meant dying to thinking and acting in terms of the old village system. Resurrection meant thinking and acting in terms of God's New Village, the Church.

Because of this understanding, Africans also believed that the missionaries needed to be saved; that they also needed to enter into God's New Village. Africans thought of missionaries as being a white tribe with their own village-based system, a white tribe which had a circle drawn around it keeping Africans out.

As revival touched Africans' lives, missionaries were surprised to find that these Africans loved and respected them, treated them trustfully as one would treat a brother or sister. Those missionaries who entered into the revival experience, confessing their pride and self-centeredness, found a special place in the hearts and homes of the African "brethren" as revival people came to be known. It was a wonderful, joyous, awesome experience for missionaries to discover themselves accepted by Africans!

How ever could the missionaries explain to the home board and their home congregations back in Lancaster what was going on? Revival had come through the preaching of Rebeka and Methuselah and others, too. These were Africans preaching to Africans in a way that Africans understood. Rebeka and Methuselah were not preaching the way missionaries preached. Probably the missionaries did not realize that the African preachers were explaining the gospel in a way that fit how Africans thought about life.

What the missionaries did understand very well was that Africans were being changed, were beginning to act differently. Africans were showing love toward the missionaries and toward each other across clan and family lines.

Missionaries tried to explain in English to people back home what they were experiencing. And they were trying to link what was happening to their Christian faith as they had experienced it back home—which was different from the African-oriented Christianity of the revival. The result was a great puzzlement in Lancaster as to what was going on.

Following are a few paragraphs from letters that Alta and Miriam wrote:

"My heart is full of praise to the Lord," Alta testified, "for giving me to understand more fully the meaning of II Corinthians 4:12. 'So then death worketh in us, but life in you.'

"Doubtless the life and power of God will be manifested to the natives to the extent that death to 'the old man'–self works in us. It is true that the 'Lord hath made known His salvation; His righteousness hath He openly showed in the sight of the heathen.'

"I believe that many natives who were at Mugango have seen, through the revealing power of the Holy Spirit, the full salvation of the Lord. I must say that some we know have accepted it, but many, though they were led to Kadesh Barnea (Numbers 32:8) have been fearful to enter into the Good Land. It is manifested through the lives of those who have given themselves unreservedly to Him, through their testimony, the Word, through the power of the indwelling Spirit. Many have seen it and even though a small percentage of the heathen have been saved we believe that His Word will not return void. God's promises are true!"

"The Lord showed me a lot of pride and self-righteousness," Miriam wrote. "There were things that I had to make right between me and others whom I had wronged. The blood had always been precious, but it became more precious over that time. Our whole outlook on life changed. There was a new freedom. Our personalities didn't change. We just saw things in the Word that we didn't see before."

Theologizing aside, it could not be denied that missionaries' lives were being changed. Clyde Shenk's response to a motorbike accident shows how the experience of revival gave him an attitude of praise to God when something bad happened.

The rope fastening his satchel to the front carrier of his little pedal motorbike came loose and tangled in the rear wheel, causing it to jam. This threw the cycle over. Clyde was surprised at his knee-jerk reaction to being dumped. He testified afterwards that instead of becoming angry over the mishap, he heard himself call out, "Praise the Lord!"

Children were getting in the revival way too. In the Shenk home, a jar of canned peaches, sent across the Atlantic in a Christmas package, fell to the floor when being opened. Packages from overseas were rare. Young Joseph Shenk thought that the crash of the peach jar must be about the same as having a rope trip up your motorbike. He also thought that to call out, "Praise the Lord!" would not be an appropriate expression for a small boy. So he said rather clearly instead, "Good!" Not surprisingly, Clyde Shenk missed the spiritual note in Joseph's loud supper-table comment.

* * *

Those were the war years which meant there was not much for the missionaries to do. There were no institutions to run, only a few church programs, and a minimum of travel. So, a great deal of intensity went into the revival experience.

War also meant there were only a few outgoing missionaries because of the need to avoid crossing the North Atlantic Ocean and the resulting circuitous route to East Africa–from an eastern port through the Panama Canal or from Los Angeles to Santiago, Chile, by ship; from Santiago over the Andes by rail and road to Buenos Aires; from Buenos Aires across the South Atlantic to Capetown; and from Capetown overland and north to Lake Victoria. Further, there were no deputations from Lancaster to the field, and no missionaries went home on furlough. It is not surprising, then, that the people back home and the Mennonite mission workers in East Africa were passing each other in the night, so to speak.

In fact, in response to requests from the field, Eastern Mennonite Board had been planning to send four new missionary couples to East Africa. But with revival in full swing, the missionaries on the field began to wonder if the new people who were being recruited would be willing to open themselves to the revival experience. So, the Tanganyika mission secretary wrote a long letter to the home board, explaining just what sort of missionary was needed. The home board was wise. They decided to wait, and not do anything for a while. The home board secretary responded, explaining the decision to stop recruiting new workers.

The missionaries were surprised and humbled by the board's letter, and they quickly sent a telegram which they followed up with a letter. They suggested the board had taken their concerns too seriously, and they apologized for some of what they had written. This is part of what they wrote:

"We regret deeply that our letter to you contained statements giving an emphasis which did not permit you to proceed with the work of sending reinforcements to the field. In rereading our letters, we feel that those letters contained injudicious statements which imposed a restriction upon your work of finding and sending workers."

Revival was making it difficult for the missionaries and home board to understand each other. Unfortunately, it also seemed to be keeping Africans away from church even more than before. Revival made it clearer what Christian faith in Africa was about. When people understood more clearly what it meant to be a Christian, many of them stopped going to church. Ray wrote:

"The revival is continuing but not without stiff opposition from the enemy. We have found that everytime the Lord takes the church deeper into the riches of His grace, the enemy counterattacks with strong attempts to bring to naught the Lord's working."

At the end of 1943, the Mugango/Jita-land churches had 76 members. There was only one baptism that year. This figure of 76 is especially sobering when we remember that seven years earlier, the Mennonites had received from AIM eight churches in Jita-land with 41 baptized members! At Bumangi in Zanaki-land, there were seven members at the end of 1943, with only three baptisms that year.

I'll See You in the Morning

The War was finally drawing to a close and the U-boat threat to Atlantic shipping fell silent. While the possibility of travelers being lost at sea was greatly reduced, people still could not travel because for five or six years people all over the world had stayed put. Suddenly everyone, it seemed, wanted to book passage. And the ocean liners were still ferrying troops. It became quite impossible to book passage. The only way to get on a boat was to go to a port city and wait for a States-bound freighter which had space for a few passengers.

In mid-1944 Eastern Mennonite Board decided that in spite of the difficulties, it was time to begin the furlough process. John and Catharine Leatherman with their children–Lois, Bill, Andrew, and Stephen–along with Phebe Yoder were chosen to be the first to go. Alta wrote, telling of the farewell party. Her letter makes it feel almost as though the ones who stayed behind were vicariously also going back to the homeland.

"On Saturday morning, August 26, 1944, the children–David, Joseph, Anna Kathryn, and John–and I went by the Buhemba lorry [a five-ton supply truck operated by a gold mine six miles beyond the Bumangi station] to the Musoma hotel. Clyde came in on his motorbike in the afternoon. We had planned this trip to Musoma in order to be there to bid farewell to the Leatherman family and Sister Yoder who were planning to leave the next day for furlough.

"The next day, Sunday, the natives who attend services in Musoma must have been surprised to see ten European adults and eleven European children in church. All of the missionaries from Bukiroba, Bumangi, and Mugango were in Musoma. After the services we white folk ate a picnic lunch in a shady spot. Later on in the afternoon we gathered together again with the group of natives who had come in from Bukiroba for a final farewell service. The last good-byes were said and the Leathermans and Sister Yoder boarded the lake steamer for the first lap of the long journey to America. We know that it was the Lord's will that they should be the first ones to go."

There were eleven Shenks and Wengers bidding farewell to the travelers that day. It would be another sixteen months before they too would together begin the furlough sojourn, ten of them traveling by rail and ship, three adults returning to what had been home–their seven children leaving home and going to an unknown place, the land of America.

* * *

Miriam had recovered fully from the collapse which nearly took her life. The cycle of her recurrent fevers was broken. By the end of World War II, prophylactic medicines had been developed, and by taking a low dose of an antimalarial medicine regularly, people pretty much stopped getting the fever.

For Ray's 34th birthday, October 27, 1944, Miriam baked and decorated a cake. She put colored sugar-icing in envelopes with a corner cut out. By squeezing the envelope, icing oozed forth, forming the decorative lettering and flowers. Ray was overwhelmed and had to be persuaded to eat any of it. "It is too beautiful," he said with his shy smile, "too beautiful to eat!"

Despite the new malaria-chasing medicines, Ray got the fever again. There was a reddish-brown color to his urine, a clear signal of danger suggesting black water fever, kidney failure. Maybe he had been driving himself too hard. He had seemed tired, but there was nothing particularly unusual about that given the size of his district and his bishop responsibilities, to say nothing of the demands on his time because of his mission-treasurer assignment.

Nyerere Itinde, an elder in the Bukiroba church, was to be married on Sunday, June 10, 1945. Ray, as bishop, was registered with the colonial government to perform marriages. It was his duty to go to Bukiroba to officiate at the wedding. Miriam was upset. "Oh, Ray," she cried, "that's our wedding anniversary. Must you go? Can't Elam come from Shirati? If you must go, can't you come home yet that evening?"

On Monday morning of that week, Ray went to Musoma on his motorbike. Clyde Shenk told of their chance meeting there.

"On Monday, June 4, I went by motorbike to Musoma more or less unexpectedly. At Bukiroba I joined Bro. Smoker and from there we went by car. On arriving at Chand's store we found that Bro. Wenger had just gotten there. Later we heard that he had also come to Musoma rather unexpectedly that morning. There were many things to talk about. After a brief conversation, we went about our duties in Musoma and then returned again to Chand's store where we had quite a lengthy conversation. One of the matters we talked about was a problem that affected the native church.

"I remember that I expressed my point of view something like this. 'We ought to pay our workmen an amount which may be described as being on the upper edge of what is considered a proper wage.'

"I felt we should guard against the possibility of taking an advantage of the people. He felt that since all of our funds came from voluntary contributions at home, we ought to use them very carefully. People who work for the mission ought to realize, like missionaries must, that in the Lord's work very often people do not get the big wages that can be earned in other jobs.

"I was so happy that we could disagree and even argue without anger or heat. We were simply seeking the mind of the Lord. I would say that this was a characteristic of Ray's. He could set forth his point of view and would not get angry nor hold a grudge if you didn't agree.

"It seemed there was a very deep love manifested between us. I felt that the Lord must be preparing us for a special blessing. Something was said about furlough. Bro. Ray was apparently looking forward to furlough with anticipation. Finally we bid farewell in the Lord. There was that last picture of Bro. Wenger standing by his motorcycle tying things on the carrier, a smile on his face and a wave of the hand as we drove away."

The fever came on Tuesday. By Wednesday afternoon Ray was experiencing some paralysis in his legs. Miriam went over to the station school where Rhoda Wenger was teaching and asked if she would take Ray to the government hospital in Musoma.

Back at the house, Miriam called the children together and Ray prayed with them, specifically commending Miriam and his children to God's care and keeping. Rhoda noticed how he looked around at the station buildings before he got into the pickup for the trip to Musoma. Miriam and the children stayed at Mugango.

The Tanganyika Mission Executive Committee was scheduled to meet at Bukiroba that Thursday and Friday. Elam Stauffer, chair, and Simeon Hurst, secretary, went to the hospital on Thursday morning, hoping to discuss some of the agenda items with Ray. They found him to be in too much distress to talk business.

On Friday Dorothy Smoker went to Mugango and brought Miriam and the three Wenger children back with her. She took the Wenger children out to Bukiroba. Miriam stayed in Musoma and got a room at the hotel.

That evening Miriam had a brief, private time with Ray. "The burden that seemed to rest the heaviest upon him was concerning the shepherding and oversight of the flock during his absence," Miriam remembered a half century later. "He did not seem overly anxious but testified that he knew everything would be taken care of. He truly carried the welfare of his spiritual children on his heart. Whether or not he had any premonitions that the Lord was calling him, I do not know."

Miriam wanted to stay at the hospital that night so as to be near. She did not want her husband to be alone. The English nurse would have none of it as it was against regulations. At 8:00 she insisted that Miriam must go. Miriam bent over to kiss Ray, "Good night."

He whispered, "I'll see you in the morning."

The next morning at 7:00, a messenger came to the hotel and told Miriam that Ray had died. "Why wasn't I called?" she wanted to know.

Ray did come home to Mugango, as Miriam had begged him to, for their eleventh wedding anniversary. That same Saturday of his home-going, people began to gather at the mission station. Miriam remembers the lonely night, lonely in one sense but in another sense it was a night of bonding to Africa and to God her Father who had brought her to Mugango. Her pillow was wet that night, the tears covenanting her to that place. "I am of these people now." During the night the inner hunger, alive for more than seven years, to visit home, to furlough, evaporated.

Miriam wrote of the funeral:

"The Body was laid to rest on the hillside, Chamakaya mountain, at the east end of the Mugango compound on Sunday, June 10, 1945, our eleventh wedding anniversary. There were approximately 500 people present at the funeral–Americans, Africans (heathen and Christian), Indian merchants, and Englishmen. The services were held outside to accommodate the people. All of the brethren missionaries who were present had part, Bros. Stauffer and Shenk had the main messages. Ezekiel Kaneja Muganda, an elder from Mugango, spoke briefly too.

"Never before have I been so conscious of my many friends. People came from the out-schools in Jita-land. Most of them walking ten, twenty, or thirty miles. Those who could not come for the funeral came later to greet me. One visit that especially touched me was the visit of two old ladies, the one a grandmother and the other a mother of fifteen or seventeen children, who walked 25 miles because of respect for the 'Askofu' (Bishop), as everyone called him, and to sympathize with and greet me.

"Before the one left she said, 'After harvest I want to come and greet you again and bring you a gift of rice for the children.' These people may be black, but they are truly friends. If this sister in the Lord returns, it will mean that she totaled 100 miles by foot, because of her respect and love. Isn't He gracious to bestow such tenderness upon His children? While these people are accustomed to more walking than Americans, still their feet get sore in the path. These two sisters stayed over one day to rest their feet. Some mothers walked 25 to 30 miles with babies tied on their backs.

"The widow, Matron Rebekah of the Girls' Home, gave me a pretty winnowing basket the day after the funeral. Several days later she came with the gift of a rooster.

"The 'why?' I will not try to answer but trust the answer to Him who overrules all for His glory."

* * *

It was necessary to furlough, to keep the scheduled travel time. The Wengers and Shenks were to leave together at the end of 1945 or the beginning of 1946. Miriam began to pack, and in her packing experienced a moving expression of African pastoral care. She wrote about it.

"One morning about two weeks ago while I was packing books, Elizabeti, an old woman who had once been a witch doctor, illiterate, who could speak little Swahili, came to greet me. She had started to go to the lake to bathe, but stopped in here just to make sure that the children and I were all well and to chat.

"As she was sitting on the porch, she began talking about the 'Askofu' (Bishop Ray) and how that now he is in the presence of the Lord. She is so anxious to go and meet her Lord and other saints gone on before. While speaking together and looking forward to that time, a silent tear came to my eye which she was very quick to notice.

"Immediately she stopped speaking, got up and came over to me and said, 'Now *Mai Miriamu* (Mother Miriam), don't you cry, don't you be sad. Stop! Stop!' And then with one arm around me she wiped each eye with the thumb of her other hand.

"I thanked the Lord for tears, for had they not come, I would have been denied the token of this woman's loving care and concern. After she had dutifully dried my eyes, she begged me to let her help with some of the packing, and so she knelt down beside me and helped to lay the books in the boxes. A woman of her age is not usually expected to work in this land, and especially not to help one as young as I.

"When all was done, she went singing on her way to take a bath."

New Year's Day 1946 found the Wengers and Shenks at Mombasa, Kenya, waiting for any freight ship going to America with room for two families. The *James Harlan*, a World War II liberty ship, (mass produced, medium-sized freighters) took them south around the tip of Africa and north to Boston. They arrived in March. Relatives met them there and drove them to Lancaster.

Miriam had been away a few days over eight years, Clyde and Alta a few days short of ten. Miriam would turn 32 in a few days.

2.

Forefathers

"It is for their faith that men of old stand on record."
                                          —Hebrews 11:2 (NEB)

Witmer Barge

As 1945 drew to a close, the Shenk family at Bumangi began packing for their long safari. They, along with the Wengers, were getting
ready to go to America, to go "home." The four Shenk
children–David (aged 8), Joseph (7), Anna Kathryn (5), and John (3),
had lived at Bumangi all their lives. If they were packing to go
"home," how come Bumangi was home? Why was "home" some
place very far away where they had never been?

Alta explained to her children that they lived in Tanganyika
because of changes in the Mennonite Church in America. These
changes began happening after her Uncle Enos Barge was killed in a
terrible accident. Uncle Enos had been her daddy's brother, Witmer
Barge's older brother.

"Enos died before he was baptized," she told her children.
"Many of the young people who knew him wondered if he was
saved and went to heaven when he died. Because of these questions, many of them gave their lives to Jesus, were baptized, and
joined the church. Then they wanted to tell others about Jesus so
that they would be saved too. This is why your daddy and I came

here to Bumangi. This is why you were born in Tanganyika instead of America."

* * *

That story was pretty sketchy. In 1990 I went to Aunt Anna, my mother's older sister, to hear the story more completely. Anna, a cheerful, talkative, tiny old lady, not quite five feet tall, 81 years old, got out the old scrapbooks and told her story.

Anna was twelve years old when she "went forward" in evangelistic meetings. It was the winter of 1921. The Witmer Barge family lived "out west" then–in Sterling, Illinois. Anna responded during a series of meetings held at their church, the Science Ridge Mennonite Church.

Being a Mennonite Christian in 1921 meant that you acted like one, and especially it meant that you looked like a Mennonite Christian. The morning after she had gone forward, Anna got up and began dressing for school. She was combing her hair in front of the mirror in the farmhouse bedroom which she shared with her sisters. Usually, Anna wore a red ribbon in her hair. "Did being a Mennonite Christian mean no more ribbons?" she asked herself.

Just then, her mother–beautiful, sensitive, caring, blue-eyed–came into the room. Mother Ella said to Anna, gently and matter-of-factly, "You don't want to wear that." The dress Anna was wearing had decorative buttons down the front. Mother Ella did not say anything about the buttons. She just took her little scissors and carefully snipped the threads. The pretties fell off into Mom's hand, leaving little fade-scars on the fabric where they had been. So it would be. Anna had gone forward. There would be no more ribbons or pretty buttons.

Anna felt different at school without buttons or her red ribbon. She needed an explanation. She went to her father, Witmer, a stocky little peasant, gruff-voiced, good humored, and shiny-bald from before Anna was born.

"Why must I be plain?" she asked him. "When I grow up, I won't be attractive and the boys won't like me. Did Mama dress so plain before you married her? Was she pretty when she was young?" Anna pressed petulantly. "If when you married Mama, she looked the way she does now, then getting married to her was like an arrangement, wasn't it? People who dress plain don't fall in love, do they?" And then Anna asked a hard question, "Were you in love with Mama?"

"Come here," Witmer said, reaching for her hand. She was a small girl, although a twelve-year-old. He lifted his second born up onto his knee, as was his custom when talking with his daughters.

"I have a story to tell you, Anna," he said, "a long story. I want to tell you about Enos, your Uncle Enos, one of my older brothers. Enos was 23 years old. I was sixteen. That was long ago, the summer of 1896. That summer, I became a Christian. I went forward in an evangelistic meeting and gave my life to Jesus. That fall, I joined the church. That was back East in Pennsylvania. I was baptized in the Strasburg Mennonite Church."

Then Witmer told his daughter the story which the local newspaper, the *Lancaster New Era*, ran in its July 29, 1896 edition:

> A fearful accident occurred on Sunday morning at 12:20 o'clock at the Pennsylvania railroad crossing at Bird-in-Hand, by which two lives were sacrificed. The crossing is a curve, and is one of the worst of railroad crossings in the country. . . .
>
> The . . . victims are Enos Barge, 24 years of age, and Miss Barbara Hershey, eighteen years old. . . . On Saturday evening, the young people left home to attend a party at the residence of John Musser, near Witmer.
>
> When they started homeward, two other teams (horse drawn buggies) were with them, and their team was between those two. Amos Landis and a lady friend, Miss Sabina Hershey, a cousin of Barbara, were in the front team, and they passed the track in safety a short distance ahead of a special east-bound train. . . .
>
> Those in the foremost team heard the engineer's whistle just after they crossed, and looking back, Mr. Landis saw the engine crash into the team occupied by his friends. The train, as testified to afterwards by the engineer, was running at a speed of about 55 miles an hour, and failing to see or hear its approach, Mr. Barge drove right in front of it. . . .

This collision was awful, the horse being hurled far from the track and killed, and the buggy reduced to kindling wood. Miss Hershey must have fallen directly in front of the engine, and was perhaps instantly killed when the engine passed over her. Her body was run over by the entire train and was found many yards east of the crossing, where it was dragged by the cars. It was literally cut to pieces, the head being so horribly mutilated that her features were scarcely recognizable. Barge was found beside the track at the crossing, while 30 feet east of him lay his right arm. He was so terribly injured that he died 23 hours later on Sunday night at the County Hospital, having been brought to Lancaster aboard the 2:20 a.m. train.

"Your Uncle Enos was conscious during much of the time between his being hit by the train and his death," Witmer continued. "Neither he nor Barbara were members of the church. None of the young people at the party were church members. They were all from Mennonite homes. Some preachers afterwards doubted whether Enos went to heaven when he died because he wasn't baptized.

"Your grandma, my mother, was with Enos during those hours of frightful suffering before he died. She was terribly distraught and at first the doctor would not allow her into Enos' room. She felt responsible for the accident because she had urged Enos to keep that date with Barbara even though he thought to cancel it. Your grandma told me that before he died Enos was praying for his other brothers and for me too. He asked that the ring on his finger be taken off so he wouldn't be wearing jewelry when he died. I think he was a Christian, even if he wasn't baptized. How can you pray for your brothers and not be a Christian?

"Enos' funeral at the Strasburg Church was big. There were more people gathered than I have ever seen in one place in my life."

The *New Era* reported the funerals of both Barbara and Enos:

THOUSANDS ATTEND THE FUNERAL OF MISS HERSHEY AND MR. BARGE, THE VICTIMS OF THE BIRD-IN-HAND TRAGEDY. The funerals of Barbara Hershey and Enos N. Barge, the victims of the terrible railroad accident at Bird-in-Hand, on Saturday night, had probably the largest attendance of sympathizing friends of any ever held in Lancaster County–certainly, the largest ever held at the respective burying grounds.

In the funeral procession that left Miss Hershey's parents' home in Paradise Township, on Tuesday, there were more than 300 vehicles, and at the Hershey meetinghouse and burying ground, in Leacock Township, a great many persons had assembled before the procession reached there. . . .

At Mr. Barge's funeral on Wednesday afternoon, at the Mennonite burying ground west of Strasburg, there were more than 1000 vehicles, and the available space in the meetinghouse yard and in the neighborhood, even into the Borough of Strasburg, was taxed most severely to provide places at which horses attached to carriages might be safely tied, the pressure finally becoming so great that John H. Brackbill and others opened their fields to accommodate the multitudes. In the meetinghouse 700 people can be comfortably seated. It was packed full, seats and standing room, and there were at least twice as many people outside, friends of the family who could not get into the building, but who eventually, by keeping everybody moving, had the opportunity to view the corpse.

"The Strasburg Church was steamy from so many people packed in. They were sitting on the benches and on the backs of the benches," Witmer continued with his story. "The young people in the back part of the church crowded in this way, two rows of people to a bench. The open windows were full of people too, and people were standing all along the side aisles of the church and in the back.

"That summer, A. D. Wenger, an evangelist [who would become Eastern Mennonite College's second president], was holding evangelistic services in Lancaster County. At that time, the Lancaster Mennonite Conference did not allow evangelists to preach in the same church more than two nights in a row. The conference leaders did not want the young people to be 'carried away' with too much emotional preaching. That is why two nights in a row was all they allowed. Anything more than that was called protracted meetings.

Conference was against protracted meetings.

"But we had what amounted to protracted meetings anyhow. Evangelists would move from church to church in one district. The churches in Lancaster County are close enough to each other that, even with horse-and-buggy transport, the same people could go to meetings even if the place of the meeting changed. That summer A. D. Wenger was preaching in the Pequea District. A. D. preached in Barbara's church and in our church, and in other churches too in the district. He came to our church, Strasburg, for two evening meetings. He came a few days after Enos' funeral. Over a thousand people came to hear A. D. preach, many more than the Strasburg Church could comfortably hold.

"It was a mass movement. Many young people were asking themselves what would happen if they died suddenly as Enos and Barbara had. Many of us began to think that we should join the church, even if we were still young people and unmarried.

"I decided that even if I was only sixteen years old, I was going to accept Jesus as my Saviour and join the church. There were many of us young people at Strasburg who were baptized that fall.

"This was a change from before. My parents hadn't been baptized until after they were married. Many people did not accept the new way. Many of my friends stayed 'gay,' or 'English,' until after they were married.

"I am happy that you accepted Jesus as your Saviour and that you will be baptized soon. Don't worry about not dressing pretty. God wants the beauty of women to be from their personalities, from their inner life, not from what they wear. Don't you think your mama is beautiful from the inside? I do. We love each other because of Jesus' beauty in us. See, my head is bald, so even if I dress fancy, I will still be bald. Your mama has to love me for what I am and not for how I look.

"There is something else I want you to know about, a decision I made when I became a Christian. It is about tobacco. The main cash crop back in Lancaster County is tobacco. I never liked working with tobacco. When I became a Christian, I began to think that a Christian shouldn't raise tobacco. Some of the preachers were preaching against it, too.

"A. D. Wenger especially preached against raising tobacco. Tobacco is a dirty crop. Raising it, drying it, sizing and packaging it, selling it–oh, tobacco is hard work and dirty. It stinks and stains your hands. You get a headache working with tobacco. And when people buy it and use it, it is bad for them.

"I decided that as a Mennonite farmer, when I grew up, I would not farm tobacco. But if you farm in Lancaster, you can't get away from tobacco. So I decided not to live in Lancaster County. That is why we live here in Sterling, Illinois. Here we farm grains. I like that better. Grains are clean and grains are food."

"Thank you, Daddy," Anna said simply. After a bit she kissed his cheek. "I like your stories. I wish it wasn't so hard to go to heaven."

* * *

In 1896 a lot of changes were coming into the Mennonite churches in Canada and the United States. In the congregations of the old Pequea District of Lancaster Conference, the deaths of Enos Barge and Barbara Hershey helped to focus and strengthen a movement which was touching Mennonites everywhere. The awakening was larger than the Barge family's experience of it.

Shortly before her death at age 94 in 1991, Myra Kendig Lehman, who was married to C.K. Lehman, a longtime Eastern Mennonite College faculty member, reminisced about what it was like when she was a girl, what it was like coming to faith at the Millersville Mennonite Church near Lancaster, Pennsylvania, at the turn of the century.

Myra Kendig, C.K. Lehman, and Clyde Shenk, who later married Alta Barge, all grew up at Millersville. Myra called herself a "96er" for the year she was born, 1896–the year of the buggy accident. She was 94 and frail, but she remembered well.

"Joining the church when I was a girl meant a whole social change," Myra remembered. "I used to wear rings and beads. But after being baptized, at the age of fifteen in 1911, I had to change everything.

"Because younger people were joining the church, Sunday schools and young people's meetings became important. Anna Landis started a young people's meeting at Millersville. Anna Kauffman was the Sunday school superintendent for many years. Later the church authorities wouldn't accept women to be in leadership like that. But when these things were new, there was no regulation and women were often in leadership.

"Mennonite women who were church members dressed 'plain' from the time Mennonites came to America," Myra knew. "But there was no regulation about dress if you hadn't joined the church," she remembered. "So women wouldn't join church until after they were married. My mother didn't join until after her marriage. For men, there hadn't been any particular dress code for church members, except that it was conservative dress. On the street, long ago, Mennonite men who were church members didn't look much different from other people. But the women who had joined the church looked different. The women dressed 'plain.'

"When younger women, and teenage girls, began to join the church, they had to look like church members even though they weren't grown women yet. They had to wear the plain dress. This was new for teenage girls to dress plain," Myra emphasized. "Then an equalizing thing began to happen. The young men were asked to dress plain too. At the revival meetings that were being held, confessing Christ meant wearing the plain uniform, the uniform of the church. Men and boys began to stop wearing neckties and to wear the plain suit when they joined the church. They didn't all wear the plain coat, but many of them did.

"I didn't like having to be plain myself," she remembered. "I didn't like it either when Chester [her husband, C.K. Lehman] began to wear a plain suit. We were not married yet when he began to dress that way. He was a church member earlier. But it was after he graduated from Princeton that he began to wear a plain suit.

"As I said before," Myra explained, "in my parents' generation, Mennonites didn't join church until after they were married. Those earlier marriages weren't church affairs. My parent's generation didn't get married in church. Couples got married in the home of the bride. Oftentimes weddings were held outside on the lawn at the bride's home. Even after Mennonites began joining church as teenagers, the practice of lawn and home weddings was continued for many years.

"The first church wedding ever at my home church, Millersville, was in 1931," Myra pointed out. "It was Kathryn Shenk's wedding. She was Clyde Shenk's older sister. Kathryn had been a Sunday school pupil of mine. She was getting married to Bob Landis. Both Kathryn and Bob had been baptized as teenagers. Then, as adults, they wanted to do this new thing, to have a church wedding. They wanted Preacher Jake Hess to marry them. Jake and his wife were favorites of the young people at Millersville.

"Well, the bishop (that was before Chester's brother Christian became the bishop)," she pointed out, "the bishop was uneasy doing this in a church and uneasy about Jake, a preacher, marrying them. But he went ahead and agreed that it could be done in the church. Now Bob, he never did wear a plain suit, then nor later. But Kathryn, of course, was plain. She wore the cape dress, black stockings, and black shoes. It was a Thursday wedding. The whole congregation sang. It sounded beautiful in the church. There were no solos or instrumental music, of course. The reception was held at Kathryn's parents' place.

"Well, the Sunday morning after Bob and Kathryn were back from their honeymoon trip, when it was time for the church service to begin, the bishop and preachers didn't come out of the anteroom to take their places on the bench behind the pulpit. The congregation sang song after song waiting for the preachers. Finally the bishop came out of the anteroom and confessed to the congregation that some of the ministry were not favorable to his having allowed a Thursday wedding to take place in the church. Poor Bob and Kathryn felt like two cents. And that is how it got started, how having church weddings got started in Clyde Shenk's home church, Millersville.

"I remember Clyde, the missionary," Myra smiled as she shifted to another subject. "Clyde was a fine young man who grew in favor with God and man. He was small as a boy. My father would often say to him, 'Clyde, stand straight because you will be a tall man.' Eventually he grew to be six feet tall. He was a fun-loving youth. His mother, Emma, was always so fussy about getting to church on time. Once they got to church so early that only two other people were there! Emma and her husband, Dave, couldn't figure out what was going on that everyone else was so late. Then Clyde let it out that he had turned all the clocks at home ahead by half an hour.

"One of the things that the plain clothing did," Myra reflected, going back to her earlier musings, "was make us exclusive. There was less and less social mixing between Mennonites and other people after the youth began dressing plain.

"But something else was going on, too," she emphasized. "Many things were changing in the Swiss-German Mennonite churches. In the East, especially in the Lancaster and Virginia Conferences, these changes were brought about by youth movements. For the most part it was lay people, not the pastors and bishops, who were leaders in the new things that were happening. The result was that many, many young people got interested in the church and got involved.

"Of course," she remembered, a frown on her face, "the changes were a concern to the preachers and bishops. The Sunday schools, evangelistic meetings, Bible Schools, the raising of social awareness as in the case of tobacco farming, early church membership, church weddings, choirs and other forms of special music, publishing houses, city missions, overseas missions, and colleges were a concern to the official church leadership. The church today," she emphasized, "is completely different from how it was when I was a girl. Almost everything that we think of as church now, we didn't have then.

"How was it possible for all these changes to happen?" Myra mused. "Well, when we as young people agreed to wear plain clothing, then the preachers and bishops were less afraid of what we were doing. They trusted us. By dressing plain, we showed them that we were willing to be obedient to the authority of the church. And it was true," she said emphatically. "We were obedient to the church's authority. We loved the church and respected its leadership. And this helped the bishops and preachers to trust us. The exciting things we were doing, as young people, functioned somewhat independently of, but in harmony with, the traditional leadership of the bishops, preachers, and deacons. Without the plain clothing, it would have been much harder for changes to happen peacefully."

* * *

During those years when Clyde Shenk was growing up near Millersville, Witmer and Ella Barge were raising their daughters–Ethel, Anna, Alta, and Elnora–in Sterling, Illinois. The

Barges were renting a 140-acre farm. They milked cows, slopped hogs, and put in 40 acres of corn as a cash crop. To make ends meet, they raised vegetables and peddled them door-to-door. As a matter of conscience, they would not sell their milk to the dairy on Sunday. They cooled it. On Monday they separated out the cream which they also then peddled as sweet cream or butter.

"We all worked together," Witmer remembered in a little autobiography that he wrote in his old age, "and that is what makes a happy home in church activities." Church, love, home, work–all were part of the package for Wit, Ella, and their daughters.

Their third daughter, Alta, sparkled as a storyteller, sometimes making up her own stories and poems. She was a cheerful lass, an attention-getter, who always had friends around her. Second-born, Anna of the red ribbon, refused to be impressed–jealous, maybe, of her younger sister–but not impressed. Once when someone said to Anna, "Isn't Alta cute?" Anna deadpanned, "That's what everyone says."

One day in the little country school which the girls attended, Alta got out of her seat against the rules. She got a scolding from the teacher. "The little thing turned, wiggled her bottom," Anna grinned, remembering, "but went back to her seat."

At a school basket-social, Alta recited a poem so winningly that the audience clapped her back. Such was her charisma that 70 years later, Anna still remembered the lines Alta gave for encore:

> Don't be what you ain't,
>> Just be what you is.
> If you isn't what you am,
>> Then you is not what you is.
> If you is a little tadpole,
>> Don't try to be the frog.
> If you're just a tail,
>> Don't try to be the dog.
> You can always pass the plate,
>> If you can't exhort or preach.
> If you're just a little pebble,
>> Don't try to be the beach.
> Don't be what you ain't.
>> Just be what you is.

When the landlady of the Barges' Illinois farm died, Witmer and Ella didn't have the $20,000 needed to buy it. So they moved back East. Besides the girls were growing up, and Witmer thought the western "fellahs" were too liberal for his daughters. It was 1925.

After returning to Lancaster, Wit got a 40-cents-an-hour job at the Dewalt Manufacturing Company. The family joined the Stumptown Mennonite Church, a sister church to Mellinger.

The Stumptown congregation decided to ordain a new preacher, using the lot. This was the first of five times that Witmer would go through the lot. It was September 8, 1926. Witmer and his seven companions sat together on a front bench in the church. Following singing, Bible reading, prayer, and preaching, eight identical new books were placed upright and side by side on the desk which served as the church's pulpit. In one book had been placed a slip of paper designating God's call to the ministry of preaching the Word. This slip of paper was "the lot." A rubber band was stretched around each book to ensure that the lot wouldn't fall out. After another prayer, the men in the class were invited to each take a book. The lot that day "fell" on Elmer G. Martin.

Working for Dewalt did not suit Witmer. With their life savings, he and Ella bought a nine-acre piece of land in Strasburg. There was a house facing the street on the property. A little barn went with the land. Wit raised vegetables on this land, farming it with a mule. From then on, the family made their living by selling their produce at a market stand in the city of Lancaster and by peddling it door-to-door.

As soon as they moved onto the truck farm, the family joined the church which Witmer had attended as a boy, Strasburg Mennonite. Wit began teaching a men's Sunday school class. In January, 1929 he went through the lot again, this time for preacher at Strasburg. Again, the lot went to another brother, Jacob Harnish.

In the spring of 1930, Wit and Ella, along with another couple, Mr. and Mrs. David High, answered the call to open a mission at Sunnyside, south of Lancaster near where daughter Alta was teaching school.

"We opened up a mission in a dance hall," Witmer wrote, "and held services there for six years. There were bootleggers there, but they soon got out of there, but there was still plenty of booze drank. In 1936 the Mission Board built us a church, and we then had a nice place to worship. We had ministers come in to preach for us until about 1945 when we asked for an ordination. Then in July 1945, I shared the lot with David High, and the lot fell on him. In 1950 David asked for a deacon, and I was in the lot with some other brothers. The lot fell on me for deacon. That was July 19, 1950. I was only one month from 70 years old when I took over the work of deacon and tended to the money matters of the mission.

"In 1954 David asked for help in preaching, and I was one of three brothers in the lot. I told Ella that I thought I was too old for the job of preacher. Ella told me that I said I believed in the lot, and that there were younger men in the class [meaning that if God agreed that Witmer was too old, then the lot would fall on one of the younger men]. The lot fell on me, and by now I was almost 74 years old."

From 1952 Ella had struggled with cancer. The Lord preserved her life through their 50th wedding anniversary–December 20, 1955. She sank rapidly the next spring. On May 17, 1956, she roused from a semi-coma, opened her blue eyes, sat up with outstretched arms and exclaimed, "Oh, it's beautiful!" She then lay back and was gone, nine days before her 73rd birthday.

Witmer continued for another twelve years, eventually wearing out in a nursing home at the age of 87.

* * *

In one old snapshot, Alta Barge is seen holding a black doll. No one remembered the occasion. But it seems somehow prophetic that a farm girl, an Illinois Mennonite farm girl, cradled a black doll.

After Alta became a Christian, she struggled continually with her mischievous, attention-getting personality. Often at the beginning of a day, she would pray for a sober minded, balanced spirit. Almost always within an hour, some flash of irritation or prankishness would bring a scolding from Mother Ella. But slowly Alta's prayers were answered and she grew into the quiet, dark-dressed, black-stockinged, hair-tightly-parted Mennonite woman whom the church could and later would entrust with missionary responsibility.

But as a young person, Alta wanted to be a school teacher. She borrowed money and took two years of teacher training at Eastern Mennonite School in Harrisonburg, Virginia. Rhoda Wenger, who would later work with Alta in Tanganyika, remembered clearly the first time she heard Alta pray. "It was at a prayer gathering in the reception room to the women's dormitory at EMS. Regularly, a number of women students would gather there after supper for a prayer time before evening study. Alta prayed with transparent sincerity, as in a normal conversational way she talked with God. Her whole manner conveyed that she was communicating with the Lord."

After graduation, Alta taught at the Temperance Home School near Sunnyside, south of Lancaster.

Preacher Dave

Miriam Wenger's father, David Landis, preached at the Mellinger Mennonite Church for half a century, 1911 to 1961. During the 50 years of his tenure, Mennonite men put on plain suits and began to take them off again. Much of the activity which Myra Lehman characterized as the new church came into its own during his watch. Preacher Dave's style of leadership helped to hold the Mellinger Church, second largest in the Lancaster Conference, together during those years of change.

David Landis was a Mennonite folk preacher–a farmer turned seed-corn salesman and a community leader who had a two-year business school certificate and was a self-taught student of the Bible. He preached without pay.

* * *

Jacob Landis, a direct line ancestor of David Landis, had purchased the first tract of land in the area where Mellinger Church now stands from William Penn on April 8, 1717. The land had been deeded to William Penn by the chiefs of the Susquehannock Indians on September 13, 1700. What the Indian chiefs did not know was that the land had already been given to William Penn for Quaker settlement by the King of England. In 1699 Penn had in turn asked London merchants to survey and hold 60,000 acres of it for colonization. Landis, a Mennonite immigrant, bought a piece of this land. Jacob's son, Benjamin, was the first preacher of the Mennonite congregation which was formed from among locally settled Mennonite immigrants. Benjamin was ordained in 1746.

Members of this Mennonite Landis family have been in the community and have been members of the Mellinger Church for more than a quarter of a millennium. David Landis was an eighth generation member of this family. His daughter, Miriam Landis Wenger, was in the ninth generation.

David married in the old style–before becoming a church member. He and Annette's (Esbenshade) wedding picture showed them tastefully and fashionably dressed. Both wore gloves. Their wedding was on a Thursday evening, December 4, 1905, at the home of the bride. They were in their early twenties. David did not wear a plain-cut coat until after he was ordained.

When David came into church leadership in 1911, a fairly high level of integration had been worked out between Mennonites and the community at large. Mennonites were leaders in the Republican Party, county commissioners, and members of the local school boards. Mennonites helped found the Lancaster County Bank. David, as a Mennonite preacher, on occasion had the baccalaureate address and prayer at the East Lampeter High School graduation ceremonies.

At the time when David Landis was nominated to be in the lot for preacher, it was expected that the nominees would be self-employed community leaders. In fact, it was considered important that preachers were community leaders.

As change swept across the church during the 50 years of David's preaching, the leaders began to be chosen more for their loyalty to the church's rules and regulations than for their stature in the community. Then, as training for ministry became more important, churches began to employ their preachers. With employment, these men were no longer called preachers but pastors or ministers. Pastors were not chosen by lot. Often they came from a distance and had no roots in the local community. Preacher Dave was regretful as he saw these changes coming. He felt that you could not know a leader, nor could a man give good leadership if he was not from within the community.

David did not follow the things that were new. He refused to preach against tobacco raising. He saw tobacco as a way to pay the mortgage. When the Brunk tent revival meetings were attracting Mennonites by the tens of thousands in the 1950s, David avoided the excitement. He thought some of the confessions in the tents could just as easily have been taken care of at home. He did not push going to Eastern Mennonite College or to Lancaster Mennonite High School when it was opened. He was not enthusiastic about his daughter becoming a missionary.

David was a middle-of-the-roader. He had balance. He did not swing far from the center. He was not against things. He let them happen. He let others have their enthusiasms, but he held to the

The David and Emma Shenk family in 1935. Taken around the time of their son Clyde's wedding, the photo includes two in-laws. (Left to right) daughter Ruth, Bob Landis (daughter Kathryn's husband), father David, son Clyde, mother Emma, daughter Kathryn, and Alta Barge (son Clyde's wife).

Clyde and Alta Shenk stand on the boat deck. They are about to sail for England on their way to Africa.

Eastern Mennonite Board of Missions missionaries in Tanganyika in 1941. (Back row, left to right) Simeon Hurst, Merle Eshleman, Clyde Shenk, Eby Lehman, Noah Mack, Ray Wenger, Vivian Eby, Rhoda Wenger, John Leatherman holding son William, and Elam Stauffer. (Middle row, left to right) Edna Hurst, Sarah Eshleman holding son David, Alta Shenk holding daughter Anna Kathryn, Elva Lehman holding sons Franklin and James, Muriel Mack holding daughter Lucille, Miriam Wenger holding daughter Annetta, Phebe Yoder, Catherine Leatherman holding son Andrew, and Elizabeth Stauffer. (Front row, left to right) Miriam Eshleman, David Shenk, Joseph Shenk (author), Mary Lois Mack, Daniel Wenger, and Lois Leatherman.

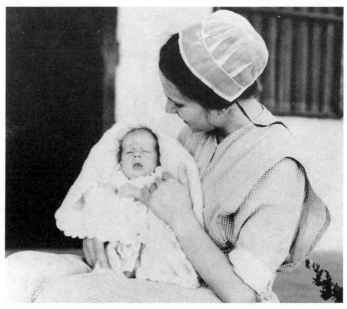

Alta Shenk holding her firstborn son, David Witmer Shenk, in 1937 in Tanganyika, East Africa.

Clyde and Alta Shenk in the 1960s with Tanzania (formerly Tanganyika) Mennonite Church leaders, Kashan Kawira (left) and Ezekiel Muganda (right).

center. This was a great gift in leadership to the church. Preacher Dave's style held things together while change was happening.

In part holding the center meant knowing when to affirm the initiative of others. George Herr was a respected Sunday school teacher for a men's class at Mellinger. At the time, it was required that male Sunday school teachers wear the plain coat. To keep the peace, George wore the plain coat, but many of his students did not, nor did they feel that it was necessary. When George died, the superintendent, Earl Groff, doubted if he could find a plain-coat-wearing brother to take George's class.

On the Sunday morning following George's death, Earl went to the room where the preachers had gathered. As Sunday school superintendent, he wanted the preachers' advice on what to do about a teacher for George's class. While Earl was talking with the preachers, Ben Herr, George's brother, came into the room and said, "George's class needs a teacher and I am going to teach it." Ben did not wear the plain coat.

Preacher Dave immediately said, "Well, I guess that takes care of that question." So, the class had a teacher who was out of regulation, but the class was satisfied and those in authority found it hard to fix the blame on either Preacher Dave or the superintendent.

David Landis enjoyed supporting interesting activities in the church community. He did not interfere with the initiatives people took. Mellinger became a church where much was going on.

Not everything that was tried succeeded. In the 1940s the young people started a church choir under the direction of a youth leader. Some of the young men got a quartet together. These efforts met with enough criticism at the district level that they had to be abandoned. Preacher Dave was grieved, but he also understood.

David believed that things would come apart if a congregation's leadership was divided. When he became the senior preacher at Mellinger, people noted that their team of three leaders (Preacher Dave; Harry Lefever, junior preacher; and John Buckwalter, deacon) always spoke with one voice on the issues. There was no sense that the unity came from arm-twisting. Rather, people felt that the three leaders were at peace among themselves. From the time of his ordination, David felt that God had called him to be a peacemaking leader.

During the years of David's leadership, a lot of authority was vested in the bishops. Congregations were clustered into districts and each district had a bishop. The bishops in turn were subject to the authority of their council–the Bishop Board.

A favorite verse of those in authority was Hebrews 13:17. "Obey them that have the rule over you and submit yourselves; for they watch for your souls, as they that must give account, that they may do it with joy, and not with grief; for that is unprofitable for you."

Older members at Mellinger tell of three occasions when Preacher Dave was required by district authority to make a public confession–when he was arrested for speeding in a 35 mph zone, when he gave parental support to daughter Miriam by attending a play in which she had a part at a public high school, and when he invited a visiting preacher who was wearing a necktie to preach at Mellinger.

David's example in making the required public confessions showed the members at Mellinger that he accepted the counsel and discipline of the larger church. This, in turn, was helpful to the young people when things which they would have liked to do, such as having a church choir, had to wait.

Over the years David and Nettie used their financial resources to help many people get a start in farming or in a business enterprise. They regarded any capital which they had as the Lord's. In their hands the Lord's money was used to make loans to help good things happen in many places. The lending of money and the repayment of loans was done in an informal just-folks way. It worked most of the time, because people kept their word and because David had good horse-sense about people, farming, and business. On the face of it, David was a lay preacher who was also a salaried store clerk selling seed-corn, but beneath that facade, he was an astute community developer.

* * *

On June 10, 1945, seven and a half years into Ray and Miriam's first term of service, David Landis received a telegram from Musoma, Tanganyika.

"RAY WENT TO BE WITH THE LORD JUNE NINE ILL FOUR DAYS BURY MUGANGO JUNE TEN DIED OF HEART FAILURE   ELAM STAUFFER"

David figured out that it was his infant grandson, Wilmer Ray, who had died. Then he got a phone call from Henry Garber, the Mission Board chairman, and it became clear that it was his son-in-law. Ray Wenger had not died of heart failure, as the cable said. He died of kidney failure, a complication of malaria and the quinine used to treat it. Elam Stauffer's wife, Elizabeth, was suffering from a chronic heart condition of which she died two years later in Kampala, Uganda. Elam no doubt was thinking of Elizabeth when he sent the cable telling of Ray's death.

David spoke briefly at Mellinger that Sunday. He took for his word of consolation John 12:24, "Verily, verily, I say unto you, except a corn of wheat fall into the ground and die, it abideth alone; but if it die, it bringeth forth much fruit." David was deeply moved. He had difficulty speaking.

* * *

Miriam and her children came home in March of the following year. She had been away for more than eight years. David found her changed. He was working in Lancaster, and Miriam gave him her worn shoes to take to the shoemaker in Lancaster to be resoled. They were badly scuffed. True to his nature, David sat down on the wood box and began to polish them so they would look respectable to the shoemaker. To Harold, his son, he said, "I don't know what has happened to Miriam. Since she has come home, it seems just any old thing will do."

David assumed that Miriam had come home to stay. But that was not so. The call she had received to be in overseas missionary service was strengthened by Ray's death. She would go back. But an extended furlough could not be avoided. Miriam was home for almost three years. A fresh youth movement developed in the Mellinger congregation during the time she was home.

Two young men, Warren Rohrer and Earl Witmer, members of the Mellinger congregation, felt their church was ready for a youth fellowship. They were concerned that the young people were not being given a Mennonite opportunity to get personally involved in Christian activities. Many of the Mellinger youth were getting involved in Youth for Christ and other interdenominational activities. Some of the Mellinger youth were dropping out of church attendance. The older members at Mellinger remembered the youth movements of the '20s and '30s, and they, too, were ready to see the young people become more active. So in 1948 the Mellinger Youth Fellowship was born.

One of the last things Miriam did before returning to Africa was to speak at the first rally of the newly organized Mellinger Youth Fellowship. That was on January 19, 1949. One hundred fifty young people were present.

* * *

In February 1949 two weeks of nightly revival services were held at Mellinger. Prayer groups had been organized and a lot of spiritual preparation preceded the meetings. Raymond Charles was the evangelist. The response was astonishing. It was felt that this was "one of the most significant times of awakening in the entire history of the congregation." Sixty-eight people made decisions to dedicate their lives to God through Jesus Christ. Many members confessed sin in their lives. Miriam Wenger's two older children, Daniel and Annetta, both made the decision to accept Jesus as Saviour.

"By January of 1950," the Mellinger 250th anniversary book says, "congregational activity had mushroomed. Practically all levels participated in some of the new ventures initiated by the youth movement. Significant strides had been taken in outreach–the Harold Thomas family had moved to the Bronx, the Shenks to Alabama, and others were exploring possibilities in Baltimore and Northern Pennsylvania.Young people in high school and college were preparing for vocations in church service having been stimulated by the time of awakening at Mellinger. The hopes and visions of the few who gathered and talked and prayed in the fall of 1948 had become reality."

What "corn of wheat" had fallen into the ground and died to have brought about such an amazing rebirth of spiritual interest and activity? Was it Ray Wenger's life? Was it Miriam packing her trunks and suitcases for her return to Musoma? Was it the efforts and dedication of Warren Rohrer and Earl Witmer? Was it Preacher Dave's acceptance of the success of others and his openness to the Holy

Spirit's continued work in his life? Was it the time given to prayer and spiritual preparation? We do not know the answer. Perhaps, many "corns of wheat" had fallen into the ground, allowing a rich harvest to take place.

Between 1948 and 1954, five new churches were planted by the Mellinger/Stumptown District. Several years before he died, Preacher Dave remarked that he "could account for over 75 persons who have gone out from the Mellinger congregation . . . as soldiers of the cross."

In 1967, the year of the 250th anniversary, members of the Mellinger Church were in Christian ministry in "many, many points in the United States and Canada, in Africa, in Europe, in the Far East, and in Alaska."

Preacher Dave passed away on May 28, 1961, at the age of 79 years. He was buried in the Mellinger Church cemetery.

3.

Alone

"Your Maker is your husband."

–Isaiah 54:5 (NEB)

As children Ray Wenger and Miriam Landis were neighbors. The Landises were farmers. Some of their income came from making butter and selling it, along with other farm produce, in a Lancaster farmers' market. For a time during his childhood, Ray had a kidney problem and the doctor ordered that he should eat no salt. So the Landises kept some butter out which they did not salt, and it became one of Miriam's weekly errands to deliver Ray's butter across the fields to the Wenger home.

Ray and Miriam went to the same school. When Miriam was in fifth grade and Ray in eighth, Ray took special notice of her. He got one of her hankies and wore it in the breast pocket of his jacket.

"When I was a girl," Miriam remembered, "we were always busy. We went to market, made butter, butchered chickens. I remember sitting down by the garden path bunching parsley. That was my job. A penny a bunch was what we sold it for on market. As a sideline, Mother raised asters and gladioli for a florist. I would walk along beside her when she cut the flowers, and she would lay them on my arm. When I got an armful, Mother would take them into the basement and lay them in the boxes.

"Mother liked pretty things. Once when we had company, she fixed the butter up like a pineapple, and I thought that was perfect!

"My mother was the oldest daughter of three in the Joseph and Mary Esbenshade family. Her name was Annette. Everyone called her Nettie. She was a good pianist. She played the hymns in *Life Songs #1*, published in 1915. It seemed to me that she could just play anything. On Sunday afternoon, or in the evening when the work was done, Mother would play the hymns. I would stand beside her and would wish that I could play. I would ask her what the songs meant.

"When Father was ordained, I wasn't born yet, but Almeda, my older sister, told me about the piano. It was against the rules for a preacher to have a piano in his home. So they were wondering what to do with it. Then the next month, the Bishop Board decided that preachers could have pianos after all. So the piano was safe.

"I remember that I begged to take piano lessons. Father and Mother said I could go to Ethel Witmore's in Lancaster for lessons. I would go when Father and Mother were at market. It cost $1.50 for a lesson, and I was ashamed to tell people what it cost. I was sure they would think it was a waste of good money. I would walk from the market over to the place. Mother walked with me a few times and then I had to go alone.

"I remember that every evening Mother would go to the kitchen table with her Bible and Sunday school book, and she would study. Sometimes she would fall asleep because she was tired. On Saturday evenings she would teach me the Sunday school lesson in preparation for Sunday. She would explain the picture cards and the scripture passage, and go over the lesson questions with me. In church she taught the old ladies' class.

"Sunday school was an important part of my childhood and later of my youth, too. It is something that missionary children miss out on. Some missionary children utterly miss out on Sunday school and Vacation Bible School. It is a great loss for them.

"When I was four or five, Mother had an operation for intestinal cancer. She was about 36 years old then.

"Father sold the farm in the beginning of 1926. Andy Rote came around and asked Father what price he wanted for it. Father quoted a price and Andy took him up on it just like that. Andy wanted to move right away, so we moved in with Grandma Esbenshade until our new house could be finished.

"It was then, after we moved in with Grammie Esbenshade, that the doctor found that Mother's cancer had come back. She died in September 1926 at the age of 42. I was 12 years old. Mother never lived in the new house on the hill at the corner of the Old Philadelphia Pike and Greenfield Road. Toward the end of September, the house was ready and we moved. Almeda was 19 then, and she kept house for us. Father remarried in November 1930.

"From as early as I can remember, I wanted to be a part of the church. I would talk with Mother and Father about joining the church, and they would say that I was too young. The winter that followed Mother's death, John Grove held revival meetings at Mellinger. He was a good preacher. We had meetings every night for three and a half weeks. The church was filled each night with people standing in the aisles. Over 100 people responded during these meetings. Grove stayed in our home during those meetings. That was in January 1927. This is when I formally accepted Jesus as my Saviour.

"My baptism was very formal. There were a lot of us from the Grove revivals. On the day for baptism, we all crowded into the men's anteroom at church and we were lectured to by the bishop. It was dry and boring, and I can't remember one thing he said.

"In high school, I decided that I would become a Lutheran. One of my teachers said something about Lutherans, and I decided that I was tired of all the plain stuff. So I decided to be a Lutheran.

"But then I began to change. Sunday school had always been exciting for me, and very interesting too. The change was that I began to understand what was happening in the church service. Father's sermons had been boring to me, but I began to understand what he was saying and to like to listen to him. Once, I went to a funeral. I had to go because a group of us sang. I thought Father's committal was beautiful.

"I began to study the Bible on my own. Father had a set of *The Pulpit Commentary* (Old and New Testaments), and I began to read those big books. I enjoyed it greatly. After high school, I took a Bible course at the Johnstown Bible School. S. G. Shetler and J. Irvin Lehman were our teachers. I enjoyed that."

* * *

Ray was the youngest child in a family of four, a quiet, serious boy, gifted from childhood with a caring spirit. Maybe that was because of his mother. Ray noticed, while still a boy, that in several ways life had not been kind to his mother. He grieved for her. That grief gave him a certain sensitivity and taught him responsibility and faithfulness. Ray was also intelligent, a self-starter when it came to work. Whatever he did was done well.

Born in 1910, Ray came of age right at the beginning of the Great Depression. He had gone to the Lancaster Business College and was an accountant by training. After graduation, he got a job at Hubleys in the office. Then, as the Depression settled in, business suffered and workers were laid off. Hubleys dismissed their single workers first, and Ray lost his job.

Not to be kept down, Ray borrowed money and bought a bread route. He made a successful business selling and delivering bread. But what is a gifted accountant doing selling bread? Soon Ray got a job at Armstrong, and he sold the bread route.

He was a member of the Mellinger church, and in due course, he rediscovered the girl whose hanky had once graced his jacket. They married in June 1934. Miriam hated being the focus of a fuss. She insisted on a quiet wedding in their new home. It was the next house along Greenfield Road from her father's place.

The Depression was still on, but Ray had a good job at Armstrong with a paycheck that met their expenses. Miriam became a home-maker and Ray "brought home the bacon."

Miriam liked how smart and business-like Ray looked as he left for work each morning in a fresh white shirt. She laundered, starched, and ironed the shirts for him—sometimes eight in a week. Ray was studying to become a CPA and took courses in the evenings. He drove a Chrysler in those days.

On Ray's free evenings, he and Miriam would often be up in Miriam's cozy sewing room on the second floor of their home, studying and talking. Ray had taken a course on the Old Testament at Vine Street in Lancaster, and Miriam had been to Bible School in Johnstown. After their marriage, they enrolled in correspondence courses from the Moody Bible Institute in Chicago. Together they did two of the correspondence courses, "World Wide Missions" and

"Scripture Memorization for Social Work."

But usually it was the next week's Sunday school lesson that they studied together. Their regular participation in Sunday school, a pattern established long before they were married, provided much of their biblical and theological training.

Missionary fervor was at fever pitch among Mennonites in Lancaster County the year Ray and Miriam got married (1934). That year an entire passenger train was chartered to take people to New York to see the first missionaries off. Everywhere young couples who were committed to the church were asking themselves whether they were called. While people seldom talked publicly about this very personal inner question, these young people knew, especially those who sensed God's tugging at their hearts, that the church would know. If God was really calling them to go to Africa, then the church would hear the same call, feel the same tugging. So they did not talk about it.

Privately, Ray and Miriam talked about Africa and about missionaries, but they did not talk about what they were hearing in their own hearts. Miriam said, "Ray and I would discuss together what it would be like on the mission field. We would be thinking that it would be impossible for us to go."

But when the call came, they were both ready to say yes. Looking back a half century later, Miriam was almost embarrassed by that "yes." Not that she ever regretted making the commitment. Her embarrassment was for the shallowness, or superficiality, of that first "yes." She and Ray had no idea whatsoever what being cross-cultural, church planters in Africa was about. Miriam remarked quietly but emphatically, "We were greenhorns! Ayee, we were *green-horns.*"

Ray never talked about how it felt to leave his promising career at Armstrong. In fact, he never talked at all about the call to missionary service. In Africa when he was chosen by lot to be a bishop, he said to Miriam, "I have felt for a number of years that I would be called to this work."

In the early years of overseas work, the Mission Board required that all of those who went would be committed to a lifetime of overseas service. Missionaries were the church's darlings.

Requiring them to be committed to do it "forever" had a way of sobering them up. They could not take the church's call lightly.

The strength of these missionaries was their culturally and historically rooted Christian faith. They were folk-missionaries sent entirely because they had credibility in their home communities. They were not trained at all in anthropology or any of the social sciences. They had very little formal training in Biblical studies, theology, or church history. What they had was credibility; they were straight shooters.

* * *

When Miriam came back from Tanganyika in 1946 without Ray, she had three children. She did not know what lay ahead. She decided that she would not move into her father's home, even though he had the room and he wished for her to live there. She also knew that she was not going to stay in the States.

It took a little while for her own home to be vacated. She and Ray had rented it out when they went to Africa. When it became available, she moved back into the house she owned and set up a single-parent household. Her father's house was just a hundred yards up the road, so he was near. Miriam had no car and did not know how to drive. Her father helped with transportation. Miriam learned to use the bus.

After a year, the Mission Board's furlough allowance stopped. Miriam needed to find work to support her family. She had not done work for pay before. It felt lonely figuring out what to do, making decisions. There were concerned people on the sidelines, hoping she would find her way, giving counsel sometimes. But she was definitely on her own. She wanted to take care of herself and of her children.

On the other side of Greenfield Road from her house was a greenhouse operation. The owners were members of Mellinger Mennonite Church, and Miriam began to work there, earning much needed dollars to buy the groceries and pay the utilities. Wilmer would run around between the rows of plants while Miriam worked. It was hard, physical work. It left her exhausted at the end of the day. But it was healing work, work with the soil, work which nurtured life–the bringing of seeds to flower.

Miriam's interest in the Bible was stronger than ever. She was teaching a Sunday school class. She missed Ray's commentaries which were stored in boxes in Africa. Her hunger to study the Bible had to be fed. She began to pray about getting a set of commentaries. Then she saw that Weaver's Book Store in Lancaster was advertising a used *Pulpit Commentary*, a complete set, the same commentary she had studied in her father's library when she was a girl.

Miriam went to Lancaster to the Weaver's Book Store, where Clyde Shenk's younger sister, Ruth, was working. She told Ruth that she would take the set. Ruth was a progressive woman and had some college education. She valued study and reading. But a woman buying a commentary, all those big volumes, did stretch her a bit. She hesitated. It was an awkward moment. Were not commentaries for preachers? Ought not a poor preacher get this bargain set? Was it not a mistake, a waste of resources, for a woman, a greenhouse-working widow to have these precious volumes on her shelf?

"You want to buy a commentary?" Ruth questioned rhetorically. *"This* commentary?"

"Yes."

"You know, they are hard to get," Ruth continued a bit lamely.

"Yes, I know."

In time Miriam also acquired complete sets of *Matthew Henry's Commentary* and *The Jamieson, Fausset & Brown Commentary on the Old and New Testaments.*

* * *

When Wilmer was old enough to go to school, Miriam felt that it was time to go back to Africa. The Mission Board was not sure how this would work. How could a single mother do a missionary's work? It was felt that if she went back, at least she should leave her children in the States. Families came forward, offering to keep the children. They would be scattered out into different homes.

Annetta was terrified when Miriam told her that there was an offer by a family to keep her. But Annetta's fright was only for a moment. Miriam assured her that they would stay together, and that they would go back to Mugango as a family.

The Mennonite mission in Tanganyika had opened a school for missionary children, grades one through eight. It was a small boarding school on the Bukiroba station with just one room and one teacher, Grace Metzler. That is how it would work. The children would be in boarding school at Bukiroba. Miriam had been asked to develop a domestic science school at Mugango. She would be living in her old house on that mission station.

The school Miriam opened offered the home economics courses in the Tanganyika Ministry of Education curriculum for grades one to eight. Every afternoon twelve to fourteen girls took classes–Bible, singing, housewifery, sewing, cooking, health, and child care. It was the first school of its kind among the Mennonites and tremendously popular.

Miriam and her family were in Africa five years on this second term of service–February 1949 to mid-1954. By then Daniel had completed two years of high school at the Rift Valley Academy, Kijabe, Kenya.

On her second furlough, Miriam realized that she would need to stay in the States until her children were on their own. That would be eight to twelve years. She needed to make a long-term arrangement for living and working. When she had gone to Africa the second time, she had offered her house to the Mission Board as a missionary home, a place where furloughed families could stay. In 1954 the house was there for her, and she made it her home again, for the third time in her life.

Lancaster Mennonite School, the local Mennonite high school, needed a matron. Miriam was offered the position. She accepted. The matron's job was to be housemother to the girls in the dormitory. Also, as matron, Miriam had the responsibility to see to it that all the girls, both day students and those in the dormitory, dressed according to the school's dress code. Miriam did not foresee the wringer that this task would put her through. No one foresaw it.

Those were difficult years for Lancaster County Mennonites. The tide which had popularized plain clothing for the conference's young people had shifted. The first eddies of overt resistance were beginning to swirl. Soon there was a strong current, turning the attitudes of the young people away from a regulated dress code. A struggle developed as conference leaders tried to hold the line against the tide. Eventually, church splits took place as conservatives and liberals splintered off from the center. And in the end, the center itself was transformed with plain suits, cape dresses, covering strings, bonnets, and black stockings giving way to popular styles.

* * *

In the summer of 1953, Clyde and Alta Shenk had an experience which illustrated the tensions of the times. They were scheduled to be reappointed for a third term of service in Tanganyika. But they were not cleared for reassignment. Several other veteran missionaries also were not cleared.

The problem broke into the open at a joint meeting of the Bishop Board and the Mission Board. A member of the Bishop Board stated the problem clearly. He said, "Our brothers and sisters that we sent to Africa have betrayed us." What had gone wrong?

As Clyde and Alta had moved among the Lancaster Conference churches on their second furlough, Clyde was frequently asked how the African Mennonites were doing in regard to the distinctive dress code which the conference practiced. Most times it was pastors and bishops asking him about this privately. Clyde told them freely and honestly that the way salvation and church membership were being experienced in Africa just did not have any connection to distinctive clothing as practiced by Lancaster Conference Mennonites. Alta had stopped wearing black stockings in Africa. In fact, she had stopped wearing any stockings although Clyde did not say this.

There was another issue which also came up during this time. Church leaders remembered hearing that back in the early '40s, a woman had spoken in evangelistic meetings in Jita-land. When Clyde was asked about this in a bishop's home, Clyde said he was in agreement with what Rebeka Makuru, the elderly African woman who had traveled with Phebe Yoder, had done. Clyde felt that God had used her. The bishop was not able to understand

Clyde's point of view. To many Mennonites of the time, these were very serious matters.

The youth movement which had taken the radical step of sending missionaries overseas had also stressed plainness of dress. The plain clothing made it easier for traditional people to trust them. And it was true that the young people who were willing to dress plain respected their elders. But it would be only a matter of time before a Clyde Shenk would say that Mennonite clothing did not have spiritual meaning for an African. Once that statement was made, it would again be only a matter of time before a pastor in Lancaster County would say that plain clothing did not have spiritual meaning for a Mennonite businessman. The bishop had reason to feel betrayed. The future was filled with uncertainty when he looked at it through Clyde's quiet witness.

Orie O. Miller, the first executive secretary of the Eastern Mennonite Board of Missions, knew that such a time would come. When the Board was first organized, he insisted that it be linked spiritually to Lancaster Conference's Bishop Board. The Mission Board was set up to be autonomous. It could act on its own—raise funds, commission workers, and perform other mission-related tasks. But the Bishop Board was given veto power—not formal, but spiritual. Regularly, the Bishop Board would gather when the Mission Board met. The bishops were free to comment on actions taken by the Mission Board. The Mission Board had agreed, from the beginning, not to move forward if the bishops were uneasy.

So with the bishops feeling betrayed, the Mission Board shelved Clyde and Alta's reappointment. Clyde did not talk about the criticisms of his beliefs and work. Instead, he prayed. Months quietly passed. Clyde and Alta waited. Keeping them in the States was not solving the problem. Finally the bishops said, "You have shown spirits of humility and faith. Africa needs you. You had better get back to your work." They sailed in December 1953. Their detention had only lasted six months beyond their regular year of furlough.

* * *

If in 1953 Lancaster Conference's traditional people were worried about what was happening in East Africa, they became even more concerned about holding the line in their own community, especially in the church high school.

The years–1955-1966–when Miriam Wenger served as matron at Lancaster Mennonite School and held the responsibility of maintaining the dress code were particularly difficult. Looking back, she said sadly, tiredly, emphatically, "Those were the years that I learned how to be hated!" How ever did she get herself into such a situation?

The night that Ray died, the British nurse at the Musoma hospital told Miriam that she could not stay with him in the hospital. So she went to the Musoma hotel. That night in her room, she read from Jeremiah. There she found Chapter 22, verse 10, "Make no weeping for the dead." Turning the pages, she came to Isaiah 54:5, "Thy Maker is thy husband." She did not know that Ray would die before she got back to the hospital in the morning. The two of them had not mentioned death to each other. Ray had simply said, "I'll see you in the morning." But that night in her innermost parts, Miriam knew that these verses were to guide the rest of her life.

She refused to look back, refused to regret or be embittered that the call, which she and Ray had followed, had left her a widow with three children. She would not weep over the past. She set her face toward the future. How would she survive in the future? God had given her the answer, "Thy Maker is thy husband." And that is how it had been. She entrusted herself to her Creator.

Then came Lancaster Mennonite School. The church was offering her employment–respectable, institutional employment. The other side of the contract was that she would be required to become an advocate for the church's dress code, a code which she regarded as legalistic and to which she had not paid a lot of attention during her second tour of service in Africa.

The church would give her security and professional respectability. She would help the church maintain its dress code. Neither she nor those offering her employment actually sat down and figured this out, but in retrospect the church relied on her. In a sense, the church became her husband.

Meanwhile, the young women at LMS were searching for meaning in their lives, searching for answers to their struggles. Miriam's prayer was that she would be able to share her faith in Jesus with them. She knew from her own experience that Jesus heals from the despair and brokenness that life brings. She wanted to share this truth, that Jesus brings meaning to life. Unfortunately, the whole premise of the LMS assignment made Miriam an enemy of those same girls. She struggled to do what the church asked her to do. This weighed her down. She lost her spiritual freedom. Many of the girls did actually hate her. She was required to act legalistically toward them, which she did not like. But she also felt that the girls were making mountains out of mole hills.

"Of course the regulations are legalistic," she thought. "But this burden of the dress code is so small a thing compared to the real-life stuff that we run into as followers of Jesus."

One area of conflict was the size of the prayer covering and how much hair it should cover. The regulation stated that girls were to have uncut hair fastened in a bun on the head. The shape and style of the bun and whether it was on the nape of the neck or higher on the head became a battle ground between the students and school administration. Miriam had a ruler for measuring the width of the frontal piece on the covering.

In the mid-'60s when the popular style was going the direction of mini skirts, the LMS regulation required that hems must cover the knee. A puzzle for the girls was how the watchers could detect when their dresses were shorter than code. Invariably, following chapel, girls whose dresses were short would get a tap on the shoulder and a summons to "come to the office." A rumor circulated among the students that the faculty, who were scattered throughout the auditorium, would check to see which skirts did not touch the floor when the students knelt during prayer.

One of the ways the girls outwitted the watchers was to have a basted hem on the skirt. After the tap on the shoulder, the girl would go by the rest room on the way to the office and pull out the basting thread, thereby lengthening the skirt by a couple of inches.

Miriam's children and her admirers in the church were having a hard time recognizing her in this role of dress regulator. She was having a hard time recognizing herself. But what could she do?

* * *

During the eleven years when Miriam was at LMS, the face of the church in Africa was also being transformed. Tanganyika became independent of Britain and changed its name to Tanzania. The Mennonite mission as an organization was replaced by the Tanzania Mennonite Church. The missionary bishops came home. Zedekia Kisare was chosen by the church to be the first Tanzanian Mennonite bishop. The African Church, through Bishop Kisare, wrote to the Mission Board requesting that Miriam return to Africa. The church had moved the domestic science school which Miriam had opened at Mugango to Bukiroba. They wanted Miriam to be Head Mistress of the Bukiroba Domestic Science School.

There was a year between when the Tanzania Mennonite Church chose Zedekia Kisare to be its bishop and his official consecration to that office. During that year, as bishop-designate, Kisare visited the United States. He encouraged Miriam to accept the church's invitation for her to return. Her children were on their own, so she would be free to pick up again on her missionary life. This would be her third tour of service. But she hesitated.

Would she be able to fit into the new patterns? It was a new day in Africa. Missionaries got their job assignments from Africans, and program budgets were controlled by the African church. Miriam had been away during the decade when these new relationships were worked out. She had known the current African leaders from the time Ray was bishop when they were first generation, new believers. Some of these new leaders had been school boys when she first knew them. Would she be able to accept their authority? LMS had made her tired of wrangling with authority.

Miriam's daughter Annetta and her husband Harold Miller were also in Tanzania. They were in the coastal, capital city of Dar es Salaam, working for the Christian Council of Tanzania. Harold was working with refugees and development. Harold and Annetta urged Miriam to come.

My family had also just taken up residence at Bukiroba. If Miriam came to Africa, we would be her neighbors. I wrote her a letter, also urging her to take the assignment.

So Miriam packed again, for her third voyage to Africa. This time she would go alone. It was toward the end of 1966.

– BOOK TWO –

Middle Voices
The Wind of Change

"The wind of change is blowing through this continent."
–Harold Macmillan

In February of 1960, Great Britain's Prime Minister Harold Macmillan gave a speech in Pretoria, South Africa. He stated that Britain's intention regarding her colonies was for majority rule: one person, one vote. This infuriated Macmillan's white Afrikaner hosts. Never before had the indigenous people, who comprised four-fifths of the South African population, been given voting power. Macmillan stood his ground with the words "the wind of change is blowing through this continent."

In the early 1960s, most of Great Britain's colonies in Africa received independence. Included were the East African countries of Kenya, Uganda, and Tanganyika. (In 1964 Tanganyika would merge with Zanzibar and become the United Republic of Tanzania.) Political independence meant church independence. The Tanzania Mennonite Church was organized and registered with the government. All assets from the Tanganyika Mennonite Mission were legally transferred and registered with the new Tanzania Mennonite Church. Everything in order, the missionaries called a meeting in 1963 to decide the future of the old Tanganyika Mennonite Mission. It was moved, seconded, and passed that the Tanganyika Mennonite Mission should cease to exist.

4.

Ancestors

"If Christian theology has not permeated our understanding of death, then we have not yet become Christians."
—Stanislaus Karuguru, Graduate of the Mennonite Theological College near Musoma, Tanzania

---

Ali

I am Ali. I am seventeen years old, a Muslim, from the Roba people. I have a job working in the house of Teacher Joseph at the Musoma Alliance Secondary School. I help Mama Joyce with the housework and cooking. I call Edith "Mama Joyce" in the custom of my people, for her oldest born is Joyce.

One day I come to work with a sore on my shin. I have fallen from my bicycle. Mama Joyce puts medicine on my leg, but my leg does not want to heal. My sore grows into an oozing ulcer. Mama Joyce does not want me to cook food with my leg like this.

Teacher tells me I must go to the Mennonite hospital at Shirati. There the surgeon, Dr. Dorcas Stoltzfus, will graft skin over the place so my leg can be well. But this I do not want to do. I am Roba, the people of Shirati are Luo, and the doctor is American. I frown at Teacher Joseph and tell him, "No."

I come back to work, but Teacher, he fires me. He says, "Ali, you cannot come into the kitchen because you have an open sore on your leg." So I pack my bundle and Teacher gives me bus fare to Shirati.

The American doctor grafts my skin over the shin-bone in my leg. My ulcer is at a place where there is not much blood, and the Doctor tells me to rest. She says I must lie on my back with my foot up and keep quiet until the graft catches to my leg.

I am anxious to go back to Musoma. I pack my bundle and find the bus to take me home. My leg begins to bleed, and the new skin slips away from my sore. I tie a rag around my shin and come again to Mama Joyce's kitchen, ready to work. Teacher Joseph, he fires me again!

Now I know I must try once more to make my leg well. I can go back to Shirati, or I can find medicine somewhere else.

One week later, I stand smiling at the kitchen door. "Look, Teacher, now my leg is well." Teacher sits on his heels to inspect my sore. He sees only a plaster covering my shin.

"Tell me," he says, "what is this brown stuff?   It looks like chewed tobacco."

Behind Teacher's house lie large slabs of granite stone, shaded by a mango tree. He invites me to sit with him beneath the tree and tell him how my leg was healed. So I tell him first how I hurt it.

My bicycle is my favorite possession. I am reckless as I ride the winding footpaths; I do not slow down but ring my bell and watch the people scatter; women with firewood on their heads, herd boys and their livestock. Goats flee from me, bleating, and squawking chickens run with their necks stretched out. One time I even killed a duck which waddled into my way as I went around a corner.

My father talks sternly to me. But flying down the footpaths is too much fun. I disregard my father's warning. Soon I fall, the bicycle swishing out from under me. I scrape my shin against a rock and for a time after that I am careful. Then my father dies, because of his age.

With Father gone, I forget that I had fallen. I go back to riding the footpaths like the wind. Soon I fall, opening my old wound. Again I fall, and again the battered place does not heal, and yet I can not stay away from my bicycle.

When Teacher fires me the second time, I am desperate. I am a religious person, a Muslim, but neither Allah nor the medicine of

Alta Shenk in 1967 with six of her grandchildren in Bukiroba, Tanzania. They are (on Alta's lap) Jonathan Shenk, (back row, left to right) Katrina Eby and Karen Shenk, (front row, left to right) Doris Shenk, Dianne Shenk, and Joyce Shenk.

Joseph (author) and Edith (Newswanger) Shenk with two of their daughters in 1966. Joseph Shenk was born and raised in East Africa. He and his wife were missionaries from 1963 until 1981, also serving in East Africa.

(Left to right) Zedekia Marwa Kisare and Ezekiel Kaneja Muganda, two influential Tanzania Mennonite Church leaders, in 1967.

The children of Clyde and Alta Shenk in a photo taken in the United States in 1972. (Left to right) David, Joseph, Daniel, Anna Kathryn, and John.

Joseph Shenk with his four daughters on a family outing in the Ng'ong Hills, Kenya in 1974. (Left to right) Joyce, Rosemary, Rebecca, and Dianne.

Several years after Alta Shenk's tragic death in an airplane crash in Kenya on July 21, 1969, Clyde Shenk married Miriam Wenger. This is a Christmas 1973 photo, showing those of the combined Shenk/Wenger families who were resident in East Africa at the time.

The Daniel and Erma (Sauder) Wenger family just before they left for Tanzania in 1976. (Left to right) Andrea, Daniel holding JoJo, Danny, Erma, and Heidi.

the Mennonite missionaries has made me well. I go to the shaman of my Roba people, a person the missionaries call a "witch doctor." I tell him the whole story.

"This is a simple problem," the shaman says. "Come tomorrow with a white rooster and a hoe."

The next day we go to the grave of my father. We first clear away the weeds from the stones which marked the grave. Then I confess my sin, confess that I was disrespectful of my father's warning and did not heed his advice. The shaman takes the rooster and cuts its throat, spattering me and my father's grave with the warm running blood. The confession finished, we go to the shaman's house where the rooster is prepared and cooked. After we eat, the shaman dresses my leg with plaster and pronounces me restored and well.

Teacher Joseph thinks my leg is sick because I hit it against a rock. He thinks I could fix my leg by going to the Mennonite doctor at Shirati.

But my leg is not sick because of an accident, no. I explain to Teacher that I was ill because I disobeyed my father. When he died, even then I did not listen. Now I have made peace with my father, and I am careful when I ride my bicycle. And now, because of the shaman's medicine and my confession at my father's grave, now my leg is well.

Joseph

In 1966 Edith and I, with our daughters Joyce and Dianne, were transferred from the Musoma Alliance Secondary School to the Mennonite Theological College at Bukiroba. Our new home was four miles up the road from the high school where Ali had worked in our kitchen. I would become principal of the Theological College, giving leadership to the training of the sixteen students enrolled there.

The Theological College shared a campus with the Bukiroba Domestic Science School. Miriam Wenger was returning to Africa to be the head teacher at the Domestic Science School. She would be our neighbor on the Bukiroba Mission Station.

I had been to Mugango, the Wengers' former home, and had visited Ray's grave, which was marked with a marble headstone engraved with lead letters. Scrubby plants had overgrown the place. A cluster of thatched houses stood nearby and the villagers–Mennonite Christians–were using the gravesite as a dumping ground.

I remembered Ali's story of how he had cleaned up his father's grave. I knew that many Africans believed that the spirit of an ancestor has power and that this power remains strong as long as the grave is tended and veneration is paid to the spirit. It is the duty of the firstborn son to care for his ancestor's grave, to keep the spirit of that ancestor strong and active.

The state of Ray's grave angered me. If he was considered the father of the Mennonites around Mugango and in Jita-land, why wasn't the church looking after the grave? Or did these Christians think of Emil Sywulka, the AIM missionary, as their father? Or did they date their spiritual birth from the revival brought through Rebeka Makuru when Ezekiel Muganda fell to the ground and was saved? Perhaps, Ezekiel, ordained in 1959 as one of the first two African pastors, was their Mennonite father.

Maybe they considered themselves radical Christians, totally rejecting any expression of respect for the dead. Maybe it was part of their Christian witness to let a Christian leader's grave go untended and become a rubbish heap.

With these thoughts churning through me, I decided to travel to

Mugango and tidy Ray's plot. Miriam should not see a rubbish heap when she returned to Africa and visited her husband's grave.

Isaiah Onyango, a friend and colleague, agreed to accompany me the following Saturday to clean up the grave. What a sight we must have been, two men on a white Vespa scooter, bumping along the rutted, sandy road. A large bucket containing two hoes and a shovel was wedged in the space between the scooter's seat and handlebars. Off we went to Musoma where we bought a sack of lime for whitewash, a brush, and some binder twine. Then south along the lake, eighteen miles to Mugango.

When we arrived at the mission station, we went first to Ray and Miriam's old house to greet the African pastor and let him know our plans.

It took the two of us five hours to finish our work. When Ray was buried, four frangipanni had been planted at the corners of the grave. We cleared away the weeds and rubbish from these small bushes and marked out a larger rectangle around them. At the corners of what was becoming a small graveyard, we dug in four large granite rocks. We dug in smaller rocks to connect them, making an enclosure. Finally, we mixed the lime and painted the rocks with whitewash.

Throughout the heat of the day as we were working, Africans stopped to watch, ask questions, and talk theology. No one offered to help. No one helped to roll the heavy rocks into place. As I noticed this, I reasoned that they must see the work as sacred, work to be done only by my friend and me. We worked through the lunch hour. No family invited us to share their food. This, too, was unusual. Perhaps they thought inviting us in would interrupt the ritualistic significance of our work.

One of the men who stood watching and talking with us had been dumping rubbish on the grave. "I thought you Christians don't respect the ancestors," he said. "It is the pagans who keep their ancestors' graves and do veneration to the spirits. But Christians pray to God and teach that it is a sin to venerate the ancestors. How is it that you, as Christians, are fixing up this bishop's grave?" Others were not so bothered by our apparent Christian heresy. They used the occasion to talk about Ray and the coming of the gospel message.

But the rubbish-dumping man persisted, noting that I was doing what would be expected if I were a Ruri following the traditional religion. "You are not the bishop's son," he said. "But the bishop's firstborn, Daniel, and you are the same age. Further, your father, Pastor Shenk, and Bishop Wenger were age mates, and they loved each other as brothers. Because Daniel is not here, it is fitting for you to act as though you were the bishop's eldest son and fix up his grave."

Onyango and I joined in the conversation as we sweated in the noonday sun. We denied that fixing up the grave meant we were going to pray to the spirit of Ray Wenger. Rather, we explained that it is not un-Christian to respect the memory of the dead. "If the bishop's grave looks beautiful, it will help us to remember his life and his witness. We know that he has gone on before us to be with God. He is waiting there for the resurrection."

Later that year, Miriam arrived at Bukiroba. During a church conference at Mugango, she visited Ray's grave. She said very little about it and did not mention if she found it tidy or not. In her heart she knew that the church belonged to Christ, not Ray. She knew that Jesus was the father of the Tanzania Mennonite Church and the focus needed to be on him.

Some twenty years later, Ray and Miriam's daughter, Annetta, visited Mugango. She told me she found her father's grave tended beautifully.

5.

Firestorms

As East Africa grappled its way toward independence from colonial rule, missionaries discovered their old network for making program decisions was disappearing. An African frame of reference was taking its place. Africans were moving to the top of the leadership pyramid.

The transition was difficult and often painful. Many "old-time white folks" were concerned that their life's efforts would get lost in history's trash bin.

Jack Shellard, an Australian missionary and World War II army officer, succinctly voiced the missionary apprehension in a conversation with me. "Joe," he said, "the things we were always afraid would happen are happening now."

Alliance–1966

After my term as chaplain and teacher at the Musoma Alliance Secondary School (1963-65), our family spent a year in New York City. I was preparing for a new assignment, training church leaders at the Mennonite Theological College at Bukiroba. Since my undergraduate degree had been in science and math education, the Mission Board decided I should earn a master's degree in religious education to be qualified for the position.

Also studying at New York University was Josiah Muganda. Josiah was the first-born son of Ezekiel Muganda who had been ordained in 1950 as one of the first Tanzanian Mennonite pastors. Ezekiel held a respected and influential position in the Mennonite Church, and Josiah would be the first Tanzanian Mennonite to earn a master's degree. He was preparing to be principal of the Mennonite Theological College. During the '65-'66 academic year, Josiah and I, both graduates of Eastern Mennonite College, met occasionally to dream and talk of being a second-generation leadership team in the new day of the independent Tanzania Mennonite Church.

* * *

The new day was thick and warm when Edith, Joyce, Dianne, and I climbed down from the DC-3 East African Airways propeller plane. It was September, 1966. I was 28 and Edith was carrying our third child, a son we would lose to a premature birth. We were arriving for our second tour in Musoma District.

Unwittingly, we walked smack into a major conflict. This conflict had in it all the issues over which missionaries and Africans disagreed as African churches took over from western missions in the late '60s and early '70s.

No church officials were at the airport to welcome their new theological college teacher, Joe Shenk. But Jack Shellard, an Anglican missionary from Australia, was there. Shellard was the headmaster of the Musoma Alliance Secondary School where I had pastored and taught for three years during my first term of service.

When the Mennonites proposed a high school in 1959, the colonial government agreed, providing that an alliance of Christian agencies govern the school and that an Anglican be appointed headmaster. It was the experience of the British government that Anglicans were successful with education in Africa. So an "Alliance" of three churches was formed–the Mennonites, the African Inland Church, and the Anglican Church Mission Society. The Alliance was to build, staff, and administer a Protestant boarding high school on behalf of the then-colonial Tanganyika Ministry of Education. The Ministry of Education would provide the capital funds and annual operating budget.

Because the school was located in Musoma District, an area

evangelized by Mennonites, the Mennonites held title for the land and buildings. As "owner mission," the Mennonite bishop of the Musoma District was ex-officio chairman of the Alliance School Board. Jack Shellard was transferred by the board from an Anglican high school in central Tanganyika (later Tanzania) and appointed to develop and administer the Musoma Alliance Secondary School.

On that day in September 1966, he stood at the airport with a proposition for me. "If you teach at Bukiroba," he began, "you will have at most twenty students, most of them with just a grade school education. They will spend their lives as church leaders in small rural churches.

"Joe, I want you to consider returning to my staff. At Alliance you will be shaping the lives of hundreds of young men who will scatter all over this nation, attaining significant leadership positions. If you want to help Africa in the transition to independence, pour your influence and energies into Alliance. Don't teach at the Theological College, Joe. Don't waste yourself."

I recognized the truth in what Shellard said and was warmed by his affirmation. But my direction had been set. My heart was in leadership training for the Mennonite Church. There would be others, hopefully Africans, to take my place at Alliance. Regretfully, I told Shellard "No."

Josiah and Grace Muganda arrived in Musoma several weeks after we returned. A great crowd gathered to welcome them. Josiah's father, pastor of the Musoma Mennonite Church, threw a tremendous party to welcome him home.

It was several weeks before the Executive Committee of the Tanzania Mennonite Church (TMC) met to decide Josiah's wage, as principal of the Theological College, and to decide which of the former missionary houses on the Bukiroba Mission Station would become his home. Soon it became clear to the committee that the church could not offer Muganda terms of service comparable to what he would get in government service. So the Executive Committee began to think about how much greater Muganda's influence would be at Alliance than at Bukiroba. The Executive Committee saw the same advantage Jack Shellard had presented to me, but in Muganda's case it would be even greater because he was Tanzanian.

At the time, Alliance had only three Tanzanian teachers; none of whom had even completed a bachelor's degree. It was expected that, before long, the government would want all high schools in the nation to have Tanzanian headmasters. The Executive Committee reasoned that if Muganda were on staff at Alliance when Shellard's current term of service expired, then certainly Muganda would become headmaster. He would be the first Tanzanian headmaster at Alliance. Not only would this move be a fair recognition of Muganda's education and abilities, it would also be a politically influential move for the Mennonite church, having a Mennonite headmaster at Alliance.

Jack Shellard had also given thought to the question of who would replace him. Matt Nyagwaswa, a Tanzanian member of the African Inland Church, was a man Shellard trusted and respected. Nyagwaswa was in California working on a master's degree with plans to return to Africa in six month's time. There was an understanding that Matt would go on staff at Alliance. While Shellard preferred that someone other than a Mennonite be headmaster after him, it was even more important to Shellard that his replacement be a brother in the East African Revival Fellowship. Matt was a brother in the Fellowship.

Many missionaries found that they were accepted and respected by Africans who were in the Revival Fellowship. Africans in the Fellowship thought of the church as God's "New Village" where brothers and sisters of all clans and races were accorded the same loyalty practiced in the traditional family-based village system.

Josiah Muganda was not in the Revival Fellowship. He explained to me that if Revival meant getting saved, then he was all for it. But Muganda felt that too often Revival had been used by the missionaries to take advantage of the Africans. "Missionaries say 'Let's pray,'" Muganda observed, "and then when your eyes are closed they make their move."

Shellard was a Revival brother, and he wanted the first African headmaster at Alliance to be part of the Revival Fellowship as well. Shellard felt Matt Nyagwaswa could be trusted to carry on what he had built.

However, four miles up the dirt road, other thoughts were taking shape. The Tanzania Mennonite Church Executive Committee concluded that I could run the Theological College. Josiah was not needed at Bukiroba. They decided that Josiah Muganda should join the staff at Alliance. The committee sent a letter to Alliance, signed by Bishop Zedekia Kisare, ex-officio chairman of the Alliance School Board.

Jack Shellard, not having been consulted, was unprepared for this turn of events. He couldn't say "no" on the basis of waiting for Nyagwaswa, so he wrote a letter to the Mennonite Church, rejecting the appointment on other grounds:

1) Alliance was fully staffed.
2) In the event that a new person be hired, the Alliance School Board would have to meet to confirm the appointment.
3) Kisare, only recently elected to be ordained Bishop, hadn't been registered yet with the Ministry of Education as board chairman and therefore could not act in the capacity of chair.

The Mennonite Executive Committee was still in session when Shellard's hand-carried letter was delivered. They responded by writing a minute which stated that on Monday morning Muganda's family and all their household effects were to be loaded onto the Bukiroba station's three-ton truck. The minute further stated that Joe Shenk would drive this truck to the Alliance campus, delivering the new staff member to Jack Shellard.

Jack Shellard was enraged by the effrontery of the Mennonites. He learned of their decision by the missionary grapevine. After considering his options, Shellard walked across the Alliance campus to the English teacher's house, who happened to be Omar Eby. Eby was married to my sister, Anna Kathryn.

Shellard minced no words. "Omar," he said, "tell your brother-in-law that if he drives that truck onto this campus, I will have him arrested and jailed for trespassing."

I was definitely in a bind. Bishop Kisare had left on a four-day trip to Jita-land, 50 miles away, and was unavailable for consultation. Missionaries at Bukiroba advised me bluntly: "Joe, the time has come for you to stand up and be counted. You cannot be a pawn for the Africans to use however they wish. Josiah was educated for the Theological College. You must not have any part in this Alliance idea. Don't you dare drive that truck to Alliance on Monday morning."

On Sunday evening I went to the home of the TMC treasurer, a friend and neighbor on the Bukiroba station. He was also a member of the Executive Committee and an ordained pastor from Bumangi, the place where I had grown up. He was a Zanaki-man. As a child, I had known and respected him so I explained the situation to him, leaving out the jail threat. "Please understand. I can't drive that truck to Alliance tomorrow morning."

"But why can't you?" he persisted. "There are not many people here who can drive. You are a driver, and right now the college is not in session and you have nothing to do. You will just be driving a truck, Joe. Driving a truck is an innocent thing to do. You must do this tomorrow, as the Executive Committee has said."

"But it isn't that simple. I can't just be 'a driver.' Symbolically, I'm not just 'a driver.' I was on Jack Shellard's staff. We respected each other. I am also a pastor–besides that, the Executive Committee has appointed me to be principal of the Theological College, so how can I be just 'a driver?' If I drive over there tomorrow, I will be making a statement. I don't want to make a statement about this struggle between the Mennonite Church and Jack Shellard."

The older man responded sadly but emphatically. "I have known you since you were a child, Joseph. Then I did not know your attitude towards us Africans. People mask their true identities, but today you have been forced to declare yourself, to show yourself as the racist you are in your heart. You have made yourself too important to cooperate with the Executive Committee. You have chosen the side of white colonialism. You have refused to do justice. Today you have been unmasked. I have seen you for the racist you are."

Few things could have shattered me the way those words did. I walked home quietly in the gloaming dusk.

The next morning the truck sat, loaded and driverless. An African Mennonite was passing through Bukiroba on his way to Musoma. He was a driver. He drove the truck to Alliance. There it sat–truck, husband, wife, children, piled up personal belongings–parked in front of the headmaster's house. Jack Shellard wasn't on campus.

Early that morning, Shellard had left and driven 65 miles to consult with the vice chairman of the Alliance School Board. The vice chairman was a Kenyan and an Anglican. He was serving in Tanzania. He was also a brother in the Revival Fellowship. Shellard explained the situation to him and asked him to write a letter talking some sense into those Mennonites. The letter was written to Bishop Kisare, informing him that the Mennonites had no right to assign Josiah Muganda to teach at Alliance. Shellard brought the letter, which was written in Kenyan Swahili, along back with him.

Not only was Jack Shellard refusing to accept the will of African Mennonites, he had now added to the conflict by having a Kenyan tell Tanzanians what to do, *and* telling them in Kenyan Swahili.

It was dusk that Monday and I was at home when Shellard returned from his trip. He stopped by the Bukiroba station to deliver the letter to Bishop Kisare's home. He also wanted to know if I had driven the truck to Alliance that morning. After finding out from other missionaries on the station that I had not, he drove down to our house. It was then dark. Lantern light shone from the windows as he pulled up outside the house. We stood there quietly in the living room. Then Jack offered, "I came to see whether you are a rat or a man. I have been told that you are a man."

We sat down, and Jack continued, "Do you remember what we used to talk about, the things we were afraid would happen? Well, those things are happening now."

I didn't know how to say what I was thinking. I wanted to explain that my decision to stay out of the truck driving business did not mean I disagreed with the local church's action. I believed Muganda could be a capable and trusted headmaster after Shellard left. But I also understood Jack's fear of watching himself become extinct—watching his work blow away before Africa's winds of change.

I shifted nervously in my chair. Then I said, "You are leaving, Jack. Soon you will be going back to Australia. But I am staying. Africa is my home."

If Jack detected naive idealism in my words, he said nothing. He did not rebuke me for feeling smugly superior to the older generation missionaries and their Western ways. Perhaps he thought of

me as a simple child, a child whose day of cross-cultural enlighten-
ment would come. He only smiled and extended his hand.

In truth I did feel a little smug about the confrontation between
the old missionary ways and the new African leadership. As a second generation missionary, I was banking on it that my life would
prove my heart. I hoped that, in time, I would be trusted by the
African leaders of the church. I was prepared to cast my lot on that
side of the issue.

Meanwhile, the Muganda family was given hospitality by several missionary families on the Alliance compound. The next morning Josiah's wife, Grace, and their children, returned to Bukiroba.
Josiah and the truck, now sidelined in one missionary's carport,
waited. Shellard ignored them.

Muganda and the three-ton truck were still on campus at
Alliance when Bishop Kisare returned to Bukiroba Wednesday
afternoon. When he learned of the standoff, he immediately sent
word for Josiah and the truck to come back to Bukiroba.

Within days of Josiah's being rebuffed, the Tanzania Ministry of
Education assigned him to be headmaster of a high school in
another region. Soon he was promoted to be headmaster of a larger school. Two and a half years later, he was transferred back to
Musoma. In Musoma he was given the powerful government post
of Regional Education Officer. Everyone called Josiah Muganda the
REO.

Within months of the Shellard-Mennonite confrontation, the
Ministry of Education nationalized all the government high
schools in Tanzania. All foreign headmasters were dismissed.
Rumor spread that the Ministry was inspired to this radical move
by Shellard's stonewalling of the Mennonites at Alliance.

Shellard was replaced by a Tanzanian Lutheran from a distant
region. The new headmaster tried to hold the school to the same
strict Protestant standards which Shellard had held. The students
rebelled, rioting and throwing stones on the headmaster's house
roof. The Musoma police were called in to patrol the campus. The
Lutheran was transferred.

Then Timothy Shindika, a member of the African Inland Church
and a man with a master's degree, was appointed headmaster.

Shindika was a brilliant administrator, sincere Christian, and skilled diplomat. He restored order and the campus settled down to its tasks of teaching and learning.

Ordination–1967

Zedekia Kisare was ordained Bishop of the Tanzania Mennonite Church by a bishop representing the Lancaster Conference of Mennonites on January 15, 1967 at Bukiroba.

This was quite soon after Miriam Wenger's return to Africa for her third tour of service–a three-year assignment. What were Miriam's thoughts on the ordination of a Tanzanian to a role her husband had held? Indeed, she accepted the passing of leadership from missionary to African with faith and good humor:

"The ordination meant much work and planning," she wrote to her sister in a letter. "I can't tell you how many people we served. I think I peeled potatoes for four hours one morning, then cut meat for two hours one afternoon. We made sandwiches, chopped fruit and served people almost by the hundreds for two and a half days. 'Tired' hardly explains the way we felt after it was all over.

"The service on Sunday morning was very impressive and the brethren gave challenging messages. The Bukiroba church was packed, and I would guess that there were at least several hundred people outside. Bishop Kisare had a very good attitude, and I am sure he feels the burden of the work."

Silver Thread of Grace–1969

In which several participants tell their stories.

John, Clyde and Alta Shenk's fourth-born child

Philip was an infant when my wife Lois became sick. We were teachers at a Kenyan high school, just finishing our three-year term. Several weeks after Philip was born, we visited my parents, Clyde and Alta, at Migori in southwestern Kenya. Lois became sick there at Migori. That night, in July of 1969, Daddy drove us across the border into Tanzania to the Mennonite hospital at Shirati. Daddy had to go back to Kenya for some church meetings which had been planned. But a Missionary Aviation Fellowship plane took Mother and me, Lois and our baby to Nairobi. We took Lois to the Nairobi Hospital. [Lois Landis Shenk tells the story of her struggle with depression and mental health in *Out of Mighty Waters*, Herald Press, 1982.]

I can't imagine what I would have done without Mother there to help me–Philip so tiny.

A few days later Lois and I with Philip got a flight back to the States. Lois was hospitalized. I was exhausted–jet-lag, weariness, sorrow.

Then I got a call that she was dead. I thought they meant my wife was dead, at the hospital. My beautiful, dark-eyed wife, my writing wife, my brilliant, shattered wife . . . No, they don't mean Lois. *Alta* is dead. *Mother* is dead. Mother? Mother, waving good-bye at the Nairobi airport. . . killed in a plane crash, flying back from Nairobi? "Yes," the caller said. "The pilot flew straight into the mountainside."

Pasaka, representative rescue-squad worker

For myself, I am not surprised that this British pilot has crashed his little plane. He is a very nice man, a sincere Christian who believes God called him to be a missionary pilot. But he takes too many risks. This crash which we are searching, for example, is the outcome of his foolishness. He should not have tried to go to Musoma today because the Ng'ong Hills are covered in fog on this side of the Rift Valley. This single motor plane does not have the instruments to fly blind in a fog. But he knew the weather patterns for this area in July. He knew the other side of the mountain would be dry and clear, even if the Nairobi side, because of the elevation, was clouded over.

I think this pilot took a bad risk. I think he flew to the northern pass to see if it was clear, and then tried the southern pass. When he found both passes fogged down to the ground, he tried to guess where this pass was and flew into the southern edge of the mountain. If he had flown a few seconds more, just 300 yards further south, he would have made the pass safely. This man's foolishness has cost him his life, and the lives of all these people.

We have found five people, all of them dead. But there is a problem. There are five bodies, but six passports—and there are six seats on the plane. In this woman's handbag we have found the passport of a little girl. It says her name is Shenk, the same as the woman. Joyce Shenk, eight years old. Her body is not here, and we wonder if she has wandered away, or if she is injured, or perhaps she has been dragged off by a leopard. Our searching has revealed nothing.

The Petersheims, missionary angels

We were living in Musoma Town at the time and were traveling to Nairobi to pick up our children from boarding school at Rosslyn Academy. Joe and Edith's daughter, Joyce, was also a student there. Rosslyn is located a few miles from downtown Nairobi. We had promised Joe and Edith that we would bring their daughter, Joyce, back with us, saving them the trip and border crossing. Joyce was in second grade.

When we got to Rosslyn Academy, we discovered Joyce's passport was still at the Kenyan Immigration Office. The school's dorm parents had decided to keep Joyce with them until her passport situation could be resolved. She could then fly home with her grandmother. Alta Shenk was in Nairobi with John, Lois, and their baby Philip. John's family was returning to the States, and Alta had a seat on an upcoming Missionary Aviation Fellowship flight to Musoma.

I looked at the little girl and could tell that she didn't want to wait one day more than necessary to see her parents again. We planned to drive back to Tanzania through the Serengeti National Park. We knew the children would enjoy the game reserve. At that time, there was no immigration post at the game park border crossing.

"We promised Joe and Edith we would bring Joyce home," we told the dorm parents. "We can get her across the border without a passport."

I remember the girl's shy smile as we all packed tightly into the tiny car for our trip home.

Edith Shenk, Joyce's mother and
Clyde and Alta's daughter-in-law

On Monday morning, July 21, the girls and I were expecting Grandma Alta to arrive by plane. She was flying from Nairobi and bringing Joyce's passport with her. She would stay with us at Bukiroba for a few days until my husband, Joe, got back from a theology conference. Then we would take her back to Clyde, to Migori in southwestern Kenya. I was looking forward to the company of my mother-in-law and was hoping she would bring good news about John and Lois.

I told my daughters to listen for the airplane. Any flight coming in to Musoma could be seen and heard from our house in Bukiroba. Planes were novel enough that at the first drone, the girls would run out to the front yard and look up, pointing at the insect crossing the blue bowl of sky.

The morning crawled on, and at noon the skies were still silent. I had lunch with the children and told them I was going for a little walk to the mission station office. Someone there had just come back from Musoma and reported that the Musoma air strip got a call from Wilson Airport in Nairobi, asking if the plane had come in. Wilson had lost radio contact and feared that the plane was down. I contacted Shirati by shortwave radio. They had also received a radio message from Nairobi, asking if the plane was at Shirati. I told Shirati to tell Nairobi that my husband could be contacted in Arusha.

I walked back to the house and called the girls to the living room. I explained that the plane was missing and might have crashed.

"You may not have a Grandma Shenk anymore," I said simply. I gathered Joyce on my lap and ruffled her hair, breathing in the smell of dust and sun.

Later on, the Africans began to come. There was no official word on anything, but they came to the house and sat quietly in the living room. After a while they would leave and others took their place. Bishop and Mama Kisare sat with us for hours, a cup of chai (tea), a word or two about how Mama Shenk was afraid of flying. Mostly we just sat together, receiving comfort in each other's presence.

Clyde Shenk

I had left Migori in the Toyota pickup with several African brethren at about 11:00 a.m. on Friday morning, July 18 for a six-day trip to visit other churches in Kenya. On Sunday afternoon, at Namanga in Karungu land, my Kenyan brethren said they wanted to go to the lake, about two miles away, to bathe. They invited me to go with them, but instead I climbed the hill just back of the village and found a place where I was shielded from the afternoon breeze and read my Bible.

I looked up a number of scriptures on prayer and saw again how the promises at some places look as though you can just ask and receive. But taking them all together it is so clear that one must know what is the will of God and ask according to His will. Romans 8:26 and 27 stood out with meaning. "We know not what we should pray for as we ought: but the Spirit itself maketh intercession for us with groanings which cannot be uttered." And further, the Spirit "maketh intercession for the saints according to the will of God." And again Jesus said He would answer our prayers so that "the Father may be glorified in the Son."

I was thinking mostly about the illness in my son John's home, but somehow, I felt led to simply open my heart to the Lord and to accept that God would help me to pray for His perfect will to be accomplished in all that concerns us. Little did I think, however, that I would need this so much as an undergirding of sustaining strength in a very short time.

We left Namanga in the morning, Monday, July 21. It was a good day. We were to go to Bande that day. En route we stopped at a fallen Christian's village to try to help him, and we had a profitable time. At another village we had food. Then some miles further on we pulled a truck out of the mud and left the driver and his people very happy and thankful. Later we stopped at another village where they were asking us to start church work, and we felt the presence of Jesus among us.

We arrived at Bande at 5 or 5:30. We had just looked at their new church–the place where Alta and I had spent eight days putting on a new roof. Then we saw Dr. Glen Brubaker and Pastor Nashon Nyambok driving in from Shirati and I wondered what brought them.

After hearing the word, I felt struck in such a way that words simply cannot describe. I think no one knows what it is like but those to whom it has happened. Yet immediately I knew that Jesus was there, and I felt a silver thread of grace sustaining me.

We decided to take the Toyota and head to Shirati. Soon we were on our way. My African brothers were a comfort to me. Their love and sympathy gave me to understand that the other members of the Body of Christ were sharing my sorrow with me. "His grace is sufficient."

Joseph Shenk

The bus is jammed with people, as buses always are, people and chickens and baskets of fish, a baby sleeping at its mama's breast. Dust filters in with the warm night air. I would like to bathe, or have a cup of chai. It will be daybreak before we reach Nairobi. I close my eyes to better see the faces of my wife and children, pictures passing randomly through my mind. My own mother's face, the covering on her dark hair, the smell of her clothing and texture of her skin. My mind begins to play with tomorrow's possibilities. Will she be grotesque and broken, lying behind the morgue's cold glass? I will have to identify her before she can be prepared for burial. Thank God there was no fire . . . she will look like sleep, eternal, peaceful rest. Or will the shock of smashing against the mist-shrouded mountain be frozen in her face? Her absence is a pain too new to understand. I push the images out, reach for difficulties easier to grasp.

The pictures filter through my mind, these last years, the disappointments. It is a hard time, God, to know what to do. Alliance. Musoma. John and Lois. And now this. She is gone–not she, Mother (I will think about that tomorrow, not any more tonight)–but she, Mama Shenk, Missionary. And Bishop Ray is gone, and "neither do men put new wine into old bottles."

I am staying because Africa is my home. I was born here, was fed on the language. I have dug the earth to plant banana trees and sweet potatoes. I have gathered the water from the rainy season to drink of all year round. There will always be a place for me here. I will preach. I will teach at the Theological College. I will be a partner with the young men returning from the U.S. with their master's degrees. We will build the new Africa together. Yet the wind of change is blowing through this country–"Else the bottles break, and the wine runneth out, and the bottles perish: but they put new wine into new bottles, and both are preserved."

I look at my reflection in the window, in the light from the driver's dashboard. I am sitting across from him, on the left side, a little further back. I can see bushes by the side of the road, out my window. I can see the potholes and washboard ridges ribbing the dirt road, light and shadow headlight illuminated. If I rest my head against my hand, bumping, against the window, maybe I can sleep a little.

Tomorrow I must identify the body in the Nairobi morgue. She must be driven to Shirati for burial. I wonder who is with Daddy now.

The driver makes a sudden noise, brakes a bit, grinds into a lower gear. He's sitting upright, looking out the windscreen at something. It's a jack rabbit, long legged and ugly, caught in the bus's headlights. The driver doesn't want to run it over, but the rabbit can't seem to escape from between the beams of light. It runs away in powerful bounds, down the road, the bus rattling along behind it. The rabbit tires. The bus slows down. Passengers begin to wake, watching. The long back feet flash white with every jump. The light shows blood through the translucent ears. The bus is crawling. With a final burst of panic, the rabbit hurtles up the tunnel of darkness between the beams; the bus follows. Exhausted, the rabbit takes one jump at a time, then crouches motionless, except its rapid breathing. The bus stops also, fixing the animal in its glaring lights.

A passenger jumps down from the bus and flashes a shadow across the scene. With a wild leap, the creature lands in the ditch along the road where the passenger drops on it, gathers it to his body. It kicks feebly a few times and then is still. The man brings it, wrapped loosely in an old shirt, onto the bus and holds it in his arms. The bus grinds through its gears and roars on down the road toward Nairobi.

Miriam Wenger

The Africans speak of planting their dead. Alta's funeral was held at Shirati. The missionary administrator at the hospital offered to hire workers to dig the grave. But it was not necessary to pay anyone to do this work. Through sun-dried earth and igneous gravel, African volunteers dug the grave with pick and shovel. They dug eight feet before hitting solid rock. It was an honor to plant someone so deeply.

A thousand and more people came, some from great distances, to mourn the woman they called Mama Shenk. Again and again they gave testimony to the power in the sacrifice of Jesus which made it possible for men and women of different races, tribes, clans, and languages to be members of God's family, God's gathered people, members of the New Village of God.

Clyde did not see his wife's body. The missionaries thought it would be too sensational to have a general viewing, and also thought it disrespectful to expose her broken body. Joe and a doctor at Shirati were the only people to see her. The casket was unopened at the funeral.

Clyde came to live with Joe and Edith on our compound at Bukiroba for a time. He caught malaria and became deathly ill. Edith told me how she and Joe stayed up all night sponging him with cool water to break the raging fever. His temperature rose to 105 degrees.

It was a mistake for Clyde not to view the body. It was difficult for him to accept Alta's death. He thought maybe authorities were hiding something from him; that perhaps she wasn't really dead at all or that her body was so battered they wanted to spare him the pain of seeing it. Joe assured him that he had seen her at the morgue, described the dress she wore and assured him that her face had not been disfigured. Slowly, over the weeks and months that followed, Clyde was healed of these doubts.

Things Fall Apart–1969

Four months after Mother's death, I learned by reading the minutes of the TMC Executive Committee that the Theological College was to be closed and that my new job was to be Bishop Kisare's driver. That was in November 1969 just before graduation.

For three years–January '67 to November '69–an older missionary couple and I had taught sixteen men, the same sixteen. Half of the students were older than I was. All but three were married, and all of the students lived in a dormitory on the Bukiroba mission station. I had become very attached to them.

For three years we dug the school gardens together, discussed Bible and theology, traveled by church pickup to weekend district conferences–eating together, bunking together, the college choir singing wonderfully. We even went on a five-day field trip to Nairobi with proceeds from our peanut garden.

The church wanted the medium of instruction in the college to be English. This was so the students would become competent in an international language. So we taught in English. But all the field experiences were done in good old comfortable, expressive Swahili. It was a blest three years.

Even so, it did not totally surprise me that the Executive Committee decided to close us down after graduation. The African district pastors–about a dozen of them by 1969–did not know what to do with the graduating class. The graduates wanted jobs. They wanted to be paid. Most of them were better educated than their district pastors. The Executive Committee decided that the graduates were to return to what they had been doing before they began studying at Bukiroba. Many of the students were upset with me for not getting them church jobs. "Why have we been here wasting our time?" they demanded. The Theological College had been a missionary idea, not an African idea. Clearly, the time to close it had come.

I had been exploring Theological Education by Extension (TEE). Set up much like a correspondence course, the students also gather weekly for a "classroom" exchange with their instructor. The more I thought about TEE, the more I felt that it answered the problems that had surfaced with the Theological College. Besides, I would much rather be running a TEE program for the church than be the bishop's driver.

In the late afternoons, between 4:00 and 6:00, Bishop Kisare usually had a pause in his day. Often I would drop by his house to greet him and chat. On one such day, I raised with him the TEE idea. He was unresponsive. I further elaborated. Still no engagement. For half an hour, I laid out the beauty of the TEE program—detailed where it was being used and how successful it was. Nothing, no feedback. Silence lay between us. I walked back to my house.

I was deeply troubled. Nothing like this had happened between the Bishop and me before. Toward evening I decided to go back and apologize.

The dusk of night was gathering as I sat again in his living room. "I'm sorry," I said. "My spirit tells me that I was pushing something with you which you were not receiving."

"Yes," he said, "today you were acting in the spirit of your missionary fathers. They always told us what was to be done. The day of you white people telling us what to do is past.

"If you are sincere in your repentance," he continued after a pause, "I forgive you. But missionaries are clever. Sometimes they will appear to repent so that we let our guard down. Then when we are relaxed, they bring their will back another way and in the end they have had their way. So I will be watching you. If this idea of TEE comes back in other clothing, I will know that in your supposed repentance today, you were only being clever."

Jack Shellard had said, "The things we were afraid would happen are happening now."

I had said, "You will soon be back in Australia. But here is my home. I will be staying."

"Servant leadership—what is servant leadership?" I wondered to myself as I walked home that evening in the early darkness. "Are servants enfranchised? Do servants have a say about what happens to them? So, well, I guess I'll be the bishop's driver."

* * *

In July of 1970, Miriam Wenger returned to the States. The missionary couple who had been my teaching colleagues at the Theological College had also gone home. The missionary administrator of the Shirati Hospital was dismissed to make way for a Tanzanian. At Bukiroba I was required to go to the church offices every morning and sign in that I had reported for work. Anything for publication in the States (prayer letters, articles for church magazines, etc.) had to be approved by the TMC executive secretary. It was a dry time for missionaries. Very few remained at Bukiroba and Shirati–the only stations which still had foreign missionaries.

Healing–1970

During the eighteen months which followed the closing of the Theological College and led up to our furlough, I began to experience healing from the firestorms of '66 and '69. Bishop Kisare became a mentor to me as together we traveled all over the territory which had become Mennonite-land–northwestern Tanzania and south-western Kenya. The Landrover cab became a school for me to learn what I thought I knew when I told Jack Shellard that I was staying.

Then one day I said to Bishop Kisare, "I am a teacher. It is my training and calling to teach. I would be happy to work again at my profession." The Bukiroba school (site of the Theological College) re-opened in January 1971. A Tanzanian, Daniel Mtoka, was appointed principal. It was re-opened as a Bible School, with instruction in Swahili. The Bible School offered a one-year course of study. I was still the Bishop's driver, but during the six months before our furlough, I was sometimes also back in the classroom again.

6.

To Love Again

"Two old believers . . ."

–Robert Frost

Clyde and Alta Shenk planted three church districts during their time in Africa. In those days a district was started by the building of a central mission station, which became the district's home-based church. Over the years and through the existing network of African relationships, other congregations would spring up in the surrounding area.

In 1936 when the Shenks first came to Africa, they opened the Bumangi Mission Station. That district eventually grew to more than twenty congregations. Then in 1954, the Shenks opened the Kisaka Mission Station on the northwestern side of the Serengeti National Park. The Kisaka District grew to about a dozen congregations. Finally in 1968, the newly independent Tanzania Mennonite Church assigned Clyde and Alta to Kenya. Mennonite-land in Tanzania reaches north to the Kenyan border, and Mennonites were spilling over the border from Tanzania into Kenya. These "Kenyan" Mennonites were asking for pastoral leadership.

The TMC applied to the Kenyan government for a right-of-occupancy to build a mission station at Migori. Only one road crosses the border from Mennonite-land into Kenya, and Migori is the first Kenyan town along the road. Clyde and Alta lived in a tiny double-axle recreational vehicle trailer parked under a scrubby tree on a hillside overlooking Migori town. They lived there for a year, shepherding the existing Kenyan congregations and waiting for clearance to start building the Migori Mission Station. The right-of-occupancy came through the week after Alta was killed. With Alta gone, all plans for building were put on hold. Clyde returned to the States.

* * *

Miriam Wenger's three-year term of service at Bukiroba ended in July 1970. Before she left for home, a correspondence developed between Clyde and her.

Miriam had committed herself, from the time of Ray's death, not to marry again. She wrote to her daughter Annetta asking, "What is a mother to do?"

Annetta answered, "If you love him, marry him."

"Love him?" Does love happen, boom! just like that? Respect? Yes, she did respect him. Miriam needed some time to pray, time to hear what God was wanting her to do.

* * *

When we received the news, I was with a group of church leaders. I told them that Clyde and Miriam were engaged to be married. The church leaders were very perplexed. A widowed African woman is never remarried. She might be inherited by her husband's brother, yes. And she might have children by this brother, but the children are accounted to be her deceased husband's children, not the biological father's children.

A pastor asked, "Is Clyde a brother to the deceased bishop, Ray Wenger?"

"No."

"Well, is Clyde any relation of his?" he persisted.

"No."

"So, what will happen when Clyde and Miriam have a child?" he queried. "Whose child will it be? Where will it inherit, from the deceased bishop, or from Clyde?"

"But, don't you see?" I pointed out, "they are both in their 50s and they are beyond the age of bearing children."

"In that case," the churchmen concluded, "this is not really a marriage. It is just two old believers taking care of each other."

Clyde Shenk and Miriam Wenger were married on August 18, 1970. It was a quiet wedding, just the two of them in the home of Paul and Ann Landis. Paul was the bishop at Mellinger which was still Miriam's home church. Clyde wanted a wedding with guests and a reception because he liked parties. But Miriam felt in her heart that the reason they were marrying was because Alta and Ray had died. The memories of those losses would not allow her to celebrate. Besides, she did not like parties where she was the center of attention.

That spring, Clyde had planted five dozen tomato plants in Miriam's garden. There were tomatoes ripening out-the-gazoo on their wedding day so Miriam spent the morning being sensible. She canned tomatoes.

For their private celebration after the marriage ceremony, Miriam prepared tuna-burger sandwiches, wrapped in foil, ready to pop into the oven. Later she found out that Clyde did not like sandwiches. He liked cooked meals. "Poor Clyde," she laughs now, "tuna-burger for his wedding dinner! I found out too that he liked tomato soup."

* * *

They returned to Africa to pick up on the work Clyde had begun with Alta in Kenya. God gave them a tremendously productive, fruitful ministry. It would be Clyde's and Miriam's last tour before mandatory retirement. They went the stretch of nearly six years without a furlough. During those years, three families of their children were resident in East Africa–Clyde's sons David and Joe, and Miriam's daughter Annetta. This was quite extraordinary–missionary grandparents getting together with their grandchildren regularly. Several months before Clyde and Miriam retired in November 1976, Miriam's son Daniel and his wife, Erma, along with their four children also came to Africa. Daniel and Erma Wenger were beginning a three-year teaching assignment at Bukiroba.

The first thing Clyde and Miriam did after returning to Kenya was to build the Migori Mission Station–pastor's house, church, all-purpose shed, outdoor showers, and toilets. And they planted dozens of trees. Once built, the station became the nerve center of the growing Kenya Mennonite Church. It seemed to Miriam that there were continual guests both from the Kenyan churches and visitors from overseas. During 1973 she kept a count of all the guest meals she served. The total came to 3,059. After that she got even busier and had no time to count!

Their Migori district stretched from the Maasai Mara Game Reserve westward to beyond Kisumu. The road distance connecting the two ends of the district was 190 miles. Continually new worship places opened up in homes and schoolrooms. Clyde and Miriam would be called to do baptisms, child dedications, and communion services. As any one congregation grew and as money was available, the missionary couple would help the Kenyan Christians to build a church. They would hitch up their house trailer to Clyde's Toyota pickup and go and live at the place where the church was being built. Every year several of these churches were built. The walls were of stone or cement block, sometimes of metal sheeting over a timber frame. The roofs were of corrugated iron sheeting. There were wooden doors and shutters on the windows. The floors were cemented and the seats were backless wooden benches. They were attractive little churches, built to last.

The Kenya Mennonite Church grew rapidly through Clyde and Miriam's leadership. By the end of their six-year term of service it had grown to a membership of some 5,000 men and women, worshipping in over 30 congregations.

Clyde and Miriam had been sent to southwestern Kenya by the Tanzania Mennonite Church. To whom were they responsible, the emerging Kenyan church or the Tanzanian church which had sent them? Repeatedly, during the last years of their service, they found themselves caught between these two interests.

The Kenyan Mennonites were pushing for Kenyans to be ordained and for the Kenyan church to be independent of the Tanzanian church. The Tanzanians, on the other hand, felt that the Kenyan church was too young. They feared that leaders might be chosen who would betray the church.

Repeatedly, in the Kenyan church councils, Clyde would be instructed to take their case to Tanzania, and repeatedly the Tanzanians suspected that Clyde was encouraging the Kenyan

Miriam (Wenger) and Clyde Shenk with members of Miriam's son Daniel's family near Migori, Kenya, in 1976.

Miriam Wenger Shenk at the home of Helon Joyce Amolo, an elder of the Machicha-Nyarombo Mennonite Church in Kenya.

Eliakim, a Kenyan carpenter, works with Clyde Shenk on the construction of the Migori Mennonite Church.

Clyde and Miriam Shenk enjoying a moment in March of 1976.

Clyde and Miriam Shenk at their farewell in Migori, Kenya, in 1976. They had kept their promises to be missionaries for life, each spending the best part of 40 years on the mission field. Their first spouses, Alta Shenk and Ray Wenger, were buried in East Africa.

Clyde and Miriam Shenk in 1985, nearly ten years after their return to Lancaster, Pennsylvania.

"secessionist" ideas. It was not until the year after Clyde and Miriam retired that the first two Kenyan pastors were chosen and ordained.

Clyde did not want to retire. Nothing would have made him happier than becoming an overseer to a half dozen, or so, Kenyan pastors, sub-dividing the work, and helping them to build up their districts. Clyde had a passion for building church structures, gathering places for the spiritual church Jesus was building. He built more churches in Tanzania and Kenya than any other Mennonite missionary. Yet, he felt that he had barely scratched the surface of the work. Why couldn't he serve four more years, or even three more? This was the crying question which burned in Clyde's heart. Again, as had always been his custom, Clyde did not talk about it; he prayed about it.

And God's voice in Clyde's soul showed him that it would not work. It was a tremendously attractive dream, yes, but it would not work. Clyde's work with Alta, and later with Miriam, was always moving on. Even while he was the pastor in a district, the local people were taking ownership in the work and giving it leadership.

So in 1976 when Clyde and Miriam were struggling with a strong desire to stay in Kenya, they came to realize that it was time for the Kenya Mennonite Church to build on the foundation which had been laid. For this to happen, Clyde and Miriam needed to let go. At Bumangi and Kisaka, Clyde had let go and moved on. Now he realized that the time had come to do the same in Kenya. He needed to pass the baton.

In November 1976 Clyde and Miriam regretfully packed for the last time and moved back to Lancaster, Pennsylvania. The giving of farewells to them by the Kenyan and Tanzanian people had begun months before. Every congregation wanted to throw a feast, give them gifts, and wish them God-speed.

At their Migori farewell, Chief Ogwada gave Clyde a Luo spear. It was a long, seven-foot, two-inch warrior's spear with an iron spike on one end and a sharp blade at the other. The Chief, a Mennonite, told Clyde, "This spear, before the coming of the gospel of Jesus, was a weapon for killing people in our warfare with the Maasai people. It is no longer a spear for killing people. As followers of

Jesus, we no longer war against people. Now we war against Satan and his evil. Because of Jesus, our warfare is different now. You have been our leader in this new warfare, in God's warfare against sin. You are to take this spear with you to America. Let it remind you of your calling. You are a spiritual warrior of our Lord Jesus Christ."

* * *

Back in Lancaster, Clyde and Miriam settled for the last time into the home Miriam had known as a twenty-year-old bride in 1934. Clyde was asked to pastor the Rohrerstown Mennonite Church, a small, dying congregation. Historically, Rohrerstown was the second-oldest gathering of Mennonite worshippers in Lancaster Conference, but by 1976 it had nearly died out.

Clyde jokingly asked me what I would advise doing to revive the congregation. I remembered that at Bukiroba we had been assigned to live for several months in a house that was infested with termites, and I had asked him what to do. After looking the house over, Clyde said with a smile, "Move!"

So about Rohrerstown I said, "I wouldn't try!"

Well, Clyde had no such idea. He and Miriam began by relating to the members who were still there in a way which encouraged them to revive their congregation. Before long, some young people joined and slowly the congregation turned around. Clyde was pastor there for eleven years.

During that decade, it seemed that Clyde and Miriam never had an evening free. Staying home was Miriam's idea of what an older couple should do, but Clyde wanted to go to everything. And he was not happy going to things alone. So they went together. Clyde took courses and taught courses. He went to meetings, and he preached at meetings. And most times, Miriam was there with him.

I asked Clyde once why he kept up such a pace. He answered, "Those 40 years I was giving out all the time. I was trying to be African in what I thought and did. Now here I am, having missed out on 40 years of learning and relating in my home environment. I have this great hunger to catch up on what I missed."

Over the years, Clyde memorized many scriptures in both Swahili and English. In his 70s, he polished up on the book of Hebrews. He could recite the entire book from memory as a sermon. Many churches invited him to do this. Clyde called the epistle "The Book of Better Things." It was always his prayer that the audience would be more in awe of the message of the book than of his ability to recite it.

Shortly after returning to the States, Clyde developed emphysema, which caused uncontrollable coughing and choking spasms. Several times he was hospitalized, but he never had an attack when he was preaching, praying, or reciting scripture. For years, he was taking ever larger doses of medications to keep his air passages open.

One typically busy week in October 1989 the congestion became unbearable again. A doctor once again adjusted Clyde's medication. At once he developed a low-grade fever. In two days he went back to the doctor for further adjustment of the medication. That evening, he went to bed early. Several hours later, Miriam heard him stir. She decided she would go to bed then so as not to disturb his sleep later.

When she came upstairs to their bedroom, Clyde asked her, "Well, Miriam, what do you think I've been doing over the past two hours?"

"Oh," she answered, "I guess you've been praying."

"No," he said sleepily, "I just recited Hebrews through twice."

In the wee hours of that morning, Miriam was awakened by a crash. She snapped on her bedside lamp. Clyde was not in bed beside her. Getting up, she found him lying on the floor. One slipper was on. He had gone home. He was 78 years old.

Our daughter Dianne said, "Grandpa always prayed for us. When Dylan was born, Grandpa and Grandma came to the hospital. He prayed for Kenton [Dianne's husband] and me, and he prayed a blessing for Dylan. I always felt safe and carefree because of Grandpa's prayers. It was like a great wall of faith surrounding all of us, the Wengers and Shenks. Now Grandpa's prayers aren't there anymore. I feel like we are alone and vulnerable, unprotected."

A few days after the funeral, Miriam got a letter from Nicaragua. It was from her grandson, Danny Wenger. He wrote to tell her how much he would miss his step-grandfather. "I enjoyed his stories and counsel always. His death is easier to accept in the knowledge of the full and rich life he has had, the many people he has blessed, and because we know that Christ has conquered death and we have faith in the resurrection."

Several months later, on the eve of the 1990 New Year, Danny was killed in Nicaragua. Searching for a metaphor, Miriam said, "I feel like Job."

On June 1, 1991, Miriam held a public auction. Her home had been sold earlier. The day of the sale, she moved to the Landis Homes Retirement Community near Lancaster. Jesus has comforted her. Even as in the past, her life continues to be filled with joy and purpose. She stays in touch with her and with Clyde's descendants. She keeps up with the ongoing witness of the church in the Lancaster area. And in Kenya and Tanzania too.

7.

Your People
Will Be My People

"Where you go, I will go . . ."

–Ruth 1:16 (NEB)

In 1976 Miriam Wenger's son Daniel with his wife Erma and their four children began a three-year term of missionary service in East Africa. They lived on the Bukiroba Mission Station near Musoma, Tanzania.

Confused, frustrated, and all knotted up inside, Erma Wenger was too embarrassed to cry. She was lost, and now she was late for the opening chapel. Swahili school was opening without her.

Erma was supposed to have been on this "road" before, but she could not recognize a thing. The farther forward she drove her Peugeot sedan, the more wrong everything looked. Her husband's directions had seemed so plain that morning; now nothing fit. On both sides of her–coming and going–streamed goats, cows, women with loads on their heads, dusty children, an occasional man on a bicycle, pedaling earnestly, bell jangling to clear the way. She rolled up her car windows to keep out the noise and dust.

Erma Wenger had set out from Bukiroba to go to the Makoko Swahili Language School. Wherever she was had stopped being even a dirt road, just cow trails and people paths which seemed, up ahead, to be leading to tin-roofed, primary school buildings scattered over a rocky outcrop. It did not look at all like the Catholic Makoko Mission Station which she had seen a week earlier on a Bible school picnic by the lake.

The path Erma was on became too rocky for the Peugeot to pass. She stopped the car and sat there feeling totally out of place. The people hurrying to town or from town and the animals going to the lake for water or forage seemed also, like her, to know that she didn't belong there. They flowed around the car as though it were a granite boulder to be noticed and left alone.

Coming towards her now were uniformed school children–green skirts and knee pants, white shirts. Trained to investigate their curiosities, the children crowded around the closed car windows. Gesturing, they showed Erma where to pass in retracing her way back toward the lake to the dirt road which had seemed to fork where she went astray. "Back at the road, turn left," they gestured, shouting all the while in Swahili, "and Makoko is just a few miles up ahead."

She did finally get to Makoko and found the language school among the many buildings on that Catholic mission station. As she walked into the school office, the American Maryknoll sister who was on duty stood up to welcome her. It was too much–a white American, welcoming her! Erma's stiff control shattered. She burst into tears. Sister Anita, knowing all about how it was in new situations when everything went wrong, took Erma to her house, got her a cup of tea, and listened.

* * *

Erma had agreed to come to Musoma with the hope that in the country of her husband's childhood, she would come to understand and love him more. But it felt that morning as though Africa would swamp her before she had any handles on how to connect Daniel to it. Daniel could have gone the nine miles from their home in Bukiroba to Makoko practically blindfolded. He could do simultaneous Swahili-English translating, and he was conversant in several tribal vernaculars.

Since their arrival in Africa, most things that happened left Erma realizing that Daniel had come to a familiar place. The culture shock

for her would have been much easier, she felt, if he were experiencing the same thing. Instead, he seemed to know everybody. He knew
how to buy goods in the crowded Musoma market and the little
storefront grocery shops. He could drive speedily over the corrugated and rutted sandy roads. He knew how to eat African foods. In
short, this place was like home to Daniel.

By contrast, Erma felt totally disoriented. The sounds and smells
and tastes, the music and languages and mannerisms, the endless
church services, the strange money, the shopping and banking, the
left side driving, the dirt roads shared equally by animals, people,
bicycles, motorbikes, cars, and lorries, the honking and dust–it was
all a wall closing her out.

Erma, a light-boned woman, slender, petite, dark-haired, had
grown up romanticizing missionaries. The stories she heard gave her
a certain mental image of them–missionaries were brave, noble, and
perfect. They were very spiritual, different from regular people.
They lived deprived lives and faced evil daily on the dark African
continent. They prayed a lot, got stuck on mud roads, preached to
under-dressed people, rescued sick Africans from death by giving
them medicine or taking them to the hospital, ate strange foods,
killed snakes, and went hunting for wild animals. Their work was
different from the work regular people did. Their work was healing,
teaching, and preaching in strange and difficult circumstances.

Daniel Wenger and Erma Sauder first noticed each other at the
Mission Board's annual Worldwide Missionary Conference held on
the Lancaster Mennonite High School campus. It was the summer of
1962. Daniel, red-haired, tall, powerfully built, fresh back from a
three-year term of bachelor service in Tanzania, was exuding missionary charisma. He had been serving in the same area where he
was born, the same place he had lived most of his life up to age sixteen. Erma heard him tell of going back to Africa as a young adult.
What a wonderful experience it had been for him! And she knew
that the level of intimacy and trust with which Daniel had been able
to relate to Africa could not possibly be reached by first generation
missionaries. Erma knew instinctively that this man was special.
Within fourteen months, they were married.

Thirteen years of marriage and four children later, the family pitched up on the Mennonite mission station at Bukiroba. Daniel had been recruited to teach in the one-class Bible School. Three of their children–Heidi, Danny, and Andrea–went to boarding school near Nairobi, Kenya, 350 miles away. The youngest, two-year-old JoJo, lived with her parents at Bukiroba.

When Erma married her MK [missionary kid], she expected that one day she would be a missionary. She felt MKs should live where they could serve best, where they knew the language and culture. During their early years of marriage, Erma became ever more aware that Daniel was wired differently from many other Mennonites. This confirmed her earlier thinking. Daniel should be working in Africa because he had intimate knowledge of Africa.

One day soon after their arrival at Bukiroba, something happened which particularly vexed her way of thinking, and she blurted out to Daniel, "That's stupid. Why would anyone do something like that?"

Daniel's spontaneous reply was a surprised, "That's not stupid. Anyone would do that."

To which Erma shot back, "No, not anyone would do that. You wouldn't do that! I wouldn't do that! Maybe an African would."

A look of surprise washed over Daniel's face. Then, thoughtfully, he said, "Yes, an African would do that."

"Oh my goodness," Erma shuddered, "he identifies with them rather than me."

And she realized Daniel saw things differently than she did. It gave her a terrible sense of desertion and aloneness. She was an alien in this place.

The Wenger children also occasionally puzzled over their father's familiarity with Africans and African life.

For example, there was an ongoing transportation problem that they sometimes wondered about. Daniel would often need to go to Musoma which was six miles away. The missionaries had a Toyota Landcruiser for their transportation. It was hard to get to Musoma if you did not have a vehicle or the gasoline to run it. So when African neighbors and friends found out that Daniel was going to Musoma, they would ask to ride along.

Having people along complicated things because each person had a half dozen things to do in a half dozen places and getting everyone together again to go back to Bukiroba would always take forever. So Daniel was a bit tight about giving rides. To the children and Erma, this came across simply as Dad not noticing the problem Tanzanians had with transportation.

Heidi remembers, "Sometimes people would ask Dad for a ride, and he would leave without them, and it would drive me crazy!"

It would probably have been easier for Daniel to deal with this problem if he had been African. Then he would have been part of the natural web of relationships which went a long way in sorting out who asked for rides. But since he was an American mission-ary–someone who was supposed to help *everybody*–there was a free-for-all atmosphere to the business of getting rides.

Daniel worked at this problem by doing a lot of his local running by motorcycle. He owned a little 125cc Honda street bike. So on a cor-rugated, rutted, and sand-ridged road, taking passengers was a prob-lem. Furthermore, JoJo was usually along on his forays to town.

Even with the efficiency of a motorbike, Daniel would often get bogged down, and the day would pass with too few things done. Africans have a saying, *"Asubuhi ni moja,"* or "There is only one morning." By this they mean that you can do only one thing in a morning or, more specifically, you should not make an early morn-ing dash into Musoma to get a Kenyan visa at immigration and expect to be back at Bukiroba in time to teach your 9:30 a.m. class in the Bible School. An African would just expect that if he was going to town, he would not be back before 1:00 p.m. at the earliest.

But we missionaries, including Daniel, would often try to do two things in a morning. We also had a saying. When the second planned activity of our morning did not get done, we would say, "A. W. A.," which meant, "Africa Wins Again!"

* * *

For her part, Erma saw that Africa was going to take a lot of get-ting used to. The daily eighteen-mile, dirt-road, round-trip to lan-guage school was an ordeal. Then there was adjusting to having a maid help with the cooking and cleaning in her home at Bukiroba. And there were the endless guests and more guests from the United States and Canada and Kenya. It seemed that all the Mennonites who visited Africa wanted to see "the work in Musoma" and that meant being houseguests on the Bukiroba station.

Over all that loomed the question of the Bukiroba Domestic Science School, a boarding school for women. Daniel's mother, Miriam Wenger, had been the school's first Head Mistress when it opened in 1967. When Erma arrived at Bukiroba, Viola Dorsch, a Canadian missionary, was Head Teacher at the Domestic Science School. Erma knew that Viola and her husband were being transferred to another assignment, and she was afraid she would be asked to take Viola's place.

In early December, the Wenger children came home from boarding school for their first four-week vacation. They had been away for three months! Erma decided that with the children home, she should drop language school for the time being. She had completed three months, about three-fourths of the course.

One of those December 1976 days while the children were still home on vacation, Viola Dorsch came to see Erma. In her arms Viola carried a pile of domestic science books and files. The time had come for the Dorsch's transfer. Needing to know who would take her place when the domestic science women came back from their Christmas break, Viola had gone to the church office in Bukiroba and had asked. She was told that Erma would replace her as the Head Teacher.

Erma had training and experience as a secretary and administrative assistant, working in an American office. She had no domestic science training and she could barely speak Swahili. There would be a staff of two—one African woman and Erma.

Erma did not feel good about Viola's message. She had strong reservations. And, furthermore, she had not been consulted. She had just been given the job. "How much say do foreign workers have in their job assignments?" she wondered. "Can missionaries say 'no' to assignments made by the local church office?"

The agreement between the Tanzania Mennonite Church and Eastern Mennonite Board of Missions was that the church could make requests to the Board that missionaries be recruited to do certain things. If the Mission Board agreed, then the Board would recruit the missionaries and send them to Tanzania. The Board would meet the costs of travel and living expenses for the missionaries. The local church would provide the program budget for the foreign workers' job assignments. In Daniel and Erma's case, it was Daniel, as a Bible School teacher, who had been recruited by the Board and sent to serve the church.

Before leaving the States, Erma had been told that her job would be wife and mother (JoJo was only two years old), as well as hostess for Bukiroba's many guests. She was told that she might become marginally involved with a church women's group and, possibly, she would get involved socially with the domestic science women. No one in the States or in Africa was worrying about who would fill Viola Dorsch's place at the time the Wengers were making their plans to go to Bukiroba. If anyone did think about it, it was not mentioned to Erma.

This was just how it was. There is a Swahili saying, "*Hivyo ndivyo ilivyo,*" the literal translation being, "This indeed is how it is." Not knowing whether she had the freedom not to teach and feeling, in any case, that she did not know how to discuss this with Africans, Erma obediently took on the responsibilities at the Domestic Science School.

In February 1977 about a month after Erma began her daily, 100-yard walk to the Domestic Science School, two administrators from the Mission Board and a Lancaster bishop paid the Tanzania Mennonite Church an administrative visit. The deputation's schedule put them in Daniel and Erma's home for an evening. Erma hoped that it would be a time to ask them for help in sorting out how she was supposed to relate to the local church.

But on their arrival that evening at the Wenger home, the Mission Board administrators announced jovially that they had had it up to their eyeballs. Had had what? Talk! An overload of talk about how African and American Mennonites worked at doing program together.

The two officials representing the Mission Board had both spent many years in Africa as missionaries, as had Daniel, in the days before things became so complex for foreign workers. The evening turned into a swapping of motorcycle stories from the good old days. While Erma could not yet get her tongue around the words, she was getting the feeling that, "*Hivyo ndivyo ilivyo!*"–that is indeed how it is.

An unexpected international wrinkle was about to further complicate Daniel and Erma's lives. The day after the deputation returned to Kenya, Tanzania closed its border with Kenya. An economic dispute had been dividing Kenya and Tanzania for several years. Back in colonial times, the three East African countries of Kenya, Tanganyika, and Uganda had a common currency and central bank. They also had a common railway, lake steamer service, and airline, as well as a common postal service.

Upon independence, the Kenyan economic infrastructure was much better developed than the infrastructure in the other two countries. With a unified East African economy, capital flowed out of Uganda and Tanzania into Kenya, and the economy in Kenya expanded rapidly. At least that was how the socialist government in Tanzania viewed what was going on. An economic war developed between capitalist Kenya and socialist Tanzania. One by one all of the cooperative systems set up in colonial times collapsed, beginning with the East African central bank and common currency.

The proverbial straw which closed the border happened in Dar es Salaam, Tanzania's capital city. In the middle of a political celebration, attended by hundreds of international guests, the Kenyan government grounded the East African Airway planes at Nairobi. This disrupted the travel plans of Tanzania's guests and was an embarrassment to the Tanzanian government. Tanzania responded by sealing its border with Kenya and impounding all of the hundreds of Kenya-registered trucks, buses, vans, and cars–as well as any and all Kenya-registered aircraft, whether publicly or privately owned, which happened to be in Tanzania that day.

The three older Wenger children were in boarding school at Rosslyn Academy near Nairobi, Kenya. February was the middle of a school term, so there was no immediate panic. But closing the border did pose quite a headache. Not only was no one allowed to cross the border by foot or by vehicle, the closure also meant that no aircraft were allowed to fly between Kenya and Tanzania. So getting the children home was going to be a big sweat.

The only way to get from one of the two countries to the other was to fly commercially by way of a third country. This was prohibitively expensive to say nothing of the fact that the border closure had also brought air travel within Tanzania to a halt because the East

African Airway planes had been grounded in Nairobi. So even if the children could get into Arusha or Dar es Salaam, Tanzania's two international airports, the only way to get to Musoma would be by overland on dirt roads. Further, both Arusha and Dar were farther from Musoma than Nairobi. What a mess!

In the weeks that followed, between the border closing and the children's three-week Easter vacation, Daniel did manage to get permission from the Department of Immigration in Dar es Salaam for the children to cross the border on foot. Someone from Nairobi brought them to the border crossing where Daniel and Erma met them on the Tanzania side.

All went well. The children came home. But on the day they were to return to boarding school, it was announced over the Tanzanian national radio that the border was being sealed tighter, that only permissions issued by the Tanzanian president's office were valid for border crossing. Daniel and Erma were on their way to the border with the children when the announcement was made. They heard about it when they got to the border checkpoint. The children were not allowed to cross over.

Thus, the Wenger family traveled almost 160 miles over dirt roads from Bukiroba up to the border crossing and back to Bukiroba. It took them a full day for this exercise in futility.

Daniel was convinced it would take several weeks, minimum, for him to get permission from the president's office for the children to cross. He decided to go the route of getting a missionary airline to secure the permissions and to fly the three children across. There were three missionary airlines–Missionary Aviation Fellowship, African Inland Mission Air, and the Seventh Day Adventists had one plane.

There were no telephones at Bukiroba, so Daniel had to go to Musoma and book his long distance calls to Nairobi to the offices of these missionary agencies to try to get someone to work on his case. The telephoning itself, working through operators in Tanzania and Kenya, took forever. Finally, one by one, he did get in touch with all three of the agencies. The recent ruling had swamped all three with work. Eventually, Daniel got AIM Air to work on his case. They said it would take two weeks.

During the next week, Daniel continued to play all the angles he could think of. Nothing would budge. The more stuck things seemed, the more he thought about the Serengeti route. From Musoma, there are only two roads going to Kenya. Daniel had tried the main one and had been turned back. Now he would try the border crossing between Tanzania's Serengeti National Park and Kenya's Maasai Mara Game Reserve. At that time, the Mennonites were building a hospital for the Tanzania Ministry of Health. This project was on the edge of the Serengeti National Park. The project had permission to cross into Kenya by truck for supplies.

This was in the middle of the rainy season and Daniel's vehicle was a Renault station wagon. He was going to try to use the hospital building project's permission papers. Hopefully, in the isolation of the game parks, the immigration officers would let them cross. What with the rains and all, it took a day and a half of travel just to get to the border point between the Serengeti and Maasai Mara. The officials there would not budge either! It took another overnight to get back to Bukiroba.

On that three-day trip, the Wengers were stuck in the mud three times and at one place forded a river where the water was hip deep. Daniel was tired and frustrated and there was no electricity or hot water to shave. He decided to keep his prickly whiskers as testimony of the hardships they had endured. After a few days of showing off his stubbly beard, he said to himself, "Why not?" and declared a moratorium on shaving until the border situation was normalized, a rash vow as it turned out.

Eventually the AIM Air connection did come through, and the children were flown back to Nairobi–two weeks late for school. As Erma watched the tiny plane fly out over the lake, she wondered when she would see the children again. Her eyes filled with tears.

* * *

Erma put herself into the domestic science teaching and administration assignment even though such a level of involvement for a new worker so soon after arrival was unprecedented. It seems people assumed that since Daniel was an old Africa hand, Erma must be too. Well, she wasn't and she struggled.

It was difficult for Erma to evaluate the effectiveness of her work. She had a hard time knowing what to emphasize or how to make her point. In her mind, she compared her work to the grading of essay questions. Everything was on a scale and should be evaluated in context. She found it most difficult to decide whether or not a task was acceptably done.

She came to understand that acceptable by African standards was different from acceptable by American missionary standards. Most of the domestic science students were more interested in sewing lots of clothes quickly than in making a few quality items.

For example, the students brought razor blades to class which they used to rip badly sewn seams because this was quicker than picking the seams out by hand. What with ripping seams, let alone doing it with razor blades, the coarse cotton cloth was soon nicked and frayed. So, from Erma's perspective, it was better to accept bad stitching than to require ripping and re-sewing. She found herself giving a "satisfactory" to work that really should have been redone.

The old treadle sewing machines the women used did not work well and sometimes the poor stitching was the machine's fault. Part of Erma's job meant that she also became sewing machine repairman.

More and more, Erma understood that the African women had a different perspective about the activity of sewing than she had. She and the women she was teaching came from very different places.

For example, the iron which Tanzanians used for pressing clothes was a boxy affair with a top that opened and closed. To heat the contraption, a charcoal fire was lit inside the iron box, and it was set outside to catch a breeze. The lid was opened and a piece of stovepipe was put on top of the box to create a draft. The box itself had a flue which was opened to draw in the air. When the charcoal inside got hot, the flue would be snapped shut, the stovepipe removed, the lid closed and latched, the handle seized, and ironing would commence. It was customary to use a blanket-draped bed as an ironing board.

Of course, such a contraption could get soot on it, or rust, and thus your clothes would be streaked black and red. So the iron needed to be cleaned each time before a fire was made in it. African peasant women had no manufactured scouring material so they scrubbed these irons with wet sand.

Erma did not know about wet sand. She was astonished when on the first day that she was to supervise ironing, the women grabbed the classroom's irons along with some water. They streamed out of the classroom and began scouring the irons with wet sand. On that day, Erma went home and cried. The gap between the African women and her seemed dauntingly wide and deep.

There were bright spots, though, and some days things went really well. "Someone must be praying," Erma would think happily. Erma's young daughter, JoJo, often went along to the sewing classes. She learned to embroider when she was only three years old and to use the treadle sewing machine when she was five.

The sewing classes continued to go better after Erma had a helper. Rhoda Koreni was able to translate for both Erma and the Tanzanian women, as well as help with the work of making sure the women were learning how to sew. Erma came to feel that her time as a domestic science teacher was a good learning experiece for everyone involved.

She even agreed to a second tour at Bukiroba after several years back in Lancaster. It was a short one-year tour, 1982-83. Daniel was on sabbatical from teaching history at Lancaster Mennonite High School. He had been recruited to pinch hit for a year as the Tanzania Mennonite Church's projects officer. JoJo and Andrea were in boarding school near Nairobi that year. Danny did his high school junior year by correspondence.

Heidi taught a preschool class of 30 youngsters. The Bible School where Daniel taught during the family's '76-'79 stint in Bukiroba had been closed. Heidi used the old Bible School mess hall as her classroom. Erma limited herself to caring for her family and station guests.

In some ways, this second tour was better integrated than the first one. Heidi and Danny sang in the Bukiroba church choir. Danny played soccer with the local team. But the church administration was more fragmented than it had been during their first tour, and Daniel found it hard to get a hold on his work.

* * *

What do "almost adult" teenagers do for excitement on a mission station in the African bush–besides play soccer and sing in the church choir? One night there was an outdoor beer party and dance out back of the Bukiroba mission station. Heidi and Danny could hear the drumming in the still night air, not far away, maybe a half mile. They decided to go back to see what was going on. After Daniel and Erma were asleep, the teenagers sneaked out of the house. An African friend had agreed to show them the way. In the moonlight, they followed the footpaths toward the sounds of partying.

When they got near, several soldiers with guns saw them. The soldiers were drunk. They came after the kids and ordered them to sit down. Heidi remembers the incident:

"The soldiers probably just wanted to show some authority over the little white missionary kids. I don't remember being that scared. Danny wasn't scared. It was just another African event, a bit of excitement. Of course, you never know what to expect, but everything turned out fine.

"The guards ordered us to sit, and Danny didn't understand, or else didn't take them seriously. He just started walking back down the path toward the mission station. But I sat down and hissed at him in English to sit too, and he did. Meanwhile, a loud argument was taking place between our guide-friend and the guards.

"In the end, we were ordered back to the mission station. Personally, I was pretty relieved to go home. None of the villagers had seen us. We were pretty sure no gossip would get back to any of the church people or missionaries. In the end, we got our excitement, which is what we were looking for, without showing our white faces at the party."

* * *

In June 1983 on the last evening before the family was to begin their return journey to the States, thieves broke into their house at Bukiroba. The Wengers had gone to another home for a farewell dinner. All their things were packed in suitcases, which were stacked in the living room, ready to be loaded in the Landrover the next morning. When they came home at about 9:00 p.m., the house was empty!

What were they to do? How were they to handle total theft of belongings, on a mission station, as a farewell experience? How were they to deal with it emotionally, spiritually, theologically?

Africans on the mission station felt especially badly. Many came to the Wenger home just to sit in the living room and to offer condolences. To the traditional African way of thinking, having their guests' belongings stolen said all the wrong things. What was going on? There were no ready answers. Did some part of the African community have a score to settle? Or was this a tear in the fabric of the Christian community? Or was it just a random happening?

It was certainly a reminder that "Peace on earth, good will among men" (Luke 2:14), although experienced in part, had not yet been realized.

To paraphrase a word from Scripture: "Men and women of faith are looking forward to the New Village with foundations, whose builder and maker is God. . . . Many are commended for their faith, yet none of them received what had been promised. God had planned something better, that the realization would not come until it could be celebrated along with those who in the future will also come to faith in Christ Jesus" (Hebrews 11:10, 39, 40).

The Wenger family left Bukiroba the next day and visited several other mission stations on their way home as had been planned. Folks in Bukiroba, Shirati, and Nairobi gave them various items of clothing to replace some of the things they had lost.

* * *

In November 1984 Daniel Wenger was at a Lancaster Mennonite High School charity auction when a doctor friend poked him in the ribs, grinning. The doctor had a ham radio, and he had just heard the word: "Tanzania and Kenya have reopened their common border." This was nearly seven years after Daniel began his bearded protest. That evening, he shaved.

– BOOK THREE –

New Voices Service

8.

Danny

---

*"When you were younger you . . . went where you want-
ed, but when you are old(er) . . . someone else will . . .
lead you where you do not want to go."*
                                                    –John 21:18 (NIV)

Road Less Traveled

Danny smelled smoke, cigarette smoke. As RA (resident assistant) of Goshen (IN) College's Westlawn Hall, he was required to
report any smoking to the dean. Sniffing his way to the other end
of the hall, he knocked on "Sam's" door. Sam was his former room-
mate and a close friend.

"Umm, guys," Danny said softly as he closed the door behind
him. "It smells like smoke in here."

The single cigarette in the room had come in behind the ear of
a visitor who had dropped into Sam's room. Carrying a cigarette
behind your ear was not forbidden at Goshen College, only the
smoking of it was. Sam had lit the little white thing and was doing
the puffing.

Caught in the act, Sam thought, "Poor RA, I've presented him
with a dilemma. He can just give me a warning, but if the higher
ups find out, they can nail him for showing favoritism."

Then he remembered something. Several years earlier, Sam and
Danny with some friends had spent a weekend in New York City.
On Saturday night they decided to go across town. On the way to

the subway, they began to wonder how their funds were holding out. There, in the station, they pulled notes and coins from their pockets, counting what they had left. They scarcely had enough money to get in anywhere, let alone pay subway fare. In a sudden burst of bravado, the lot of them jumped over the turnstiles and headed for the trains. But Danny hesitated, dug in his pockets again, and dropped change for the cost of a ride into the token vender. Sam knew that Danny would report the cigarette smoking.

* * *

Danny began his college years as a math major. From his early childhood, statistics, chess, calculations, and most things having to do with numbers fascinated him. During his years in college, though, a growing interest in making people the focus of his life's work nudged him out of math into economics and international relations.

Introverted, shy, quiet–especially in new situations–Danny thought about things, sorted out the issues, tried to get the big picture. He would find and enter quiet spaces in which to search out the pattern of things, which when discovered excited him immensely.

Somewhere along the way, he decided that in God's ordering of things, it was intended that people be joyful–that all of the complex web of heredity and environment and accumulated relationships and experiences were, in God's purpose, to result in joy. He knew, by faith, that fitting himself to the purpose of God in his life and being part of this human adventure with God did indeed bring joy. When Danny saw these intersections happening, he became very excited.

* * *

Like his father before him, Danny was a missionary kid. He had spent four years with his family in Tanzania where soccer was as important as baseball is in the States. At Goshen College, he was naturally drawn to the game. His own skills, abilities, and achievements were of little interest to him. The team–that was what mattered. Dwayne Hartzler, Goshen College's soccer coach the years

Danny was there, remembered coaching him:

"When Dan came to Goshen, he wasn't, and never became, a really good athlete, not particularly fast or quick. No, with Dan it wasn't a kind of 'fire in your eye' intent that he's going out there to prove himself. But he was committed. We played him at about any place. He was fullback, mid-field, forward, scoring goals, giving assists, playing defense. That was Dan.

"I carry in my mind's eye, several little video shots of him. As a sophomore, he scored a goal in overtime against St. Francis to win the game. As a senior, he created the only goal of the game against Grace to not only win the game, but to win the conference.

"But the one that practically everyone at Goshen who's connected with soccer remembers happened in his junior year in a game against Bethel College. He hit a cross in a flat out, diving header, and put his nose right down in the dirt to score a spectacular goal. It was captured on film, and is part of the Goshen College promotional videotape.

"It's not that goal against Bethel, the diving header, that I remember most vividly. What I remember is Dan, after he scored it. He came sprinting back by the bench, grinning from ear to ear. He wanted me to know, as if I didn't, that *our team* had just scored the goal of the year."

* * *

Danny made a public commitment to Christ when he was a student at Lancaster Mennonite High School. He was baptized at the Mellinger Mennonite Church when he was fifteen years old. That was in 1981. During 1982-83, his junior year in high school, he was with his family in Musoma, Tanzania, on their second term in Africa. After their return from Africa and during his senior year at LMHS, Danny attended a series of renewal meetings at Mountville Mennonite Church where his step-uncle, David Shenk, was pastor. Richard Landis was the evangelist. At those meetings, Danny rededicated his life to Christ. Richard told Danny that he felt God had his hand on him for a special ministry. Danny recognized this call, and Richard prayed with him that the Lord would fulfill this ministry in his life.

* * *

When Danny went to college, he took along a pair of grass green pants which he had bought in New York City. Wearing those pants seemed to be his way of announcing that he was not part of the mainstream. Just to emphasize the point, Danny insisted on wearing his LMHS sweatshirt, a distinct embarrassment to any appropriate collegiate wardrobe. He also often showed up for soccer practice in glaring white shoes.

Danny's differentness reflected a desire to be on the "road less traveled." His bright green pants and zany ways acted as a lure, calling others to check out life. He loved one-on-one conversations and small group discussions about politics, life, philosophy, faith.

If two opposing sides developed, he was usually at the place where the two sides intersected–on the edge of both issues. He would position himself between things, taking the role of interpreter-mediator. For young Dan Wenger, life, the living of it, was an investment. He said, "The more you live, the richer you will be."

At Goshen College, it was popular to be even-handed about faith. Faith was personal and private, good, and to be affirmed. Faith could be shared, expressed, discussed, but many students felt uneasy about seeing Christian faith as "The Way." There was a lot of doubt about the missionary enthusiasms of 50 to 100 years earlier which planted the seeds of Christianity around the world. To work as a missionary was sometimes considered imperialistic, an imposition of the North on the South, of the West on the East. It was popular to think anthropologically about faith, not evangelically.

Goshen College required all of its students to have an extended cross-cultural experience. Danny chose to go to Costa Rica. He joined a group of students who lived, worked, and studied in that Central American culture for several months. As part of the experience, each student actually lived in a Costa Rican home. As they began to understand Central American history, many concluded that the western Christian church and its missionaries were imperialistic and insensitive.

Here, too, Danny took the road less traveled. Something about the way he had experienced and thought about Christian faith made him see Jesus Christ as the universal Saviour. If Jesus came to save North Americans, then he came to save Costa Ricans too. Danny did not believe that sharing Jesus, by definition, was imperialistic.

Amy Miller, one of his classmates, was struck by Danny's line of reasoning in their Cultural Anthropology class. An annual feature of the class was a discussion on how Christians from the developed world should relate to the so-called third world or to traditional societies which had other-than-Christian belief systems.

"The discussion was known and prepared for as the big 'Missionary versus Anthropologist Debate.' We were all able to choose our sides. Out of a class of 40 or more, Dan and one or two others were the only ones who took the missionary side. I remember Dan did most of the arguing. The rest of us, 35 or more, had a terribly difficult time arguing with him. It almost felt like arguing with Jesus, because everything we said, he had an answer for, and it was a good answer. It was a very frustrating debate, and it got a little heated at times, but Dan was definitely the winner. I had twice as much respect for him after that."

What was it that Danny said? Well, after college, Danny signed on with the Mennonite Central Committee (MCC) for a three-year stint in Nicaragua. From there he wrote a letter to an American friend.

July 19, 1989: "Chris, you've referred to me in a few letters as missionary, and I think I've responded that I don't see myself that way. I am starting to, however. My MCC country directors, Jim and Ann Hershberger, stress people development over economic development, which probably all MCCers do. But it's only now really starting to take hold deep down within me that I can't judge the success of any project by the number of jobs provided or the number of people reached by a particular project. What it's about is helping people to discover a sense of service to everyone, not just their family or their church. And it's about strengthening their ability to have healthy human relationships. This kind of approach just seems to make a lot more sense, or is easier to do, from a Biblical standpoint.

"I suppose I'm really getting a handle on this question from the wrong end. A good missionary would probably say that we need to share the Gospel first of all, and then out of that Gospel message, come all of our other development activities. For me, I would say that my good intentions, as a development worker, have certainly had at least a loose connection to my religious beliefs. But I'm now beginning to understand that the sharing of my religious beliefs may be more important than my development work."

* * *

Just before Danny left for Nicaragua, he got a letter from Ann Hershberger, reminding him to bring his accounting textbooks. Danny may not have known that his grandfather, Ray Wenger, had been recruited at age 27 in 1937 to be an accountant for the Mennonite mission in Tanganyika. Danny was 22 when he packed his own college accounting books and turned south toward Nicaragua.

Grandmother Miriam did not want him to go. Central America was too dangerous, too conflicted. Danny wrote in his journal, "Grandma is very obviously not happy about my going to Nicaragua. I guess she thinks it's too much for me, or I should be married, or I'll get shot."

Just before Danny left for Nicaragua, his step-uncle, David Shenk, invited him out for breakfast. At that breakfast, Danny confided, "I recognize that the Contra War might put me at risk, but I am confident that going to Nicaragua is God's appointment for me. I am at peace with whatever the consequence might be. But pray for me; I feel that I am a rather weak Christian."

Danny would be in Nicaragua from February to December, 1989.

Perspective

During his eleven months in Nicaragua, Danny kept a journal. He tried to connect the situation in Nicaragua to what he was reading and to what he believed about life and God. His story is of interest, not because it is more insightful, more exciting, more purposeful than any other story. Rather, his story is useful because of who he was. Danny was a third generation missionary. He was from a family of church leaders, stretching back to the early 18th century when the first Mennonites settled in Lancaster County, Pennsylvania. Danny was an eleventh generation descendant of the Landis family of settlers who built the first Mellinger Mennonite Church.

In the years following the arrival of the Mennonites in North America, the church experienced a great many changes. Among those changes was the spreading of the church, through evangelism and church planting. When Danny Wenger's great-grandfather, David Landis, was a boy, Mennonites worshipped in German, Dutch, and English with the exception of a small church in Indonesia planted by Dutch Mennonites.

Four generations later Mennonites worshipped in some 120 languages worldwide. In the summer of 1990, a Mennonite World Conference was held in Winnipeg, Manitoba. Christians from Mennonite and Brethren in Christ churches from 56 countries gathered for that celebration. During the three generations when most of these changes happened, Danny Wenger's family had been at the center of this work of God.

* * *

Danny's involvement in the cross-cultural mission of the church was different than the work done by his parents, and it was especially different than the work done by his grandparents. Partly this was because Danny chose to go to a place where the church had already been planted in contrast to his grandparents who were pioneer workers. But the shift in tone between the time of Danny's grandparents and his time was probably more directly related to differences in world view. The way of being God's people in mission was different for Danny than it was for Ray and Miriam Wenger. However, in spite of changes, the Gospel remained the Good News about God's work on earth through Jesus the Christ. So while Danny's story, on the surface of it, was very different from his Grandfather Ray's story, the stories of these two men, separated by 50 years, were in many ways the same story.

* * *

One day Audelia, Danny's Nicaraguan "mother," asked him why he was always writing in his notebook. Danny answered that he was journaling in the hope that what he was experiencing would be helpful to others some day.

It is clear from the journals that working out of the conscious events of a very young life, Danny was beginning to understand the Nicaraguan picture, beginning to understand what this meant for him.

In Nicaragua Danny was bumping into a lot of new ideas. He was working with people who figured out life differently from how he had it figured out. Danny gave these new experiences and his new friends a fair hearing. Again and again, he would go to the edges of his own belief system in order to hear a Nicaraguan out. And he was prepared to change if he saw that his point of view was not right. But he did not change recklessly. He stayed in touch with his roots–Mellinger Mennonite Church, Goshen College, East Africa, and the Landis-Wenger-Shenk families. He used his background for footing as he worked at absorbing the new material which was swirling around him.

* * *

Danny Wenger's journals have about them a moroseness which many of his Goshen College friends found uncharacteristic. Especially in his senior year at Goshen, he was remembered as being flamboyant, a person who put 150 percent into both work and play. He had obviously figured out Goshen. He felt at home. He felt secure, and in that security, he went at life with abandonment.

The journals, written as he was trying to figure out how to fit into his new life in Nicaragua, reflect a different kind of Danny.

They have a down side. But as he began to acclimate to the Central American environment, his journal entries started to show flashes of his Goshen College, soccer field exuberance. Sadly, for those who knew him, the process was frozen too soon.

Orientation

MCCers typically arrive in a country all pumped up in the anticipation of digging right into all the work. However, their experiences usually begin with a week or two spent in listening, processing, reflecting. This time is called orientation.

During Danny's orientation in Managua, the capital city, he found that many things were changing in Nicaragua. The revolutionary socialist Sandinista government, under the leadership of President Daniel Ortega, had been in power for ten years. They had come to power militarily in 1979 when they overthrew the capitalist Somoza dictatorship. During the 1981-1989 Reagan administration in the United States, great efforts had been made on the part of the United States, some of them covert, to destabilize Nicaragua's socialist government. The U.S. government did this by funneling support to the Contras, guerrilla armies which represented the capitalist interests of the long-ruling Somoza family.

The changes Nicaragua was experiencing when Danny arrived in 1989 were partly due to the fact that the new Bush administration in the United States had stopped fueling the Contra guerilla armies. A second cause for change was that the presidents of the Central American countries had been meeting periodically since 1987 to develop a comprehensive Central American peace plan. Besides Nicaragua, two other Central American countries, Guatemala and El Salvador, had civil wars going on. The Central American presidents agreed on a plan to stop these wars. The leader of the group, President Arias of Costa Rica, was awarded the 1987 Nobel Peace Prize for his work.

It wasn't hard for Danny to see that the Nicaraguan economy was in disrepair. Why had the economy collapsed? The socialist Sandinistas had taken the property of the Somozan capitalists, who represented about ten percent of the population, and had redistributed it, without killing or locking up the formerly-rich ten percent of the population. The formerly-rich people were still around and they were angry. They worked against the socialist government's economic programs. And they constantly lobbied the United States for military support of their Contra armies. Also

The Daniel and Erma Wenger family in 1988, several months before son
Danny left for a Mennonite Central Committee (MCC) assignment in
Nicaragua. (Left to right) Andrea, Heidi, JoJo, Danny, Daniel, and Erma.

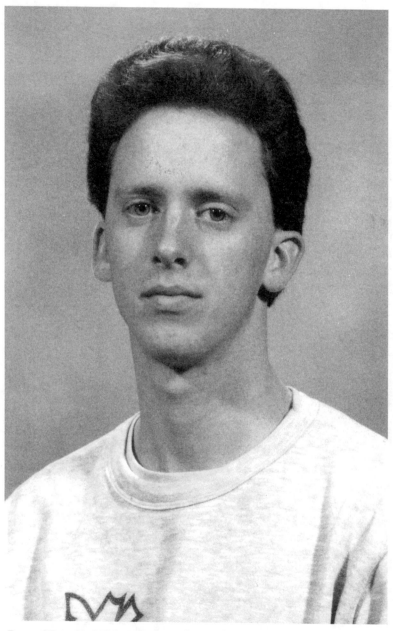

Danny Wenger's MCC orientation photo taken in early 1989. A color copy of this photo hangs in the Daniel Wenger Documentation Center in Managua.

Danny Wenger with MCC friends on the back of a pickup truck in Nicaragua. This truck is similar to the one being used at the time of the accident.

Danny Wenger with Hosanna friends in 1989. Lissette (with arm out-stretched) sits next to Danny.

A photograph taken at the November 1989 Central American MCC retreat in Honduras. Danny stands at the top right. The MCC country representatives in Nicaragua, Jim and Ann Hershberger, are near the bottom center of the photo. Ann is seated front row center holding daughter Rachel. Jim is seated directly behind her holding daughter Rebecca.

some of the redistributed wealth was not reinvested well. Some of it was lost.

While Danny felt that the socialists had done the right thing by distributing land to the peasant farmers, he also recognized that it had been economically disruptive, resulting in angry landowners and continued guerrilla warfare.

"Is there no way to help the poor without causing all this strain and anger?" Danny wondered. "Probably not. Cuba apparently took care of the dilemma by shooting dead all the rich guys. That's it; no more opposition. Get on with the new society. Thank God the Sandinistas chose another way, but it's not easy."

At first right after the socialist victory, the revolutionary government was able to subsidize everything. "The poor people could then afford basic necessities," Danny observed. "But the government and producers could not meet the demand. Shortages developed, resulting in astronomical inflation, causing the government to change its policies, cut subsidies, and embark on a new, recessive strategy. Now most things are available in stores, but people don't have the money. Inflation has eroded purchasing power and I've seen in the paper, over and over, stories of people being laid off."

Despite the deteriorating economic situation, the Sandinista government was still very popular with the people. Visitors could feel this popularity at national political rallies where there was little or no apparent security.

"We went to the Sandinista rally today in front of the National Palace," Danny wrote. "Security was in fact lax. We could have shoved our way up close to President Ortega without ever being checked. The rally really seemed to indicate an openness with the people, a shared confidence, or sense that the government was of and for the people.

"It's incredible how much contact Ortega has with the people," Danny marveled. "There is no obvious security up close."

Another day Danny went to an open-air rally where Bishop Desmond Tutu, a South African clergyman who won the 1984 Nobel Peace Prize, addressed the people.

"Desmond Tutu was good," Danny felt. "He spoke of hope and the inevitable victory of the poor over oppression. The evening before, he had spoken of Shadrach, Meshach, and Abednego (Daniel 3:1-30), and how even in the fire, nothing happened to them because God was with them–likewise Nicaragua, likewise South Africa."

* * *

Throughout Danny's eleven months in Nicaragua, he struggled with questions of what it meant to be a Christian. Was it or was it not the business of Christians to work at the problems of oppression and poverty? And if Christians were to confront oppression and poverty, how should they do it? During his first week in Nicaragua, he wrote, "I saw Bill Moyer's video "God and Politics" on the liberation theology versus conservative evangelism debate within the Methodist church. Very intriguing."

Danny concluded that the conservative evangelicals in the video "were correct in placing emphasis on a personal relationship with Jesus Christ . . . but their politics stank. The liberation theology side tended to be purely political . . . minimizing personal spiritual well-being, but their politics were right on. True, the liberationists were correct in rejecting a grin-and-bear-it attitude towards life on earth because there'll be pie-in-the-sky by and by. We do need to work towards the Kingdom here on earth. And we do need to assume the vantage point of the poor.

"I believe a true Christian approach is to integrate spiritual ministry with service. Social action and faith-building go hand in hand. I'm skeptical as to whether either half can be accomplished effectively if the other half is denied. I think Mennonites have gone a long way here toward emphasizing both word and deed."

Liberation theology's home is Latin America. The liberation theologians believe God is on the side of the earth's poor people. They believe God is at work helping the poor to free themselves from the oppression of the rich. The oppression of the poor by the rich is what liberation theologians call sin. When the poor accept oppression, that is also sin. Refusing to accept repression is to do good.

In contrast missionaries from the United States tend to believe that God is at work to free people from "sins" in the more traditional sense of the word. For many missionaries being rich or poor is beside the point of salvation.

On March 1 Danny wrote the reference "Isaiah 16:4b-5" in his journal. He had been in Nicaragua's capital city, Managua, for a month. During that month he had worked hard to see in his mind's eye how God was accomplishing His agenda in that impoverished, war-torn country. Danny wanted to see the pattern of God's activity so that he could fit his attitudes and style of involvement to God's way. What does Isaiah 16:4b-5 say?

> The oppressor will come to an end,
>> and destruction will cease;
>> the aggressor will vanish from the land.
> In love a throne will be established;
>> in faithfulness a man will sit on it–
>> One from the house of David–
> One who in judging seeks justice
>> and speeds the cause of righteousness.

With confidence, Danny wrote at the beginning of his second month, "Oppression will end. God will rule with justice. This is the plan for earth. Will we join Him in doing His will?"

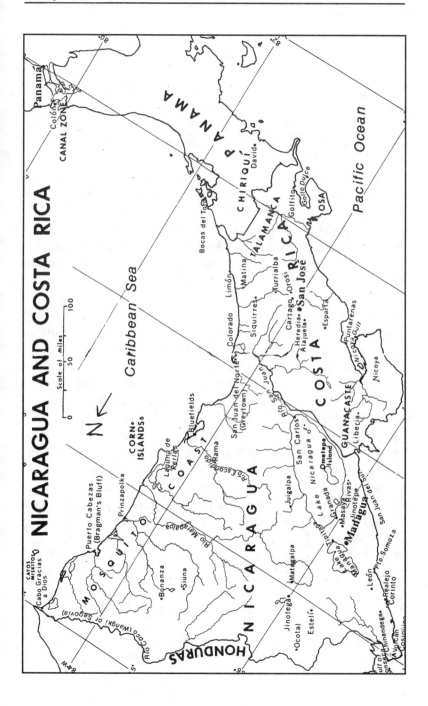

Audelia

Danny's home base was in the capital city of Managua. Within a month of his arrival, Jim Hershberger, MCC co-country representative, took Danny to visit several homes which were open to having an MCC boarder. They settled on Audelia's house as a suitable place for Danny to live.

Danny's room in Audelia's house was small with a big bed. The bed took up all but about 30 percent of the room space. The roof leaked at both ends of the bed. On the day he moved in, Danny was annoyed that his room had not been tidied up for his arrival. There was one toilet in the house, and it had no seat or toilet paper. The TV was on all the time. From his bed at night, he could hear music blaring from the radios of several neighbors.

In the morning before the day filled with noise, Audelia could be heard conversing with or yelling at her brother from her house to his house next-door. "As for privacy," Danny journaled, "what is privacy?" He called his street "an intimate community."

Audelia had a son, Jonathan, eight years old. Right off, Danny set about working on a relationship with this "little brother." Before long, Jonathan had accepted his mother's new boarder.

"Jonathan really seems to have taken to me more in the last few days," Danny wrote. "He's been attacking me with hugs, and always tries to jump on my back or something. We've been playing chess, which probably doesn't have much to do with it."

Audelia certainly was Danny's kind of woman, always ready to get into a serious, deep conversation. Of course, in the beginning, Danny had a language problem. "Sometimes," he wrote, "there is a lull in what Audelia is saying, and I'm forming something to say. But it takes me too long, and Audelia launches another lengthy discourse before I get going."

Jonathan was the subject of one of her get-acquainted, one-way "conversations" with Danny. Audelia was widowed. Danny summarized her speech:

"Audelia has feared for the proper development of Jonathan, given the lack of a male role model in the family. She was very glad that I was here, and thought I was a good model for him—very encouraging words." Danny's response was in action rather than words. "This afternoon I took Jonathan for a ride on the MCC motorcycle, which he very much seemed to enjoy. He's really a fun guy, it would seem.

"Audelia's candidness is very refreshing," Danny observed. "She said this evening how there had been talk since the Sandinistas came to power of the *hombre nuevo*, the new man. But it's embarrassing for her to see that this *hombre nuevo* exists largely only in theory in Nicaragua. Most individuals in post-revolutionary Nicaragua 'serve-their-country' selfishly for personal gain. True service, she thought, should be done sacrificially for public gain. It's quite a challenge to hear a poor, Nicaraguan Baptist housewife talking about service in this way. For me service is almost a luxury, not such a sacrifice. Three-years-in-Nicaragua looks good on a resume.

"I mentioned to Audelia that the *hombre nuevo* becomes possible through Christ, and that revolutions do not change people's hearts in a sweeping fashion. She agreed and suggested that her church has not emphasized Christ's work enough but has talked mostly, in the revolution's terms, of service and social action." To be a Christian was to be a better socialist.

Supporting the Sandinista revolution was the main focus of Audelia's Baptist faith. The revolution for her was personal and immediate. She told Danny about her brother, Santos, who lived in the next house. Santos "was a medic and was shot in the back by the Somosa soldiers during the fight for liberation when the Sandinistas came to power. His back was not operated on and it still hurts him badly on occasion. His son, Audelia's nephew, was captured by the Somosa soldiers, had acid thrown in his face, and died at the hands of his captors."

Several days later Danny wrote:

"I just spent some time talking with Santos, Audelia's brother. At age seven he began *machete* work, cutting sugarcane in the fields for money, and kept at it until he was eighteen years old. Then he came to Managua and took some classes to learn how to read. Eventually, he became a medic.

"He said the landowners during the time of the Somozas exploited the laborers and paid very little, although it did not take much to buy things then either. He thought the economy was probably best, in terms of purchasing power, during the capitalist Somoza era, peaking just before the earthquake which leveled Managua in 1972. Then again, following the 1979 socialist revolution, he saw some gain in the real wages of the working class. But since the mid '80s purchasing power has been completely eroded. Interestingly, he places a lot of blame on the IMF (International Monetary Fund) and World Bank, not the Nicaraguan government or the ongoing Contra war.

"Audelia says Santos is emotionally ill due to the death of his son. His wife left him because of it. He has experienced a lot of pain in his life. He has almost a plodding deliberateness without much vigor.

"Audelia says that people cover their pain with laughter. 'Sometimes I feel like a clown or jester,' she told me. 'Laughter is a gift from God to people for dealing with pain. In the night I cry tears in my pillow for the death of my husband. Both my children do not know of my tears because I laugh and I can coax laughter from others too. Laughter allows us to be in touch with pain. We do not need to forget because we can laugh.'"

* * *

Lissette came home during the second week that Danny was in Audelia's home. Lissette was Jonathan's big sister, Audelia's daughter. Audelia was afraid her daughter would be fat. When she came, Lissette was full-figured, but not fat. She was 20 years old, a social work student in the University and an extrovert like her mother.

"She seems very friendly, outgoing, easy to get to know," Danny observed of his new "sister." "I think I'd feel fairly comfortable going some place with her. She's already invited me to several different happenings. She's concerned about service and maintaining ties with religion and the church, but she's also very earthy. She even smokes. She seems to have some good ideas on development.

"The night she arrived, I sat out at the table in the living room and did homework while she wrote a letter. Neither of us got real far because of our talking." Lissette knew a little English. Spanish was the language they used between them.

Lissette had just broken up with a fellow she had been engaged to, and she began to be at home a lot. She took Danny on, from the beginning, as her intellectual sparring partner–she the full-figured, Spanish-speaking Nicaraguan, extroverted, say-what-you-think Baptist, liberation-theology, university-trained feminist and social worker; he the slim red-haired North American, quietly-introvert-ed-reflective-thinker, Anabaptist, peace-theology, MCC change-agent.

Besides talking–she fluent, liquid-tongued; he hesitantly search-ing for the right Spanish word or phrase–Lissette and Danny went to a lot of places together. They got around on foot, by jam-packed public bus, and on Danny's little MCC motorbike. Through Lissette, the Spanish world of Nicaragua opened up for Danny.

Belonging

Danny thought of himself as an "MCC worker." For him, the ideal person, the *hombre nuevo,* would be in the mold of an MCC worker. One day he tried, tongue-in-cheek, to explain this to Lissette.

"The MCC worker is a great cross-cultural interactor, a facilitator/educator for community development. He or she spends a lot of time with his/her kids, lives frugally, is a pleasant person to be around, is articulate, has a strong spiritual base, knows the Bible, integrates Christian principles into his/her life, and is as much committed to education and change in North America as to the country where he/she is working."

Danny wanted Lissette to hear this because she could not understand the Nicaraguan Mennonites she knew. For his part, Danny had some problems with the Nicaraguan Mennonites, too.

Three different Mennonite mission boards or church agencies from North America had planted churches in Nicaragua. Because he was a Mennonite and because part of his job description was to help the Mennonite churches create jobs by starting small industries, Danny felt duty-bound to at least attend a Mennonite church. But it was rough going. After four months, he wrote:

"Mennonite church is really quite boring. Today was really bad. I hardly understood anything of the Sunday school lesson. Why am I continuing to attend? Supposedly to build Mennonite contacts and get familiar with the Mennonites. To avoid guilt and suspicion, too, I suppose. The fact is, it is not that easy to simply get to know them."

Of course, Audelia and Lissette took him to the Baptist churches. Baptist preaching and teaching had a way of making him feel guilty. He would journal, guiltily applying the Sunday school lesson or sermon to his own life.

On Danny's second Sunday in Audelia's home, he went with Lissette by motorbike to Managua's First Baptist Church. "Sunday school," he wrote, "centered on Ananias and Sapphira who died on the spot after claiming they had given all to the church. Why did they have to suffer such a drastic fate? They lied and passed themselves off as better than they were. I too deserve the same fate it would seem, for I am dishonest and dislike revealing my weaknesses and imperfection. I don't know why they should have met such a fate, and not I, but I think that it must be the awesome grace of God that allows us to continue life despite our pride and our black hearts."

One Saturday Lissette took him to the University to attend a Bible study–a group of about 50 students which called itself *Hosanna*. Danny's first impressions were rooted in his life understandings. He commented that Goshen College students would not find this crowd all that stimulating.

"They were a real happy and simple bunch, which I tend not to go for. It is to their credit that they can get their jollies singing children's songs and so on. I was happy that they weren't a stuffy Bible-beater bunch. I shouldn't use 'Bible-beater.' They were quite relaxed, earthy, and open."

Given these first impressions, it is a particular irony that this group became Danny's spiritual home in Nicaragua, a place to belong. *Hosanna* turned out to be about much more than singing children's songs. In 1979, the year of the socialist revolutionary victory, several Christian medical students at the University had covenanted together to use their medical training in the service of the poor. They began to study the Bible and worship together.

Several years later when the first of the students became doctors, they formed a medical society which they called the *Accion Medica Christiana* (AMC, meaning Christian Medical Service). The two groups–*Hosanna* and *AMC*–functioned separately but attracted many of the same people. From the beginning, AMC members looked to Bible study and worship, which they found at the *Hosanna* meetings, for direction and power in their medical service to the poor.

Danny soon became quite involved. Lissette often coordinated the food at *Hosanna* get togethers, and she drafted Danny to help her. He participated in skits and other group activities. Before long, he found himself drawn into one of their MCC-type projects.

"They want to start a project in a poor barrio where there's a fair amount of prostitution going on. I went to the meeting last night to hear about it, and got drafted onto the task force to do a feasibility study.

"This project is still wide open. Our group of five is to study the needs and resources and present a proposal of action. To do it right, it will take a good bit of thought and maybe time as well."

The *Hosanna* Sunday worship services were also soon stretching his thinking. A Cuban theologian, René Costellanos, usually did the preaching. René was a 76-year-old professor of theology at the University who also taught folk dance and psychology. He was also a vegetarian. His sermons were in Spanish, but Danny got into them and was often moved by René's messages.

About one sermon, Danny wrote, "The whole thing brought up several questions for me. How do we distinguish between good and evil forces, right and wrong uses of parapsychology? Is a Ouija board directly tied to an evil force, or is it generally called evil out of fear of the unknown or does it have only bad results because of the way it's used? And why won't God accept those who throw devils out in God's name? Aren't we supposed to recognize men by the fruits of their work? And how do I know if a thought that pops into my head is the truth or 'the work of the devil'?

"Another question: do I have some mountains that I should be faithing away? It's not been my style, to faith away obstacles. In fact, lately I've been turning away from that mystical stuff. I was trying to make my prayers more a matter of lining myself up, rather than asking God to do all the work. But I do also believe that there is an inexplicable power of prayer and other unscientific things, and we shouldn't just limit our world ties to the material things we can make sense of."

While Danny loved the intellectual stimulation he got from *Hosanna*, he also began to look to them "for community, for camaraderie." Could a transplant such as he, an American Mennonite living in Nicaragua, find camaraderie in a foreign culture? Could Danny really find buddies in Nicaragua? Some days he would think, yes, this culture and these people were becoming second nature. On other days, he was filled with despair over the impossibility of being able to take root fully in Nicaraguan soil. In early October, his ninth month, Danny wrote:

"Last night was the *Hosanna* send-off for University medical students going to the Atlantic Coast for one month of field work. It was really a beautiful time by the lake, eating good food, swimming, joking around, singing. There was a real sense of togetherness. It seemed even a notch better than many of the groupie times I've had back in the States.

"Yet I felt very much out of it. They were not my people. I only knew the names of about half of them. They did not speak my language. I miss a lot of what is said when it's free-for-all joking around. It was very difficult to join in all the fun. I made a few attempts, a couple of which brought momentary success. But in general, I was left with a big aching feeling, a longing for connectedness to these people."

Lissette also occasionally contributed to Danny's feelings of being different, of being an outsider. "Another thing that hurt last night," Danny continued, "was Lissette's exclusion of me from the joke-telling. When her joke got towards the punch line, she whispered it to those in the back of the van and afterwards to the one beside her. She thinks I'm so straight! She limits herself, blaming it on me. I think I would welcome a touch of vulgarity in our relationship. I don't think I have any reason to limit her; why should she limit me?"

* * *

On a Sunday evening soon after Danny had moved into Audelia's house and during the first months of his time in Nicaragua, Lissette took him out–a bus ride to the end of the line and a leisurely walk back to their home. "It felt good to talk with a peer about whatever, just a light time, joking around in Spanish." When they were closer home, Lissette surprised him by asking him what he thought of her. Later he exclaimed in his journal, "Ohhh palleeze! Give me a break."

By May of 1989, Lissette had raised the question of whether they should become *novios.* To be *novios* would mean that their being together was not just a professional association. It would mean they were dating.

Danny had never been in a serious romantic relationship with a woman, never been in love. He had a number of women friends, some of whom he found especially attractive, and he corresponded somewhat regularly with several women. He loved conversing with women, loved the intellectual give and take. He believed that sex was for marriage and that it would be a physical expression of intellectual-spiritual admiration and commitment. He refused to see women as sex objects.

Lissette seemed to see Danny through the eyes of her recently failed relationship and seemed to look to him for affirmation of her physical femininity. Danny saw her as an intellectual and professional colleague. Each found the other strange and difficult. In spite of Danny's misgivings about them becoming romantically involved, Danny and Lissette began to spend more and more time together.

* * *

Another social reality of living in a capital city was the ebb and flow of international peoples. Nicaragua's Sandinista socialism and the government's conflict with the Contras attracted many seekers. Many were students. Danny occasionally wrote of meeting these people and socializing with them—young people from around the world comparing notes. It was a place where he felt he belonged.

"Up in San Judas [the section of Managua where Danny lived], we've got an international brigade hanging out. We have a Dominican and an Argentinean here in Audelia's house. Last night Lissette and I had a fairly lengthy talk with them as well as with the Brazilian and the Puerto Rican who are staying in Santos's house next door. All of them were talking about the divided church, the poor struggling against the government, harassment of church people, imperialism, etc.—universal problems, it seems."

Although Danny did not make the comparison, AMC was quite similar to MCC, an MCC in Nicaraguan clothing. Later, as Danny began to do extended visits on the Nicaraguan Atlantic Coast in connection with his job in food distribution for MCC, he often encountered AMC doctors "in the boonies," putting their faith into practice. As a social worker, Lissette also was occasionally on assignment over on the Atlantic Coast where she related to AMC.

In addition, Danny spent time with Jim and Ann Hershberger, the MCC co-country representatives, receiving his work assignments and playing with their children. He admired Ann, taking her as the model for his idealized "MCC worker." He did his monthly MCC reports and joined the regular social gatherings of MCC volunteers working in Nicaragua. He attended a week-long MCC retreat in Honduras.

But it is clear that Danny didn't find his primary friendships among his fellow MCCers. He was a third-generation "missionary." Sometimes such people are called Third-Culture-Kids (TCKs). As a TCK it was natural for Danny to look to educated Nicaraguans for his primary social and spiritual relationships. Lissette, Audelia's home, and the *Hosanna* folks became Danny's primary home away from home, his primary place to belong.

Jobs

What does an MCC worker do overseas? In the 1980s and '90s, a typical assignment involved job creation and food aid. Danny worked on these types of projects. Neither of these were easy tasks. In fact, they were tough assignments.

Several Canadian Mennonite missionaries had set up a group of small manufacturing cooperatives among Nicaraguan Mennonites. Because MCC has access to mountains of used clothing, they had conceived the idea that MCC-Nicaragua could import some of this clothing and set up women's groups in the congregations to sort and market the clothing, remaking or altering it if necessary.

Most of the Protestant churches in Nicaragua, of which the Mennonite groups are a small minority, had gotten together and formed the Association of Nicaraguan Evangelical Churches (CEPAD) to be their joint relief and development agency. MCC worked through CEPAD to import and warehouse the bales of used clothing for the Mennonite projects. Around the time of Danny's arrival, the Canadian missionaries retired from missionary service, and Danny was assigned to take over their work with the clothing project. Ann Hershberger had been close to the work, and she helped him get started.

From the beginning, Danny set limits. He agreed to work as an agent for the churches, doing the paperwork with CEPAD to get the used clothing shipments out of the warehouse. He also served as a production and marketing consultant.

Danny wrote pages and pages in his journal about hassles with the warehouse, related to security systems, paperwork, misunderstandings about scheduling, transportation, and the product itself. But his toughest problems in this particular jobs-creation assignment developed at the consultative end of it, not at the warehouse. His first meetings with the various congregational clothing cooperatives went very well, but he soon realized that a lot of what he thought was useful dialogue had been window dressing. He found himself unable to work with the problems without getting caught in the cross-fire among the various interest groups. He had stepped into a long-standing situation, and some people were not sure they could trust him. It was a difficult time.

In June, his fifth month, he wrote, "I ran into mistakes and mis-understandings and disappointments and conflicts with the clothing projects. Thursday I felt very humbled and discouraged."

In July he wrote, "Today we had a meeting about the clothing cooperatives. One thing that came out a lot was personality conflicts and various feuds and rivalries. Right now I could name about eight feuds or personality conflicts among individuals or groups of the Mennonite churches, which includes Mennonite missionaries and MCCers. It's really a sad story. I wonder how many feuds are going on back in the U.S."

In August he wrote, "Yesterday we had a marathon clothing cooperative meeting. I thought it was a very good meeting in terms of the problems discussed and the agreements reached. But nobody was designated to carry out the good decisions that were made."

A few days later he wrote, "I feel terrible! There are major problems with the clothing stores and I don't have time to deal with it."

As Danny came to understand the situation, he began to talk confidentially with several people about what he thought was wrong and what could be done. He felt some of the activity bordered on corrupt business practices. His search for solutions soon developed into some people seeing him as being part of the problem. In September he was distressed because what he had said, supposedly in confidence, had become public. An older MCCer confronted him.

"It appears I may have misjudged the ability to keep a secret and avoid gossip," Danny confided to his journal. "We need now to do some quick thinking on damage control. [The older MCCer] said very forcefully that what I was doing, spreading things around, wasn't appreciated. The harshness of the rebuke and the reality of the problem hit me hard, and I got depressed pretty quickly. It seems like I've done as much damage as help in this whole thing. Exactly what do I think I'm doing here anyway?"

That evening Danny confided to Lissette. "I laid everything out in front of her and we talked it out and she gave some advice which I felt was right on the mark. I felt fine. My troubles were lifted. Free as a bird! I have never made the switch from a foul mood so quickly in my life. I choose to call it a miracle of grace. Thanks to God."

But that did not solve the clothing co-op problems. Two days later he wrote, "Today I learned that one of the stores had dumped the slips, not just for one day, but a lot of them have been thrown out. Now there are real questions about how the money is used.

"I feel real low. I have completely failed in my responsibility to stay on top of things. Why have I not done more? I don't like feeling like a spy, checking in on every little thing. It seems imperialistic to have the foreigners checking in on everything. Nothing works when we are seen as the eye-in-the-sky."

An October entry shows that things were not improving. "I'm disappointed with the clothing shops. The people see MCC as something to be milked for their own good. They want to protect their own turf and see only as far as their own interests. Problems are to be shoved under the rug and denied. MCC is seen as an enemy and not as a co-partner. Although they speak differently, MCC is not welcome."

Always looking for a bright side, Danny pictured a "values" balance sheet in his mind, but was forced to conclude that maybe it was time to liquidate, a step which he did not have the authority to take. "Are we doing any good?" he asked himself. "Yes, some good is happening. Poor people are getting cheap clothes. Supposedly at least some of the money is or will be used wisely. But what are we doing for the spiritual and social development of the church? Maybe [the older MCCer] is right when he says we should 'cut off the clothes.'"

Danny's last entry on clothing cooperatives was made in early December. The gossip he had so regretted back in September had, without his prior knowledge, been included in an MCC report which the Nicaraguan clothing co-op directors then read.

The "directors found out in a vague, roundabout way about my concerns," Danny lamented. "Not good. I don't know what would have been best. Problems must be handled to some extent, but the tendency to speculate, make rumors, is real and only creates more damage."

Food

In addition to the used clothing, jobs-creation business, Danny was also asked to work with MCC food shipments from Canada. In both of these tasks, Danny stood between the importing agent (MCC) and the implementing Nicaraguan agencies.

But there were differences between his "Jobs" and "Food" assignments. The clothing stores were small Mennonite projects, and Danny was close to the grass-roots managers of the projects. In the early days, the clothing stores had been managed closely by North American missionaries. The missionaries were turning leadership over to the local church, and, in some cases, Danny was dealing with the management vacuum created by this transition.

But with food distribution, MCC was relating to inter-denominational agencies–the AMC doctors and The Protestant Council of Churches (CEPAD). In fact, the MCC food shipment and distribution could happen without an MCC representative in Nicaragua. But MCC wanted the food to have a peace-church connection. MCC wanted to be able to assure its donors that the food was reaching needy people. This was Danny's role, to be Mr. MCC at the distributing end. With both AMC and CEPAD, Danny worked with Nicaraguan professionals who in turn worked with the grass-roots people. Throughout his year in Nicaragua, Danny got along quite well with these Nicaraguan professionals.

He did the food paperwork in Managua, the capital city, which is on the western, Pacific Coast side of the country. But since most of the food distribution work was over on the eastern, Atlantic Coast, Danny made five trips across the country to the Atlantic side, visiting the areas where most of the food was going.

This eastern, wet, flat-land side of Nicaragua is nicknamed the Mosquito Coast. The area is lightly populated with Native Americans and descendants of the black folks who had been brought from Africa to work the colonial banana plantations. There are few roads on the Mosquito Coast. The land is crossed by many rivers, some navigable, running eastward out of Nicaragua's central highlands into the Atlantic Ocean.

The year before Danny's arrival, the Mosquito Coast had been devastated by Hurricane Joan. The area had also been disrupted ten years earlier at the time of the Sandinista revolution. Many Native Americans had gone north to Honduras or south to Costa Rica to avoid forced service in the Sandinista army. Now with the Contra war slowing down, these Native Americans were moving back to their old homes and MCC food was tiding them over until they could get their own peasant farms going again.

On the Mosquito Coast, Danny encountered racial and cultural prejudices between the inland people from Managua, who were Spanish-speaking, and the people who were getting the food aid–English-speaking blacks and Native Americans.

* * *

Danny made his first trip east in April. He went with the CEPAD administrator for the Mosquito Coast. Their destination was Puerto Cabezas, the northernmost of Nicaragua's two Atlantic seaports.

"I'm taking off for the Mosquito Coast," he wrote, "and feel okay about it really. I'll be on my own."

"What a trip!" he wrote the first evening out. "Took off for Puerto Cabezas at 4:45 a.m. and made it to Rosita, a small town about three-fourths of the way to the Atlantic Coast. I've never been so grungy in my life. It was total dust. The road was fairly bad too, some places just rocks. Getting stuck behind convoys going 20 kph was a big drag too. Then there were the river crossings. At one place, Darwin went right into a holding pond for a bridge construction. The jeep filled with water. Chepe had to get out into water up to his chest so he could lock the front wheels into four-wheel drive."

At both Rosita and Puerto Cabezas, Danny spent time finding out what CEPAD was doing with the food they got from MCC. Things were pretty slow-paced on the coast, and Danny became irritated with all the waiting around and endless talking.

"Darwin is an interesting guy," he observed. "He likes to joke around a lot. He also led in lengthy Bible studies the two nights we were in Rosita. I'm not sure how much he prepared, but he just went on and on. I've been impressed generally with the style of talking that a lot of Nicaraguans have. They just keep going and going repeating things endlessly."

By the fourth day of Danny's trip, the excitement of travel had worn thin. He had planned to fly back to Managua but the flight was cancelled. He wrote:

"Right now I'm feeling pretty down on Puerto Cabezas. (1) Hot, humid, little breeze, (2) extremely lazy, slow-pace, (3) the ocean, though beautiful, has not been fit for body surfing (yeah, that's important), (4) immigration, which monitors in-country travel, and the airline flights have been uncooperative, (5) the electricity just went out, leaving me in the dark, (6) no running water, and (7) outhouses that stink. Fortunately, I've been constipated since I left Managua. I'll take some misery points, thank you."

To kill time, Darwin drove Danny north to the Honduras border to the town of Waspam on the Coco River. That lifted his spirits briefly.

"Waspam," he wrote, "was a beautiful place overlooking the Coco River and the lush fields in Honduras on the other side." But driving back to Puerto Cabezas, he went into his grump again.

"I got really annoyed on the trip back from Waspam," he fumed. "Darwin was driving super-slow over washboard roads. He had turned off the air conditioner and persisted in driving on the main road when the track alongside was much smoother. My back hurt. I was not happy. Life was terrible. I'm having fun writing this!"

That night, his fifth on the road, the cork blew. "I got the runs bad last night and had to fly to the outhouse at 7:00, 1:00, 5:00, and 7:00."

* * *

Danny's next trip to the Mosquito Coast came at the end of June. A ship with over 800 tons of MCC Canadian food arrived at Puerto Cabezas on June 28. Things quickly became a mess. A local shipping agent called it *'Todo fue desastre'* (everything a disaster). Yet everywhere he looked, Danny could see relatively simple ways to improve the operation.

"We've had big problems in handling the shipment here in Puerto Cabezas," he wrote with satisfaction. "It's been kind of exciting and interesting to uncover all the problems and see and hear what's going on, which makes me feel a little guilty 'cuz I shouldn't be getting an ego trip over all the yuck that's happening. Actually, it's just plain unfortunate what's going on.

"Stealing happened at all stages of the process," Danny went on. "On the dock it was basically the workers stealing. The general population stayed off the dock for the most part. But during transport from the dock to the warehouse, at least one truck was stopped by a barrier as knife-wielding locals carried off some sacks. At the warehouse, the people slipped knives through the slats of the parked trucks, tore open bags, and collected the grain as it spilled out. Even after it was in the warehouse, at night, people slipped knives under the door and cut a few bags. A few attempts were made to break into the warehouse; fortunately they were unsuccessful."

Why all the stealing? A good part of it was because the local native population had no respect for the local black CEPAD administrator or the Spanish CEPAD administrators from Managua. The natives thought all the CEPAD administrators were fat cats.

Whenever the Nicaraguan government brought in a shipment of food, the army was called out to keep order. But the only force that CEPAD had were the local police. They were also natives with much the same attitude as the local population–that the CEPAD people were fat cats.

In the end, Danny calculated that less than one percent of the shipment had been lost and about five percent had been damaged. It was a shipment of wheat flour, corn, rice, oil, meat, and beans. He made a number of suggestions on ways to do the next shipment better.

In spite of the hassles on the docks, Danny had a great time with the CEPAD fellows who had come over from Managua. "We spent most of four days working, eating, and doing practically everything together," he wrote. "I got a good dose of Nicaraguan slang from these guys. Now when I see them in their Managua offices, we can joke around a little before getting down to business, so that's been a positive development."

* * *

Danny wanted to get the big picture, wanted to find out what was happening downstream with the MCC food. So he arranged to return to the Mosquito Coast for the third time. He spent ten days on the Coast, visiting the nine communities which had been receiving MCC Canadian food.

This time Lissette decided to join him. As it happened, she was on a social work assignment at Sahsa, Danny's first stop on the trip. On his first trip to the Coast, Danny and Darwin had driven through Sahsa, dropping off medicine for the AMC doctor at the same clinic where Lissette was now working. On that trip, Sahsa had seemed like the end of the world to Danny. "Poor doctor," he thought, "out here working with a different culture without other Spanish people around, living in the middle of nowhere, completely isolated."

But after being in Sahsa several days on his third trip to the Coast, Danny wrote, "Sahsa doesn't seem like the middle of nowhere anymore. I don't pity Dr. Samuel so much now. He has good relationships and seems to be doing well."

On this trip Lissette helped Danny to see things through the eyes of a Nicaraguan social worker. Every day they were at a different place, trying to understand the community. Why was MCC food aid necessary? When would it no longer be needed?

Danny kept careful notes on each place they visited and wrote a detailed report. He had especially good things to say about the work of the AMC doctors. "I had a sense of pride," he wrote, "that MCC is part of their work, and we should consider it a great privilege to be able to support them in their ministry."

The fact-finding and reporting was only part of Danny's food distribution work. Beyond that, he was putting a human face to the MCC logo and its motto, "In the Name of Christ." At one place, Danny was asked to do a devotional meditation.

"I said a little bit about the challenge of sharing everything when I tend to be selfish. Then I talked about MCC being a way for North American Mennonites to share. I feel uncomfortable talking about MCC this way, mostly for fear of sounding paternalistic and imperialistic. I asked Lissette about my talk afterwards. She has many questions about Mennonites and about MCC. I'm not quite sure what her problem is. Maybe I need to differentiate between MCC and Mennonites in general."

Halfway through Danny and Lissette's ten-day tour, they were traveling between communities in an open-bed pickup truck. Danny evidently was riding in the back, and Lissette was probably in the cab with the driver.

"I had a fun trip in on the pickup today," he wrote. "I wasn't especially comfortable when it poured down rain, but my spirit was high. I was contemplating various aspects of life, few of which I recall at the moment, and it was a very positive, uplifting experience."

When the trip came to an end, Danny was sad to have to go back to Managua. Food and drink for him, spiritually, was getting to know people by exchanging personal ideas and observations. On this trip for the first time since coming to Nicaragua, he had been in a situation where he could spend quality time getting to know people through unhurried, in-depth conversations.

"Last leg of the trip," Danny wrote at dawn on his last morning in Puerto Cabezas. "I'm waiting to be picked up to go to the airport. In a way, I don't want to go back to Managua. Why? Perhaps I want the excitement of traveling to new places, dealing with the big development and aid questions, and talking to and learning about new people. Perhaps more than that, I want intimacy. With Lissette along on every step of the trip, I could not escape it.

"Scott Peck, in *A Different Drum*, says intimacy and vulnerability bring pain, but are rewarding. I've seen that. I've had bittersweet talks lately about myself and my work which were troubling talks. It was painful and discouraging for me, yet I feel that relationships have grown through this. I feel a slightly greater sense of community. I don't want to go back to relationships which are largely superficial and broken up into ten-minute segments."

During this trip a certain level of intimacy developed between Danny and Lissette. On the last evening before Danny's flight back to Managua, they spent several hours sitting on the wharf at Puerto Cabezas sorting out their relationship. They had been together for over a week. In terms of his work, Danny had been treating Lissette as a professional colleague. At home his personal relationship to her had been one of brother and sister—Audelia was mother, Jonathan was little brother, and Lissette was grown-up sister.

Though they spent a great deal of time together, his journals indicate that he continued to see her as a colleague and sister. But Lissette seemed not to be able to keep herself from feeling more for Danny than the boundaries which he had set would allow. She was 20; he was 23.

"I feel sorry for Lissette. She says she's done everything possible to not like me, but she can't help it. She hasn't gotten much from me in return. She's disappointed with me for not sharing my soul, and that makes it difficult for her."

Danny was often self-critical; an introvert. Lissette was open, extroverted, and self-accepting. Again and again in his journals, Danny noted that his silence and hesitancy frustrated Lissette. She was frequently getting on his case for being the way he was—too quiet, too North American, too unresponsive. This bothered Danny and he made several journal entries about how she could "make me feel guilty, then flip me out by being nice."

She wanted to know what was going on inside him. He needed quiet time to know that even for himself. While Danny could be and often was fun loving, Lissette knew this was the superficial part of him. She wanted to know the inner Danny. Now and then she saw glimpses of that inner self, a man whom she was beginning to love.

After their evening together by the sea, Danny wrote "I am moved by the fact that she cares for me so much, especially since I feel I haven't done much to deserve her care. In the past little while, I have thought that it would be possible for me to love her and that scares me. I am perhaps a little scared of the unknown for my own sake, but I have been in a frame of mind lately for new things. I am more scared for Lissette. I believe she is still hurting from breaking up with her last boyfriend, and I'm afraid of putting her in the position for the same kind of pain."

* * *

Danny was back home in Managua for less than two weeks before it was time to take another trip, his fourth to the Mosquito Coast. This time he went to Nicaragua's southern seaport on the Atlantic, the old town of Bluefields. A request had come to MCC to provide food aid in the communities inland from Bluefields as a way of encouraging the Native Americans to begin some development projects. Danny went over to the Coast to examine the prospects. This fourth trip to the east was filled with grace. Danny was alone—no hassles from Lissette or any of the other folks who regularly took his energy. He did a lot of creative thinking over that time.

* * *

His fifth and last trip east to the Mosquito Coast came near the end of his time in Nicaragua. It was an extended visit, three weeks plus, connected to an 840-ton food shipment. He was over on the Coast from October 28 to November 21, a total of 24 days.

On this last trip the off-loading at Puerto Cabezas went smoothly with none of the mayhem which had characterized the July shipment. Many of Danny's written suggestions had been acted on.

Only part of this shipment was off-loaded in Puerto Cabezas, the balance was being taken to Bluefields. During the five days the ship was in Puerto, Danny became friends with the Danish captain who invited him on board for the voyage down the coast. The "cruise" was a wonderful experience—his first time on a real ship.

Shipboard luxuries included Danny's first hot shower since the morning of February 3 when he had left his home in Lancaster. The European food was a welcome change from standard Nicaraguan fare. The captain even invited Danny to phone home, on the house. He made a call to his parents. Danny found it "fun checking out all the equipment and maps on the ship's bridge and talking about religion, politics, and shipping with the captain."

Once in Bluefields, Danny spent the days hanging out on the ship watching the off-loading. In the evenings, he spent time with people. Lissette came over for a few days, and since Danny had been in Bluefields before, he was happy and feeling quite at home.

"Bluefields is a fairly small place so, walking on the streets, I kept bumping into old friends or work acquaintances which was fun because that never happens in Managua. Lissette and some friends came down from Managua for a couple of days and all of them introduced me to their friends and sweethearts, so it was a great social time."

The off-loading completed, Danny's intention was to follow the food shipment inland from the port to observe its distribution. Trying to get inland shattered his peace of mind. It seemed that a large unseen hand was blocking every effort he made.

The food was shipped out of Bluefields on slow diesel boats. The route was back up the coast to Pearl Lagoon and then inland by river. Danny did not want to get stuck on one of the "barges." He arranged instead for a boat with a gasoline, outboard motor to take him around. Then, "whaddya know there's no gas in town. The diesel boats have left, loaded with food while I am stranded in Bluefields."

Instead, Danny hitched an overland ride to Pearl Lagoon to spend the weekend with the AMC doctor there. On Monday he went back to Bluefields where some Cuban friends lent him gas. He did get off on Tuesday, but the outboard motor soon broke down.

"This has been really frustrating. I can't get anything done! I'm sick of repacking and unpacking and lugging my bags around. The grass-flea bites are driving me crazy. I never know what's going to happen next."

He began to think about home. "I am really getting to miss Managua. I think of Lissette and the family and of Jim and Ann and their daughters. It would be great to shoot the breeze with Ann while Rachel [a Hershberger toddler] climbs all over me, or have a leisurely breakfast with the Audelia family, having just as much coffee, bread and cream, and bananas as I want."

That night about fifteen gallons of his Cuban-supplied gasoline was stolen! On Wednesday he managed to get another boat and set out again. The lagoon was choppy but the boat driver plowed ahead at full throttle, pounding the boat on the waves until Danny feared it would break up!

When he finally caught up with the food shipment, he had some of the most significant days of his entire time in Nicaragua. He wrote to a friend, "I've never had to talk about the Mennonites so much in all my life." He used Walter Klaassen's *Anabaptism, Neither Protestant nor Catholic* as his primary resource in explaining to the Native Americans who Mennonites were.

The shipment of MCC food out of Bluefields was being received

The Audelia family where Danny Wenger lived during his year in Nicaragua. (Back row) mother Audelia, daughter Lissette. (Front row) son Jonathan, step-daughter Diana.

Danny Wenger explains the MCC philosophy to a group of Nicaraguans as part of his food distribution work on the Mosquito Coast.

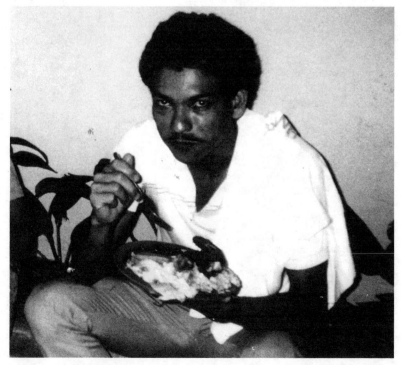

Danny's friend, Hernaldo, several months before the tragic accident on December 30, 1989.

Danny's friend, Lissette, with his mother, Erma, some months after Danny's death.

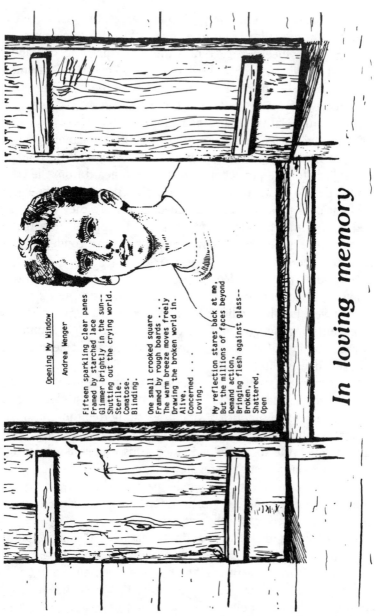

Opening My Window

Andrea Wenger

Fifteen sparkling clear panes
Framed by starched lace
Glimmer brightly in the sun--
Shutting out the crying world.
Sterile.
Comatose.
Blinding.

One small crooked square
Framed by rough boards . . .
The warm breeze moves freely
Drawing the broken world in.
Alive,
Concerned . . . .
Loving.

My reflection stares back at me,
But the millions of faces beyond
Demand action,
Bringing flesh against glass--
Broken,
Shattered,
Open

In loving memory

The cover of the program distributed at Danny Wenger's funeral, Mellinger Mennonite Church, Lancaster, Pennsylvania. The poem was written by Danny's sister, Andrea.

by eight different communities. Danny managed to visit seven of them and arranged for town meetings in five of these communities. The town meetings gave him the opportunity to talk about MCC and the Mennonites as well as to share how the Mennonites viewed food aid. Since this was the first time these communities were receiving MCC food aid, Danny Wenger was the first Mennonite the Native Americans had met.

One of the towns "had major problems with the handling of the food." At that town meeting, Danny talked for a half hour about MCC's goals for the project and what he had heard from the community people about their poor leadership. He talked about the problems of dependency and the need to work so they would not need to continue getting the external food supplies. To a friend Danny wrote, "I felt like the powerful, intervening, condescending *gringo* preacher."

To his journal he confided, "I gave quite a speech, kind of proud of myself. I had fun doing it for the most part and I think it was received well. It's always difficult talking about creating dependency and encouraging them to work. I'm conscious that I might sound like a preachy foreigner who lacks respect for the local people and who really just doesn't understand."

When he returned to Bluefields, Danny spent the evening before his trip back to Managua with a group of visiting students from England and North America. While most supported the Sandinista socialist revolution, there was considerable complaining about the ways in which the socialists had failed. This was unusual–foreign students grousing about the revolution.

"It is great to know that some people aren't blind to the Sandinista faults. Generally North Americans who visit here don't seem to be at all critical of the revolution."

Danny listed some of the Sandinista faults: "(1) narrow, politicized education in the schools; (2) lack of distinction between party and government; (3) sacrificing the best development decisions to political considerations; and (4) wealthy, powerful, intimidating presence of the ruling elite in humble, rural communities, not to mention all their past cultural insensitivities towards blacks and Native Americans and their political/military mistakes."

Making Sense of It

Danny Wenger's personality compelled him to look for the over-all pattern of things–to search for the big picture. He read lots of Henri Nouwen and M. Scott Peck. He began to take MCC's philosophy very seriously and his appreciation for his Mennonite missionary family roots began to grow.

Early in his Nicaraguan experience, Danny worried a lot about his responsibility to his home congregation, the Mellinger Mennonite Church. MCC wanted its overseas volunteers to work at bringing about change in North America. Danny figured that Mellinger was supportive of him. But he was pretty sure that many of the members wouldn't understand how he felt about Nicaragua. It felt to him that the differences between Lancaster County and Nicaragua were too great for meaningful communication to happen.

How could he work toward making his experience useful to his supporters back home? Danny concluded that probably the best way would be to think of people back home in two categories. Some people would have had experiences similar to his and they would understand him. Others, probably a majority, would accept that whatever he did in Nicaragua was okay. They wouldn't be that interested or concerned about the details.

Another early concern was what he would do after his three years in Nicaragua. "Seminary? Barcelona for the 1992 Summer Olympics? A nine-to-five job where he could get rich and escape the world's problems? Graduate school in a large American city? Another three-year stint with MCC? Live in the United States without a car to save the environment and money?"

As his job responsibilities and his relationship with Lissette pulled him deeper into the Nicaraguan world, worries about his church back home and re-entry to the U.S. stopped chasing themselves around in his head. He thought and wrote a lot about community.

Genuine community would not happen among people until they trusted each other enough to let others know who they were inside. The road to genuine community required a lot of sharing, which meant pain, and a lot of adjusting. Community demanded a high level of commitment and openness. Danny realized it was hard work to relate to Nicaraguans. "I'm still not comfortable with letting my guard down around Nicaraguans."

During the months after Danny and Lissette's ten-day trip to the Coast in July, their friendship intensified. It almost seemed that he was her project. She worked continually to bring him into the Nicaraguan frame of reference. She was critical of his silence and introversion, his slowness to express himself emotionally–characteristics which made him seem strange to her. For his part, Danny was committed to taking Lissette seriously in spite of his hating "those talks" she would have with him. He believed it was a start toward Nicaraguan community, "a whopping community of two."

Danny wondered sometimes whether she was as committed to community as he was. Once after a particularly intense "spat," Danny confided to his journal, "She still needs to learn to accept my past, recognize the good in it, and accept me as I am."

* * *

Community wasn't the only topic that interested Danny. In many pages of his journal, he sorted out his thoughts on God, Jesus, Christianity, peace, spirituality, prayer, and faith. He picked up these ideas, turned them over, asked questions, noted what the Bible–especially Isaiah–and others said. Then he planned the direction of his own thinking.

It took lots of quiet time to do this, something Danny did not get much of in Managua. However, his fourth trip to the Mosquito Coast, when he spent a number of days alone in Bluefields, offered him some free time. His journal entries over this time were extraordinarily creative.

"I am using some of my time here to read, relax, reflect, organize, dream, and pray–things I've not done that much of lately.

"It is conceivable that a few months or years down the road, the Contras will die. Hostilities will cease. But deep fractures will still exist in this country. Peace seems almost around the corner, but shalom (peace) seems but a dream.

"Let us dream then. I dream of a Nicaraguan National Reconciliation Project. It would seek to heal the political wounds of this nation, but would go beyond that to welcome and encourage reconciliation between non-political entities that are in conflict. It would culminate in a day or week of activities that would be full of symbolic gestures such as handshakes, gift giving, cooperation in festivities, even foot washing, ending with communion feasts and wild celebration.

"The concepts on which the Project would be built include forgiveness, repentance, *shalom*, community, cooperation, unity in diversity. The Project would not seek to change ideology, culture, religious belief, etc. It would ask us to transcend these, to recognize the legitimacy of being different, and to commit ourselves to working with instead of against those who don't agree with us.

"Can any part of this dream be made real? It is not realistic in its entirety. For one I doubt the participation of the U.S. Embassy. Secondly, there are so many conflicts at so many different levels, that one project could not have success at accommodating them all, certainly not in the same time span. But I believe there might come a day when many would be willing to undertake such a Project.

"What should the plan of action be? Perhaps MCC Peace Portfolio could draw up a proposal." After struggling through several pages on how MCC might implement such a Project, Danny allowed himself to be doubtful as to whether his peace vision with its focus on celebration might not be missing the point.

"Am I substituting a project for true reconciliation?" he wondered. "Would implementing the Project hamper genuine reconciliation efforts or try to move them along too quickly? Reconciliation could be sought on a case-by-case basis in a quiet, private fashion.

"But a public effort with public support and public celebration," he insisted to himself, "would have a marvelous impact on the mood and spirit of the people!"

Lissette had also been dreaming about a peace project. Her perspective was quite different from Danny's. Peace, in her dream, would happen when women would no longer be dominated by men. Lissette believed there was a direct connection between capitalism and male *machismo*. She saw male dominance as the pri-

mary destructive force in society. In her view, it found its highest
development in capitalist societies.

Shortly after Lissette and Danny met the first time, they had a
discussion about this. Danny insisted that male dominance was
everywhere and predated capitalism. Lissette refused to budge.

This subject became the focus of her thesis at the University.
After Danny got back from his Bluefields trip where he had
dreamed of a Peace Project, Lissette gave him her thesis to read and
critique. Her peace ideas, with the core belief that socialism
reduces male dominance, sparked "a pretty tough conversation"
between them.

"I went over her thesis paper and balked at the word 'guarantee'
being used to describe the effect of the revolution on conditions for
women's liberation. I feel the only guarantee is Christ, that we can
improve a lot here on earth, but the perfect society will be reached
only after Christ's second coming.

"Lissette thought the Nicaraguan socialist revolution would
bring about full equality between women and men. I thought 'Why
be a Christian if the revolution can do all that?' and asked her why
she was a Christian then. So she thought I was doing what the capitalist Ligia does, which is claim that Christianity and revolution
are incompatible, and that really upset her."

The more they talked, the more polarized they became. "I felt
this wall go up between us during the discussion, and Lissette felt
it too. She was very disappointed to find it there. She is also very
disappointed about the fact that I haven't changed my views or
ways of thinking so much in the nine months I've been here."

The deeper Danny was immersed in the Nicaraguan world view,
including the way people thought and felt about Christianity, the
greater despair he felt about trying to explain Nicaragua to people
back home.

Clouds

When the MCC country representatives–Jim and Ann Hershberger–had asked Audelia if she would be willing to have Danny in her home, they expected that Lissette would be gone much of the time and that her student's path would not intersect with Danny's to any extent. As it turned out, Lissette was home a lot, and she was free socially.

Furthermore, no one expected that *Hosanna* would become socially and spiritually significant in Danny's life. MCC did not know that Danny and Lissette were being thrown into a very close relationship, where they spent a lot of time together at home and where their professional, social, and religious lives intersected frequently. No other MCCers lived in the part of town where Danny lived, and he seldom talked about Lissette when he was with MCCers.

Lissette and Danny had an intense relationship with each bringing to it quite different life experiences. They also had some things in common. They both had university-trained minds. Lissette could read English. The language of their relationship was Spanish. They were both Christians. They had both recently become adults.

But having a girlfriend in Nicaragua, whether North American or otherwise, was not what Danny had in mind. His journal is clear that he was not at all ready to think about marriage or a relationship that might be pointing toward marriage. As the weeks and months slipped by, however, and as Lissette and he were doing more and more things together, he began to realize that "supposedly we aren't *novios,* but I am having trouble seeing the difference." Still, taking the step of acknowledging to others what their friendship had become frightened him.

Lissette eventually concluded that Danny was just an old conservative. Not understanding her, he fumed, "Lissette has this idea that I'm conservative, which really bugs me. I don't consider myself conservative." Especially after their July trip together to the Coast, the *Hosanna* people began teasing them.

Finally, Danny agreed to admit to himself and others that he and Lissette were dating, that they were *novios.* On November 23 he told Jim and Ann. They were taken by surprise and reacted with shock and displeasure. This, in turn, shook Danny up.

"I was taken aback with the seriousness with which Jim and Ann took the news. I have seen this as a limited commitment. I see obstacles to a dedicated relationship if it would move toward marriage, and I have been clear that I want to have the freedom to cut off at some juncture. Lissette has assured me of that freedom." Both Danny and Lissette were so knotted up inside that they had a good, therapeutic cry. Danny had not cried for five years.

Jim and Ann made it clear that if Danny and Lissette were *novios*, then it was wrong for Danny to continue living in her home. They wanted him to move out of Audelia's house. After discussions all around, it was agreed that he would move. But Audelia insisted that he not move until after the Christmas and New Year's celebrations. Together, they decided that Danny would move on January 2, 1990, a Tuesday.

* * *

Christmas was coming, a time of peace. Danny was always looking for examples, or indications of progress toward community and peace. But that December, it seemed that all the peace indicators were nose diving. He and Lissette were particularly shaken by the response to their announcement.

Danny had also become concerned about the family situation next-door in Audelia's brother's house. In mid-December, there was a late-night incident between two of Lissette's male cousins.

"A fight broke out. Lissette and I went over and intervened, trying to calm the guy down. In the process, he hit Lissette and got her upset. Then there were strong words between her and the other guy. Finally the police came, and Lissette was angry with the police for not taking the two guys to jail.

"Lissette was extremely upset, partly because of the fight, but more because the two men had been offended by her intervention. So I spent several hours consoling her, trying to ease the tension so she could sleep, since she had a big weekend ahead of her. I don't think I have ever given so much of myself. I felt drained by the time I went to bed. I didn't sleep well, and in the morning, Lissette was still distraught."

A few days before Christmas, Danny wrote, "I want to see Lissette and her cousins reconciled. . . . Doesn't the Christ child give hope for complete reconciliation . . . ?"

Danny also was following the gathering storm in Panama closely, "This Panama situation is getting scary," he had written in May. "The papers are all full of American CIA plans for invasion and of Bush-bashing. . . . I talked with Lissette this evening about the possibility of an invasion of Panama by the U.S. Lissette seemed to sparkle with excitement at the prospect of Nicaragua, Cuba, and other countries going down to Panama to take on the big bad U.S. bully. I must admit myself that it certainly sounds exciting. Why should peace be more boring than war?"

Then on December 20, just before Christmas, Panama was invaded, "The U.S. has invaded Panama! Presumably hundreds of civilians have been killed in this senseless attack.

"At times it seems the invasion is just what you might expect of the U.S. Yet at other times I am incredulous. It is so insensible. 'To protect U.S. lives,' Bush says. And how many Panamanians have died already? And Bush says it's worth it. The Panamanian lives don't even figure in. 'Because Noriega is a drug-runner,' Bush says. Since when does the U.S. government really take drugs seriously?"

The situation with the Contras in Nicaragua also did not look good in December. Danny wrote: "Contra attacks have been on the rise since August, prompting President Ortega to end the 20-month-old ceasefire the Nicaraguan government had put into effect unilaterally. Many suspect the U.S. Embassy here is encouraging a violent, polarized atmosphere."

In the midst of all of this, however, something very nice happened. Danny was asked to be in charge of the devotions for a Christmas party at one of the clothing stores, a store where he had experienced a lot of difficulty.

"Christmas has always been a fun time of vacation, friends, family, gifts, turkey, etc. A jolly time, basically. This year it's been harder to be jolly because there's so much pain in Panama, Romania, even next-door in El Salvador. How can we celebrate amid so much suffering?"

These were the concerns and issues which were uppermost in Danny's mind when he wrote a New Year's form letter to family and friends. He keyed the letter into his computer on December 29 but never scripted it. Unfinished, it waited for the New Year when Jim Hershberger punched the "Enter" key on Danny Wenger's computer and got a printout.

Natalia's Question

In early November a young Nicaraguan woman, Natalia, got into a conversation with Danny. She wanted to know about MCC. She thought MCC must be a good agency, but she had a difficult question.

"The other evening Natalia was asking about MCC. From the little she knew, she liked it except that we don't have more Nicaraguans. After so many years, why haven't we developed the abilities in people to take over the work? I had no good answer. I want to find out why MCC Nicaragua hasn't had Nicaraguans on staff.

"It also made me question what I'm doing here. I think there must be many Nicaraguans capable of doing what I'm doing. What sets me apart may be my North American education so that I can send information on our work to the U.S. Maybe it is my peace position; I don't know what else. Not real convincing arguments for me."

* * *

On December 30 a Mennonite church in Corazo, about 25 miles south of Managua, arranged to use the MCC Toyota 4 x 4 double-cab pickup to take its youth group, some 30 of them, to the mountains for an overnight retreat. Danny was appointed to drive the pickup. In Nicaragua it is drivers who are insured, not vehicles. MCC did not want people who might not be insured driving its vehicles. Since Danny was an insured driver, he was appointed to do the driving for the youth retreat.

There were too many youth for everyone to get aboard the Toyota, so they had to make two trips. Danny took half of the youth group up to the retreat center. He returned for the second half soon after noon. He found that the second bunch of youth had not all assembled yet.

Lissette was also at the staging area, and she got into the cab of the pickup with Danny. She wanted him to go over to Hernaldo's house where he could get something to eat. She also thought Hernaldo could be persuaded to go along on the retreat.

Hernaldo was one of the AMC medical students at the University. Lissette and Danny knew him well. He was home from the University at the time because his mother was very sick. It was expected that she would not live.

Lissette and Danny did not want to go to the overnight youth bash "alone." They would be the only two there who were older than the kids they were transporting. Both of them wanted Hernaldo to go along. Hernaldo did not want to leave his mother. She was very low. In the end Lissette and Danny prevailed and Hernaldo packed an overnight bag.

For Danny's lunch Hernaldo gave him a shish kebab of meat. Lissette urged Danny to let Hernaldo drive. They needed to get on back to the youth staging area. Danny could eat while Hernaldo drove. It was just a quarter mile. Why not? Hernaldo drove over to where the kids had gathered.

The young people quickly piled into the open back of the pickup. There was a frame of galvanized pipe over the truck bed. The youth were standing up in the back. There were more than fifteen young people crowded into the back, many sitting on the end gate, sort of hanging onto the back of the truck bed. Soon everyone was ready to go. Danny, sitting in the middle of the truck's front seat, had not finished his shish kebab.

"Let Hernaldo drive," Lissette urged. "You're not finished eating yet. He can drive. He has a driver's license."

Maybe Danny remembered Natalia's question, "Why hasn't MCC developed the abilities in people to take over the work MCCers do?" His response to the question had been, "I think there must be many Nicaraguans capable of doing what I'm doing."

Hernaldo did have a driver's license. In fact, an MCCer had taught Hernaldo how to drive, nothing formal, no learner's permit. It was just a sort of, "Hey, Hernaldo, try this! I'll teach you how to drive." Then one day at a Sandinista fair, at a booth which issued driver's licenses for a small fee, Hernaldo bought a license for himself. He did not, however, have insurance.

Of course, if the pickup had been owned by a Nicaraguan agency, a designated, insured Nicaraguan would have been assigned to drive. In such a case, Lissette would probably not have thought to ask that Hernaldo drive. But in that cross-cultural space between a Nicaraguan Mennonite church outing and MCC, no commonly assumed rules applied. It seemed natural to her, "But of course, we do not need a North American to drive us to the retreat. There are Nicaraguans who can drive."

Danny stayed where he was. After the kids were loaded, Hernaldo got back into the driver's seat and off they went.

Immediately, Danny sensed the instability of the vehicle. He asked Hernaldo to stop. Both men slid out the driver's door and Danny insisted that four of the youth get into the second seat of the double cab. But the young people would not break up their group. No one would come inside. So Danny had them crowd forward in the bed of the pickup, no hanging over the end gate!

In the meantime, Lissette slid over into the middle of the seat. Danny got back in on the passenger side and sat against the door. Within a mile, the truck went out of control. It rolled over completely twice. Young people were scattered all over the road. Danny was thrown out. He was crushed between the pickup and the trunk of a leafless, broken-off tree.

Epilogue

HERNALDO

"You have to go to school; you have to go to school; you have to go to school!" His children could not help but know what father believed–father, the peasant cutter of sugarcane. School was the way to the future. Church too, church was important, school and church.

Hernaldo grew up going to the San Jose Mennonite Church and the public schools in his rural community. The San Jose Church is neighbor to the Los Cruces Mennonite Church, both south of Managua. Both were planted by Canadian Mennonite missionaries.

Hernaldo believed as his father believed; it was good to go to church and school. He grew into a strikingly handsome youth. The Canadian missionary pastor at church came to love this tall, sinewy boy with the warm, deep-set eyes–a brightly intelligent lad, faithful in church attendance and growing in his Christian faith. The missionary began to hope that this young man might one day become the pastor of his family's church. He arranged for Hernaldo to go on with his studies after he finished high school.

The Sandinista revolution helped make the missionary's dream a possibility, helped make it possible for bright youths from poor peasant families to get college educations. The revolution forced the National University to base entry requirements on academic ability, not on the ability to pay the fees. The missionary arranged for Hernaldo to go to Managua to take the university entrance exam. Hernaldo qualified to enter the medical college. Having qualified, the potential divinity student became instead a medical student.

While the Sandinista revolution made possible tuition-free, university education for qualifying students, room and board and other living expenses were on the student. Hernaldo, being a poor peasant, was not able to pay for room and board. A Mennonite couple from the Canadian mission who were living in Managua offered a room in their home to the young medical student.

When the couple returned to Canada, Hernaldo needed a home in the middle of his quest for a medical degree. Jim and Ann Hershberger came to the rescue and invited Hernaldo to live with them. At the time of the accident, Hernaldo had been living with the Hershbergers for two years.

Shortly after Hernaldo became a student at the University, the *Hosanna* Bible study group discovered him. They were his kind of people, and he quickly became involved in their activities.

After moving into Jim and Ann's home, Hernaldo told them about *Hosanna.* By then a number of the medical students in the group had graduated and formed Acción Médica Christiana or AMC. It was through Hernaldo that MCC learned about *Hosanna* and AMC. When Danny arrived in Nicaragua, he was the first MCCer to work with AMC in the field. In fact, it was because of Hernaldo that Danny was assigned to work with them.

Hernaldo had just finished his studies in December of 1989. He went home at the end of the month to be with his mother and to be her doctor. Hernaldo did not want to go with Lissette and Danny to the Mennonite youth retreat. His mother was very sick. But Danny and Lissette's arguments against his not going eventually prevailed. Hernaldo agreed to leave his mother and spend that one overnight in the mountains.

In the accident, Hernaldo's left arm was badly broken. He was hospitalized in Jinotepe and was there in the hospital the next day, Sunday, when his mother died.

Hernaldo's grief was almost beyond endurance. He healed slowly and was in the hospital several weeks. In fact, a week after the accident, his arm had to be repinned as it had not been set properly the first time. During this surgery, his heart stopped beating, and it was with difficulty that the doctors revived him. They believed it was grief which nearly took his life.

There were many people terribly angry and terribly hurt by the accident. One by one they needed to express their anger, as well as receive and give forgiveness. They did this in various ways. Slowly, the fabric of the community stretched to cover that healing wound.

When Hernaldo was eventually well enough to begin his internship at the University Hospital, Jim and Ann invited him to come back to his old living arrangement. Hernaldo found it hard to believe that the leaders of the agency whose worker had died and whose vehicle had been totaled with no insurance coverage would keep the door to their home open to him.

It seemed to Jim and Ann that Hernaldo was doing penance that year by demanding of his body that it receive the pain which would allow it to recover. He forced his body to get well so he could be of service to God. A therapy regimen had been prescribed for him which required that he push weights with his injured arm.

"He would push that weight, silently, persistently, against great pain," Ann observed. "He would push on and on. The cold sweat of concealed anguish wet his hair and dripped from his forehead."

After his internship, Hernaldo volunteered for service with the AMC on the Mosquito Coast. He was posted to a small island, Rama Cay, off of Bluefields. This island is where the remnant of the Rama Native Americans live, only some 800 of them. There is a small clinic on the island.

Besides his work on the Cay, Hernaldo visited villages on the Mosquito Coast inland from Bluefields. His work routinely took him up three navigable rivers because there were no roads. It took a week to ten days to do one river. Then he would be back on the Cay for a few weeks before he would do another round. He made about four cycles per year over the areas he served.

On any one trip, he would see 600 to 800 patients. Besides treating illnesses, Hernaldo worked at immunizations and preventative measures for TB, malaria, and malnutrition. He also worked at identifying and resourcing village people who were trained as lay health workers.

In addition to the one-on-one care which he developed with the Native Americans, Hernaldo kept a log of what he saw and did on each trip. As soon as he got back to the Cay after a trip, he radioed his log to the AMC Documentation Center in Managua where the information was keyed into a growing data base. This was the first time in history that a data base was being developed on these Native American communities. AMC hoped that the information collected through the research would be useful to Native American leaders working to improve the welfare of their people.

By 1991 there were four AMC doctors on the Mosquito Coast doing the sort of thing that Hernaldo did. And there were three MCC volunteers working with AMC, continuing the involvement which Danny Wenger had pioneered.

At the time of the accident, the documentation center was only an AMC dream, only a hope. The AMC leaders hoped for a library where medical students could come to study, and they wanted a computer to develop a medical data base.

Soon after Danny's death, AMC decided that when their center did become more than a dream, when it actually opened, it would be named the Daniel Wenger Documentation Center.

AMC asked Jim and Ann Hershberger what they thought. Then when Danny's family–his parents and three sisters–visited Nicaragua some time after the accident, the AMC leaders asked Danny's parents directly if they would consent to this use of Danny's name.

Not only was the Wenger family happy to agree to the AMC proposal, but they were also able to make seed money available to get the center started. At the time of Danny's death, a memorial fund had been set up in the States and some $4,000 of this money was forwarded through MCC for the AMC center.

In December 1990 Daniel and Erma Wenger visited Nicaragua a second time. Their visit coincided with the first anniversary of the accident. On that day, they also attended the dedication of the Daniel Wenger Documentation Center.

By mid 1991 the center had several computers. A program was in place to collect and store medical data from the AMC fieldwork. The center also had a small library, a clinic, and a residence. Future dreams included a satellite hook-up with medical information services in the United States and the purchase of Spanish-language medical texts for the library.

After his work in the field, Hernaldo returned to Managua, married, got a degree in epidemiology, and became the AMC administrator.

* * *

Lissette escaped serious physical injury in the accident. She graduated from the University and began a one-year assignment, working with AMC on the Mosquito Coast. During this time, AMC sent her to Honduras for a workshop. While at the workshop, she wore Danny's Goshen College T-shirt. A young Mennonite man, son of the president of the Honduran Evangelical Mennonite Church, was also at the workshop.

Flores noticed Lissette's T-shirt and introduced himself. In March 1991, they were married in Lissette's home church, Managua's First Baptist. Lissette and Flores spent the 1993-94 school year at Hesston College, a two-year Mennonite school in Hesston, Kansas.

In 1995 they led a Mennonite Central Committee youth discovery team which toured in Colombia and the United States. Thus Lissette and Flores became MCC workers as Danny had been. They have returned to Central America where they continue their involvement in church work in Honduras and Guatemala.

About the Author

Joseph C. Shenk was born and raised in East Africa, the son of missionaries who served in Tanganyika (now Tanzania). Shenk and his wife, Edith (Newswanger) Shenk, also were missionaries in East Africa, serving in Tanzania and Kenya from 1963 through 1981.

The Shenks, who have four grown daughters, now live in Harrisonburg, Virginia. They are co-pastors at Weavers Mennonite Church in Harrisonburg.